Simple Models
of Group Behavior

Simple Models
of Group Behavior

OTOMAR J. BARTOS

COLUMBIA UNIVERSITY PRESS

NEW YORK AND LONDON 1967

Otomar J. Bartos is Professor of Sociology at the University of Pittsburgh.

To Joan

PREFACE

The literature on mathematical models is found scattered through numerous books and articles, most of which presuppose a certain level of mathematical training. Since many social scientists do not have an adequate background, this increasingly important type of theoretical endeavor remains inaccessible to them. This book attempts to remedy the situation by bringing together some of the most promising attempts in this field, while presenting at the same time the mathematical theory needed to understand them.

The very fact that the book is intended to introduce those with very little mathematical training to a field which relies heavily on mathematics creates a dilemma. If the text emphasizes mathematical theory to the extent necessary to provide a thorough understanding of the subject, most of those for whom the book is primarily intended will be lost as readers. If, on the other hand, only the bare essentials of the theory are given, then the objection may be raised that a little knowledge is worse than none.

There is no escape from these two alternatives—a choice must be made. My choice was to keep the discussion of mathematical theory to an absolute minimum, taking the calculated risk that even such minimal knowledge will, in the long run, prove beneficial. My experience in teaching classes using the material as presented here gives me reason for optimism. A student introduced to the applications of mathematics for the first time seems to regard them as a challenge rather than as a *fait accomplis:* More often than not dissatisfied and curious, he strives for a deeper understanding of the material. Only rarely have I encountered a student who completed the course and went away feeling that he then knew all he needed to know.

To say that the discussion of mathematical theory is kept to a minimum is not to say that a reader without mathematical training will find it easy to understand. In my opinion, failure to make adjustments in reading habits is responsible, more than any other single factor, for the fact that many social scientists have started and then given up attempts to comprehend mathematically oriented research. The reader should expect difficulty at the beginning and should be prepared to read over and over again any section which at first seems obscure. Above all, he should do the exercises which follow most of the chapters.

The book may be used as a text for undergraduate or graduate courses in the social sciences. Although acquaintance with finite mathematics, as presented for example in Kemeny, Snell, and Thompson (1957) *Introduction to Finite Mathematics*, is a definite advantage, the text can be studied profitably even by those without this background. Depending on the preparation of the students and on the amount of supplementary reading offered, the book can be used as the text for a one-semester or a two-semester course. If it is used for a two-semester course, then Parts I and II covering Markov chains and their application may be used for the first semester, Parts III and IV dealing primarily with the theory of games, for the second.

I wish to thank those who have read the manuscript and often offered valuable suggestions: Leon. J. Gleser, Burkart Holzner, Paul F. Lazarsfeld, Omar K. Moore, Forrest R. Pitts, Anatole Rapoport, and many others. Thanks are also

due to the Social Science Research Institute at the University
of Hawaii for help in preparing the manuscript; to the Air
Force Office of Scientific Research for supporting my research
which is reported in Chapter 14; and to Mrs. O. A. Bushnell,
Bernard Gronert, and Linnae Coss for invaluable editorial
help. Last but not least, my thanks go to many of my students
whose comments and criticisms have helped to increase the
readability of the text.

OTOMAR J. BARTOS

Honolulu, Hawaii
May, 1967

CONTENTS

PART ONE

MATHEMATICAL BACKGROUND

The social scientist who is interested in using mathematical models usually starts by asking some rather basic questions. What is a model? What is the place of model construction among other approaches to the study of human groups? And what in particular are its advantages and disadvantages? Why *mathematical* models? And if the idea of mathematical models is accepted, which ones should be chosen? Before these questions can be answered in a thorough fashion, of course, a certain degree of familiarity with models and their construction is required. Hence we shall offer only preliminary answers in Chapter 1, reserving a more detailed discussion for the last two chapters of the book.

For reasons which will be considered briefly in Chapter 1, we shall limit our discussion to two types of models: those based on the theory of Markov chains and those based on the theory of games. Pursuing the objective of acquainting the reader with those, and only those, parts of mathematical theory that are necessary for an understanding of the models discussed in this book, we devote space in Chapter 2 to some of the fundamental concepts of matrix algebra. Chapters 3 and 4 build upon these foundations, giving the fundamental definitions and theorems of the theory of Markov chains. This background is sufficient for an understanding of the models covered in Part II and also provides a good starting point for the discussion of the theory of games in Part III. Additional mathematical theory will be included in subsequent chapters as the specific need arises.

For the most part, our discussion of mathematical theory will consist mainly of a survey of the more important definitions and a few theorems. Furthermore, we shall as a rule present theorems without proof, asking the reader to accept them on faith. Clearly, such a procedure cannot be expected to provide a thorough understanding of the subject, and therefore we urge the reader to seek additional information in any one of the excellent introductory texts. Perhaps the best single text for this purpose is that of Kemeny, Snell, and Thompson, *Introduction to Finite Mathematics* (1957).

CHAPTER 1

Mathematical Models

About a century ago, the so-called organic analogy began to influence sociological thinking. The analogy was based on a belief that a society is similar in many important respects to an organism. It was believed that a society and an organism both grow in size and complexity, both have several systems of organs (sustaining, distributing, and regulating), both strive to maintain an internal equilibrium.[1] Guided by this worthwhile analogy, sociologists gained an intuitive understanding of the functioning of a society as well as, at a later date, a set of specific hypotheses to work with. Some of these hypotheses proved to be tenable, others did not, but the concepts derived from the analogy are even today a significant part of sociological theory.[2]

Two aspects of the organic analogy are worth noting. First, the model used in the analogy, the organism, was easily understood by the sociologists of a century ago. All men can contemplate the functioning of an organism with relative ease since a prime example, the human body, is familiar to everyone. Moreover, the development of biology made such contemplation even easier for the educated,

[1] See, for example, Spencer (1877).
[2] The so-called functional theory is often viewed as a sophisticated restatement of the organic analogy.

since various charts and graphs depicting the functioning of the human body were available. The second point concerns the impact of the organic analogy on sociology. Essentially, familiarity with biology made it possible for sociologists to formulate hypotheses about society. At first these hypotheses bore a clear earmark of their origin by referring to such things as societal "growth," "organs," "backbone," and "death." Moreover, the early hypotheses tended by and large to view a society as being similar to an organism. At a later date, however, biological terminology was discarded, and the differences between societies and organisms were emphasized. It was shown that some hypotheses which hold true for an organism do not apply to a society, and that the organism-derived hypotheses are not sufficient for an understanding of group behavior. For example, the hypothesis that a society fights all disruptive practices in the same way that an organism fights all infections was discarded by most sociologists, and indeed some felt that internal conflict, damaging as it may be for an organism, is important and often beneficial for a society. Thus, as time went by, the organic model was clarified and its proper function within the sociological theory was ascertained.

1.1   CHOICE OF A MODEL

In this book we propose to do much the same thing as did the early sociologists. The chief difference between their approach and ours lies not so much in the method used—although we can afford today to be methodologically more advanced than they were—but rather in the choice of the model. They used an organism; we shall use two distinct mathematical theories, the theory of Markov chains and the theory of games. They believed that a society functions as an organism; we shall view some social processes as probabilistic Markov chains or, in some instances, as systems which maximize some property or properties.

Some readers undoubtedly will feel that there is considerable difference between the use of an organism as a model and the use of a mathematical theory as a model. After all, they will say, the main value of the organic analogy lies in the fact that it gave the sociologist something tangible to work with—an organism—while a mathematical theory gives nothing of the sort, and cannot be considered a model at all. We do not agree. What made the organic analogy valuable was not its tangibility but the fact that scientists were well acquainted with it. Whether or not a mathematical theory can serve as a model for sociology thus depends not on the "tangibility" of the theory but rather on whether the sociologists are acquainted with it. We propose to add to the growing number of texts designed to acquaint the sociologist with mathematical theory, many of which are listed in the Bibliography, by describing in some detail in Chapters 3 and 4 one of the two theories to be used, the theory of Markov chains. The theory of games is dealt with in somewhat lesser detail in Part III. It is our belief that once sociologists become acquainted with mathematical theory as intimately as the nineteenth century sociologists were with biology, mathematical theory will become as fruitful to sociology as was the organic analogy.

We have chosen for consideration two distinct mathematical theories, the theory of Markov chains and the theory of games. The practical applications as well as the philosophical implications of these two theories are quite different. The theory of Markov chains is especially valuable for *describing* social processes such as voting, resolution of conflicts, formation of friendships, or social mobility. The theory of games, on the other hand, can be used for *prescribing* how an intelligent person should go about resolving social conflicts, ranging all the way from open warfare between nations to disagreements between husband and wife.

1.2 ALTERNATIVE APPROACHES

Our decision to consider only models that utilize the theory of Markov chains or the theory of games calls for some justification. Why choose these models rather than others? Are these approaches superior to others? We do not wish to make any such sweeping claim. We merely feel that the approaches we have chosen will provide an ideal introduction to mathematical social theory, because they are simple enough to be understood by the beginner and at the same time yield models that can hold their own under more advanced examination. As we shall attempt to show, such models can represent rather faithfully at least some aspects of social life. The strengths (as well as the weaknesses) of our two approaches are most obvious, perhaps, when contrasted with some of the alternatives.

The most obvious alternative, of course, is a *nonmathematical* theory. Until very recently, as we have already observed, sociologists have managed very well with the organic model, or even without any model whatsoever. We do not wish to add to the already voluminous literature on the merits and demerits of mathematics for the social sciences.[3] Let us say only that, while plain English may have a flexibility at times denied to the language of mathematics, this is not an unmixed blessing. Sometimes flexibility results in vagueness of such magnitude that the assertions of the theory itself actually become unclear. Mathematical theory, on the other hand, abhors lack of precision. This too, no doubt, can be a fault.[4] But precision, as a crucial element in the spirit of mathematics, has the advantage that one can require conclusive proof that a certain assertion does or does not follow from the theory. As we shall show, mathematical models usually have a number of logical implications, some of which may be testable empirically. If the implications are refuted by the facts, then the model itself is shown to be deficient.

The other chief advantage of mathematical language, in our opinion, is its ability to express complex ideas through simple, and therefore easily understandable, symbols. The reader is invited to try to express in plain English the relationship between X and Y (X being interaction, Y being liking), when the relationship is quite simple mathematically, $Y = A + \sqrt{X}$. The equation is graphed in Figure 1.1. Would one say, "Starting from a certain level, as interaction increases, liking increases, but at an ever decreasing rate"? Assuming that one has adequate understanding of both the English

---

[3] For a good sampling of the opinions representing those who do and do not advocate the use of mathematical models by the social scientist, see Charlesworth (1963).

[4] When one tries to be more precise than is justified by the data one is able to collect, then precision can amount to self-delusion. For an example, see the discussion of the application of the theory of games to warfare, Sec. 11.2, "The Battle of Avranche."

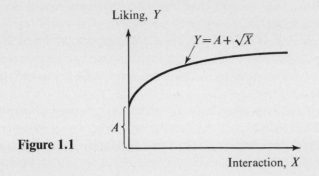

Figure 1.1

language and of mathematics, which of the two expressions is easier to deal with, the English sentence or the mathematical equation?

But even if the reader were to accept our argument—that the language of mathematics is better suited to handle complicated theoretical notions than is plain English—he still may not agree with our choice of the mathematical approach. The reader trained in calculus and differential equations will have almost no opportunity to apply his knowledge in reading our book. Instead, he will have to become acquainted with matrix algebra, probability theory and, on occasion, the theory of difference (as opposed to differential) equations.[5]

The distinction between the mathematical skills a reader is likely to have and those required for understanding the Markov chains theory is related to the fundamental difference between the so-called deterministic and stochastic approaches to model construction. A *deterministic* model—of which the various "classical" economic models[6] are a prime example—yields, as a rule, predictions of single outcomes; a *stochastic* (i.e., probabilistic) model, on the other hand—the Markov chains belonging to this category—normally predicts a whole distribution of outcomes. To cite an example, in Chapter 7 we shall discuss a model of conflict. This model, being of the stochastic type, predicts merely the probability that a person will conform to group pressure. If the model were deterministic

[5] A good introductory text on difference equations with applications to social science is Goldberg (1958).

[6] For an excellent introductory discussion of economic models see Beach (1964).

rather than stochastic, on the other hand, it would predict whether a person will or will not conform.

It may seem to the reader that our argument so far favors the deterministic over the stochastic approach. Is it not better to be able to predict behavior exactly rather than merely in a probabilistic fashion? In principle, yes. But if one deals with simple models, as we do, then one must expect to encounter a discrepancy between exact prediction and observation. Now the question is: Which is better under such circumstances—to have a model that predicts exactly but is almost always wrong, or a model that predicts with less exactitude (but nevertheless with complete precision[7]) but is almost always correct? We prefer a model which aims at doing a modest job and does it well to a model that fails—in principle—in an ambitious undertaking.

This does not mean, however, that we shall be using only stochastic models in this book. The last section of the text, Part III, deals with the theory of games, and therefore uses the probability theory in a secondary role only.[8] But our departure from the stochastic approach is not from choice but by necessity. We shall indeed argue that certain portions of the theory of games would be improved if they could be made stochastic (see Chapter 14, section titled "Experiments with Bargaining Games"), but for this introductory text we have to accept the theory of games as it is, for deterministic models are generally much more manageable mathematically than are stochastic models.

Which brings us to another alternative bypassed in our choice of models, the alternative of *simulation*. We bypassed it for the same reasons that led us to use the essentially nonstochastic theory of games although, in principle, we prefer stochastic models: Deterministic models are simpler than stochastic ones, and the models we have chosen are simpler than those normally used for simulation.

[7] A stochastic model although predicting merely the probability of behavior, is nevertheless conceptually quite precise: It predicts precise probability distribution of behaviors. Thus it is possible to test, in a very precise fashion, whether the prediction is or is not correct; if the predicted and the actually observed distributions differ, the model is incorrect.

[8] Probability theory enters into the theory of games in two main ways. It is an integral part of the very concept of "utility," and it is used to define so-called mixed strategies. However, the main approach of the theory of games is deterministic, since the objective is to identify one and only one solution of the game.

This difference follows from the very definition of simulation. According to Pool et al. (1965), "simulation is a technique that is appropriate when so many variables are simultaneously in operation that simpler methods of calculation fail."[9] Since there are many variables and much calculation to be done, a high-speed electronic computer is usually employed to do the job. For this reason, simulation has become identified with computer application.

The models which we shall discuss are simple in at least two ways: First, they usually involve only a few variables; second, it is possible to solve them through mathematical reasoning, thus reducing considerably the amount of computation needed for any special problem. But the difference between our models and simulation tends to disappear at times, for it is possible to use an essentially simple model in a complex way. For example, the simplest Markov chains model involves a 2×2 matrix i.e., a matrix with two rows and two columns (see Chapter 3); the simplest game is also represented by a single 2×2 matrix (see Chapter 9). But it is possible to consider matrices of any size. When, however, very large matrices are used, the mathematical reasoning fails to be advantageous and the researcher often has to resort to "brute force," that is, he has to forego a search for a general solution and be satisfied with finding a specific solution for the specific case he is considering. This he often accomplishes by using a computer (see Chapters 7 and 8).

It should be emphasized, however, that simulation is more than using essentially simple models in a complex way; the difference is often one of research strategy. Implicit in our discussion will be the belief that social scientists can benefit from applying existing mathematical theories (such as the Markov chains theory) to actual behavior. Implicit in much of simulation is the belief that the mathematical formulation has to be tailormade to fit the specific problem at hand, that the existing mathematical theories often are not applicable.[10]

---

[9] Pool et al. (1965), p. 2.

[10] For example, Dawson (1962) says: "Many simulation processes are relatively free from complex mathematics.... The lack of dependency upon complex mathematical analysis not only has the advantage of making simulation comprehensible to the mathematically unsophisticated, but it also can be used in studying situations where mathematical methods capable of considering all of the desirable factors are not available." (p. 13).

A number of philosophical as well as practical problems is involved in these two beliefs, but we shall not consider them here. Let us merely state that it seems better to investigate whether available mathematical theories in fact are not applicable, than to merely assume that they are not. And we propose to do just that in this book: to investigate whether two mathematical theories, the theory of Markov chains and the theory of games, are in fact applicable as models of group behavior.

1.3   TERMINOLOGY

Our statement that we intend to use the Markov chains theory or the theory of games as models for studying group behavior is not entirely accurate. Stated more precisely, these theories become models when they are applied to the study of group behavior. Thus, strictly speaking, one should distinguish between a "mathematical theory," a "model," and "actual behavior." These three concepts can be arranged hierarchically, in the order of decreasing generality:

Mathematical theory (e.g., Markov chains).

Model (e.g., a model of social conflict).

Actual behavior (e.g., behavior in Asch's experiments). (See Chapter 7.)

It should be obvious that the two mathematical theories we have chosen for consideration are really not models, but meta-models. Only after specific assumptions are introduced,[11] so that the generality of the mathematical theory is reduced, do we obtain a model in the proper sense of the word. However, to avoid awkwardness of language, we shall not always observe these distinctions rigorously in our discussion.

---

[11] The specific assumptions are of several kinds. For example, when applying the Markov chains theory, one has to decide on the size of the matrix, whether any components are zero, and what the various mathematical "states" stand for as far as the group behavior is concerned. Ultimately, one often has to determine the values of the transition probabilities p_{ij} (see Chapters 5–8).

CHAPTER 2

Matrix Algebra

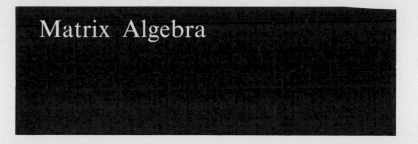

As in much of mathematical theory, the basis of matrix algebra is a set of conventions which, if adhered to, make certain types of operations easier to perform. More specifically, by treating a collection of numbers (a matrix) as a unit (for instance, by using it in addition and multiplication) one can grasp many results which would otherwise be quite difficult to comprehend. The applications of matrix algebra are many, ranging from statistical theory to specific problems such as the kinship structure of preliterate tribes.[1] For our purposes matrix algebra is the essential foundation not only for further theoretical formulations (e.g., Markov chains theory), but also for the development of some specific models to be discussed in the later chapters (social structures in Chapter 5 and games in Chapters 9 through 14). We shall start our discussion by considering a simple and rather homely illustration.

Example 1. Suppose that a housewife goes shopping, and that she buys 2 lb of steak and 5 lb of apples. How much money does she spend, if 1 lb of steak is $1.10, and 1 lb of apples is $0.20? Let us

[1] See, for example, Kemeny et al. (1957), Chapter 7, or Horst (1963).

start by rewriting the above information:

amount of steak purchased $= a_1 = 2\,\text{lb}$
amount of apples purchased $= a_2 = 5\,\text{lb}$
price of steak, per 1 lb $= b_1 = \$1.10$
price of apples, per 1 lb $= b_2 = \$0.20$

It is clear that the total amount spent, T, by the housewife is

$$T = a_1b_1 + a_2b_2 = 2\,\text{lb} \times \$1.10 + 5\,\text{lb} \times \$0.20 = \$3.20$$

Now in order to "translate" the above example into matrix notation, we have to agree to the following conventions:

1. We will write the amount of steak purchased and the amount of apples purchased as a "row vector," A:

$$A = (a_1, a_2)$$

2. We will write[2] the price per pound of steak and the price per pound of apples as a "column vector," B':

$$B' = \begin{bmatrix} b_1 \\ b_2 \end{bmatrix}$$

3. We agree that whenever we write AB' where A is a row vector and B' is a column vector, we mean to indicate the following operation: $a_1b_1 + a_2b_2$. In other words, we define the so-called inner product, AB', as

$$AB' = a_1b_1 + a_2b_2$$

Applying these conventions to the present example we write:

$$A = (2\,\text{lb}, 5\,\text{lb}), \qquad B' = \begin{bmatrix} \$1.10 \\ \$0.20 \end{bmatrix}$$

Now, if the reader contemplates for a moment the definition of the inner product AB' [as given by (3) above], he will agree that we can write that $T = AB'$:

$$T = AB' = (2, 5) \begin{bmatrix} 1.10 \\ 0.20 \end{bmatrix} = 2 \times 1.10 + 5 \times 0.20 = 3.20$$

[2] The decision to write the quantities as a row vector and the prices as a column vector is arbitrary: The same results would hold if prices constituted a row, quantities a column vector.

Note that we have omitted the symbols "lb" and "$." This omission is by no means necessary, but it is customary since it simplifies the notation.

Whether or not one uses matrix notation, the results are the same. But by using matrix notation we have gained one advantage— economy of expression. Instead of the cumbersome

$$T = a_1b_1 + a_2b_2$$

it is sufficient to write

$$T = AB'$$

Of course this gain has its price—the necessity of memorizing the conventions governing matrix algebra. We shall now present the most important of these conventions.

2.1   BASIC DEFINITIONS

A *matrix* is a rectangular array of numbers, such as

$$\begin{bmatrix} 7 & 8 \\ -4 & 0 \end{bmatrix} \quad \text{or} \quad \begin{bmatrix} 17 & 0.4 & 2 \\ 0.1 & 12 & 3 \end{bmatrix} \quad \text{or} \quad \begin{bmatrix} \frac{1}{2} \\ \frac{3}{4} \\ \frac{1}{4} \end{bmatrix}$$

Each matrix consists of rows and columns. So, for example, the first matrix has two rows and two columns; the third has three rows and one column. It is customary to call the first matrix shown a 2 × 2 matrix, the second a 2 × 3 matrix, the third a 3 × 1 matrix, thus indicating the number of rows and columns.

It is customary to denote the individual components of any matrix A as a_{ij}. The subscript i indicates the row in which the component is located, the subscript j the column. Thus, for example, any 2 × 3 matrix can be written as

$$A = \begin{bmatrix} a_{11} & a_{12} & a_{13} \\ a_{21} & a_{22} & a_{23} \end{bmatrix}$$

Notice that the subscript for rows, i, always appears first. Thus a_{23} refers to the component located in the second row, third column of matrix A.

A *column vector* is a matrix which has several rows but only one column, for example,

$$A' = \begin{bmatrix} 7 \\ 0 \\ -3 \end{bmatrix}$$

A *row vector* is a matrix which has only one row but several columns, for example,

$$A = (400, \tfrac{1}{2}, 7)$$

Note that the column vector is always designated with a prime, A', while the row vector is without it, A. Furthermore, in subsequent chapters we shall distinguish between a matrix and a vector by using small letters, such as a and a', to designate vectors.

2.2   BASIC OPERATIONS

Matrix Addition.   When two matrices, A and B, have the same shape (the same number of rows and columns), they can be added by adding the corresponding components. For instance,

$$\begin{bmatrix} 7 & 0 \\ -31 & 8 \\ 4 & -1 \end{bmatrix} + \begin{bmatrix} 0 & 3 \\ -2 & 14 \\ 7 & 5 \end{bmatrix} = \begin{bmatrix} 7+0 & 0+3 \\ -31-2 & 8+14 \\ 4+7 & -1+5 \end{bmatrix}$$

$$= \begin{bmatrix} 7 & 3 \\ -33 & 22 \\ 11 & 4 \end{bmatrix}$$

Matrix Multiplication.   To define matrix multiplication, we first consider a product between two *vectors*, a row vector R and a column vector C',

$$R = (r_1, r_2, \ldots), \quad C' = \begin{bmatrix} c_1 \\ c_2 \\ . \\ . \\ . \end{bmatrix}$$

The so-called *inner product* of the two vectors, RC', is defined as

$$RC' = r_1c_1 + r_2c_2 + \cdots$$

We already have had an opportunity to show how the inner product can be used to compute the total bill of a shopper: If a housewife buys 2 lb of steak at \$1.10 per pound and 5 lb of apples at \$0.20 per pound, we can compute her total expenditure by vector multiplication:

$$(2, 5) \begin{bmatrix} 1.10 \\ 0.20 \end{bmatrix} = 2 \times 1.10 + 5 \times 0.20 = 3.20$$

Notice that:

1. The term "inner product" refers to a product between a column vector and a row vector. It is not possible to multiply a row vector by a row vector, or a column vector by a column vector.
2. To indicate vector multiplication, the row vector R is always written first, the column vector C' second; $C'R$ is not a permissible expression!
3. The result of multiplying two vectors is not a vector but an ordinary number.

The product of two *matrices*, A and B, is similarly given by obtaining a matrix the ijth component of which (i for rows, j for columns) is the inner product of the ith row of A by the jth column of B. For example,

$$\begin{bmatrix} 1 & 0 & 2 \\ 0 & 3 & 4 \end{bmatrix} \begin{bmatrix} 1 & 0 & 2 & 3 \\ 0 & 3 & 1 & 2 \\ 1 & 2 & 0 & 1 \end{bmatrix} =$$

$$= \begin{bmatrix} 1 \times 1 + 0 \times 0 + 2 \times 1, & 1 \times 0 + 0 \times 3 + 2 \times 2, \\ 0 \times 1 + 3 \times 0 + 4 \times 1, & 0 \times 0 + 3 \times 3 + 4 \times 2, \end{bmatrix}$$

$$\begin{matrix} 1 \times 2 + 0 \times 1 + 2 \times 0, & 1 \times 3 + 0 \times 2 + 2 \times 1 \\ 0 \times 2 + 3 \times 1 + 4 \times 0, & 0 \times 3 + 3 \times 2 + 4 \times 1 \end{matrix} =$$

$$= \begin{bmatrix} 3 & 4 & 2 & 5 \\ 4 & 17 & 3 & 10 \end{bmatrix}$$

The reader may find it useful to note that multiplication between
A and B proceeds as if A was a set of row vectors, B a set of column
vectors. Furthermore, notice that:

1. Matrix A can be multiplied by matrix B only if A has exactly
as many columns as B has rows. In the above example, A has three
columns and B has three rows—hence multiplication is possible.

2. The resulting matrix has as many rows as matrix A and as
many columns as matrix B.

3. The product AB is not "commutative," that is, the product AB
is usually not the same as the product BA. To give a very simple
illustration, let

$$A = \begin{bmatrix} 0 & 1 \\ 1 & 0 \end{bmatrix}, \quad B = \begin{bmatrix} 1 & 1 \\ 1 & 0 \end{bmatrix}$$

Multiplying, we obtain

$$AB = \begin{bmatrix} 1 & 0 \\ 1 & 1 \end{bmatrix}, \quad BA = \begin{bmatrix} 1 & 1 \\ 0 & 1 \end{bmatrix}$$

and see that $AB \neq BA$.

2.3   ADDITIONAL CONCEPTS

While matrix addition and multiplication are the two basic operations of matrix algebra, the following concepts are of considerable
importance:

Transpose of a Matrix.   The matrix obtained from matrix A by
interchanging the rows and columns of A, so that the component a_{ij}
is transformed into a'_{ji}, is called the "transpose of matrix A" and is
designated by A'. So, for example, the transpose of matrix

$$A = \begin{bmatrix} 2 & 0 & 7 \\ 1 & 4 & 2 \end{bmatrix}$$

is

$$A' = \begin{bmatrix} 2 & 1 \\ 0 & 4 \\ 7 & 2 \end{bmatrix}$$

Note, for example, that the first row of A became the first column of A. It should be also noted that the convention whereby a row vector is designated by a (without a prime) while a column vector is designated by a' (with a prime) is really a convention that all vectors are *row* vectors unless otherwise specified (by adding a prime).

Power of a Matrix. In ordinary algebra, a^n denotes the number obtained by using number a as a factor n times; similarly, in matrix algebra a matrix A can be raised to the nth power. For example, if A is given by

$$A = \begin{bmatrix} 1 & 0 \\ 2 & 1 \end{bmatrix}$$

then

$$A^3 = AAA = \begin{bmatrix} 1 & 0 \\ 2 & 1 \end{bmatrix}\begin{bmatrix} 1 & 0 \\ 2 & 1 \end{bmatrix}\begin{bmatrix} 1 & 0 \\ 2 & 1 \end{bmatrix} = \begin{bmatrix} 1 & 0 \\ 4 & 1 \end{bmatrix}\begin{bmatrix} 1 & 0 \\ 2 & 1 \end{bmatrix} = \begin{bmatrix} 1 & 0 \\ 6 & 1 \end{bmatrix}$$

Notice that only a square $(m \times m)$ matrix can be raised to the nth power.

The Expression $A = B$. If A and B are two $n \times m$ matrices, then $A = B$ means that the corresponding components of the two matrices are equal. For example,

$$\begin{bmatrix} a_{11} & a_{12} \\ a_{21} & a_{22} \end{bmatrix} = \begin{bmatrix} 7 & -3 \\ 0 & 4 \end{bmatrix}$$

means that $a_{11} = 7$, $a_{12} = -3$, $a_{21} = 0$, and $a_{22} = 4$. Note that this convention means that $A = B$ can always be written as a set of $n \times m$ relations, $\{a_{ij} = b_{ij}\}$.

Determinant of a 2×2 Matrix. If A is a 2×2 matrix, i.e., if

$$A = \begin{bmatrix} a_{11} & a_{12} \\ a_{21} & a_{22} \end{bmatrix}$$

then the determinant of A, usually denoted as

$$\begin{vmatrix} a_{11} & a_{12} \\ a_{21} & a_{22} \end{vmatrix}$$

is defined as

(2.1)
$$\begin{vmatrix} a_{11} & a_{12} \\ a_{21} & a_{22} \end{vmatrix} = a_{11}a_{22} - a_{21}a_{12}$$

For example,

$$\begin{vmatrix} 2 & 1 \\ 0 & 8 \end{vmatrix} = 2 \times 8 - 0 \times 1 = 16$$

Notice that:

1. The determinant of matrix A is denoted by using different (straight) brackets from those used for the matrix A itself.
2. Only 2×2 matrices are discussed here. However, all square matrices have determinants.[3]
3. The reasons for ever wanting to know the determinant of a matrix have not been indicated as yet. One of the reasons is given below, in the discussion of the inverse of a matrix.

Identity Matrix.   A matrix is an identity matrix, I, if it is a square matrix and if all components on its main diagonal are 1, and all the remaining components are 0.

For example

$$\begin{bmatrix} 1 & 0 & 0 \\ 0 & 1 & 0 \\ 0 & 0 & 1 \end{bmatrix}$$

is an identity matrix, I.

Inverse of a Square Matrix, A^{-1}.   In ordinary algebra the inverse (or reciprocal) of number a is defined as a number b such that $ab = 1$. Similarly, in matrix algebra it is often useful to find the inverse A^{-1} of a square matrix A. A matrix B is called the inverse of a square matrix A if the product of A and B is the identity matrix I. In other words,

(2.2) $B = A^{-1}$ if and only if $AB = I$.

---

[3] The definition of a determinant for large matrices is too complex for our introductory text. For such a definition see, for example, Horst (1963).

The following observations can be made about the inverse of a matrix:

1. We are discussing only the inverse of a square matrix.

2. Not all square matrices have an inverse. It can be shown that a square matrix A has an inverse *if and only if its determinant is not 0*. For example, consider matrix

$$A = \begin{bmatrix} 2 & -3 \\ 4 & -6 \end{bmatrix}$$

The reader should try to compute inverse of that matrix by using the procedure described in Example 2 below. He will arrive at the following system of four equations:

(i) $\qquad\qquad 2b_{11} - 3b_{21} = 1$

(ii) $\qquad\qquad 2b_{12} - 3b_{22} = 0$

(iii) $\qquad\qquad 4b_{11} - 6b_{22} = 0$

(iv) $\qquad\qquad 4b_{12} - 6b_{22} = 1$

It is obvious that this system of equations cannot be solved because it is contradictory. For instance, when (i) is multiplied by 2, the left side of (i) becomes identical with the left side of (iii), but the right-hand sides of these two equations are not identical. It can be shown that such an unsolvable system of equations will be arrived at whenever the determinant of A is zero.

3. If A has an inverse, the inverse has the same shape as A, i.e., A^{-1} is a square matrix with the same number of rows as A.

Example 2. Find the inverse of the following matrix:

$$A = \begin{bmatrix} 4 & 1 \\ 0 & 3 \end{bmatrix}$$

First we find the determinant of A to discover whether A has an inverse. Since the determinant is nonzero ($4 \times 3 - 0 \times 1 = 12$), we conclude that A has an inverse, and we proceed to find it. Given the above matrix A we can use eq. 2.2 to write $AB = I$:

$$\begin{bmatrix} 4 & 1 \\ 0 & 3 \end{bmatrix} \begin{bmatrix} b_{11} & b_{12} \\ b_{21} & b_{22} \end{bmatrix} = \begin{bmatrix} 1 & 0 \\ 0 & 1 \end{bmatrix}$$

which, in turn, becomes

$$\begin{bmatrix} 4b_{11} + b_{21} & 4b_{12} + b_{22} \\ 3b_{21} & 3b_{22} \end{bmatrix} = \begin{bmatrix} 1 & 0 \\ 0 & 1 \end{bmatrix}$$

However, since we have an expression which equates two 2×2 matrices, we can write the following set of $2 \times 2 = 4$ equations:

(i) $\qquad\qquad\qquad 4b_{11} + b_{21} = 1$
(ii) $\qquad\qquad\qquad 4b_{12} + b_{22} = 0$
(iii) $\qquad\qquad\qquad\qquad 3b_{21} = 0$
(iv) $\qquad\qquad\qquad\qquad 3b_{22} = 1$

The above is a system of four linear equations with four unknowns, and we proceed to solve the system. From (iii) it follows that

(iii') $\qquad\qquad\qquad\qquad b_{21} = 0,$

and from (iv) that

(iv') $\qquad\qquad\qquad\qquad b_{22} = \dfrac{1}{3}$

Substituting (iii') into (i) we write

$$b_{11} = \dfrac{1}{4}$$

and substituting (iv') into (ii) we obtain

$$b_{12} = \dfrac{-1}{12}$$

Thus we have computed the components of matrix B:

$$B = \begin{bmatrix} \frac{1}{4} & \frac{-1}{12} \\ 0 & \frac{1}{3} \end{bmatrix}$$

Now if it is true—as it should be if our computations are correct—that $AB = I$, then B is the inverse of A, $B = A^{-1}$. In other words, it must hold true that

$$\begin{bmatrix} 4 & 1 \\ 0 & 3 \end{bmatrix}\begin{bmatrix} \frac{1}{4} & \frac{-1}{12} \\ 0 & \frac{1}{3} \end{bmatrix} = \begin{bmatrix} 1 & 0 \\ 0 & 1 \end{bmatrix}$$

It is easy to see that this equality indeed holds true—hence B is the inverse of A:

$$A^{-1} = \begin{bmatrix} \frac{1}{4} & \frac{-1}{12} \\ 0 & \frac{1}{3} \end{bmatrix}$$

EXERCISES

1. For the matrices (vectors) A, B, and C, write their transposes A', B', and C':

$$A = (4, 3, -1) \quad B = \begin{bmatrix} 3 & 2 \\ 8 & 9 \end{bmatrix} \quad C = \begin{bmatrix} 7 & -1 & 9 & 0 \\ -1 & 4 & 7 & 10 \end{bmatrix}$$

2. Write the sum $A + B$ for:

(a) $\quad A = \begin{bmatrix} 30 & 4 \\ 17 & -6 \end{bmatrix} \quad B = \begin{bmatrix} 1 & 1 \\ 1 & 1 \end{bmatrix}$

(b) $\quad A = \begin{bmatrix} .3 & .7 \\ .5 & .5 \end{bmatrix} \quad B = \begin{bmatrix} .2 & -.2 \\ -.3 & .3 \end{bmatrix}$

3. Perform multiplication AB whenever possible:

(a) $\quad A = \begin{bmatrix} 2 & 0 & 1 \\ 4 & 1 & 8 \end{bmatrix} \quad B = \begin{bmatrix} 2 & 3 & 1 \\ 0 & 1 & 0 \\ 2 & 1 & 4 \end{bmatrix}$

(b) $\quad A = \begin{bmatrix} 7 & 1 \\ 2 & 4 \end{bmatrix} \quad B = \begin{bmatrix} 1 \\ 0 \\ 1 \end{bmatrix}$

(c) $\quad A = \begin{bmatrix} .4 & .6 \\ .8 & .2 \end{bmatrix} \quad B = \begin{bmatrix} 1 & 0 \\ 0 & 1 \end{bmatrix}$

4. Compute AB and BA for

$$A = \begin{bmatrix} 2 & 1 \\ 0 & 3 \end{bmatrix} \quad B = \begin{bmatrix} 1 & 3 \\ 4 & 4 \end{bmatrix}$$

Are the two products identical?

5. Compute the inverse of matrix A whenever possible:

(a)
$$A = \begin{bmatrix} 3 & 2 \\ -1 & 1 \end{bmatrix}$$

(b)
$$A = \begin{bmatrix} 3 & 2 \\ 6 & 4 \end{bmatrix}$$

(c)
$$A = \begin{bmatrix} .2 & .8 \\ .6 & .4 \end{bmatrix}$$

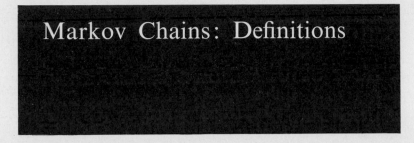

CHAPTER 3

Markov Chains: Definitions

A behavioral scientist is often interested in studying such social processes as voting, social mobility, or the formation of friendships. There are several branches of mathematical theory which can be used for the study of such processes but, for reasons given in Chapter 1, we shall be chiefly interested in theories which, when applied, lead only to probabilistic predictions of behavior. One of the most promising of such theories is the theory of Markov chains.

3.1 STOCHASTIC PROCESSES

It will be helpful to begin our discussion of Markov chains by coordinating our intuitive notion of a process with a rigorous definition that can be given within the context of the Markov chains theory. Imagine that time t is an integer-valued variable, $t = 0, 1, 2, \ldots$, and that at each time t we perform an experiment which can have a number of outcomes. For example, consider a series of presidential elections in the United States. The behavior of a voter during such election is our "experiment"; since presidential elections occur regularly every four years, our time (when we wish to start with the 1960 election) is $t = 1960, 1964, 1968, \ldots$, or, simply

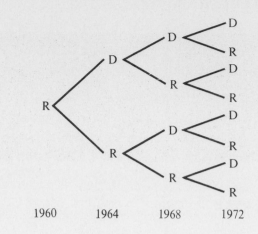

Figure 3.1　　　1960　　　　1964　　　　1968　　　　1972

$t = 0, 1, 2, \ldots$. Note that we assume that $t = 0$ is identical with $t = 1960$, $t = 1$ with $t = 1964$, and so on.

Suppose that we wish to consider only the two major parties, Democratic and Republican, then the possible outcomes of our experiments are "voter votes Democratic" and "voter votes Republican." It is possible to represent all of the possible outcomes of a sequence of experiments by a "tree of logical possibilities." Assuming that our voter was a Republican in 1960, all the possible ways in which he can vote in the three subsequent elections can be given by the "tree" illustrated in Figure 3.1. Of course, the tree represents the possible ways (always remembering that we are considering only Democratic and Republican votes) in which the voter can cast his ballot for the president after 1960. His actual voting will clearly be only one path of the tree, as shown for example in Figure 3.2, where his actual votes (if he voted Republican in 1960 and 1968, Democratic in 1964 and 1972) are shown by the solid lines.

With these basic concepts in mind, we can now define the process rigorously. Suppose that we associate with each branch of the tree of logical probabilities a *transition probability* $p_{ij}^{(t)}$ such that the sum of $p_{ij}^{(t)}$ for a given experiment is 1; then a *stochastic process* is a series of experiments the outcomes of which depend on the relevant transition probabilities $p_{ij}^{(t)}$. It should be added that $p_{ij}^{(t)}$ designates

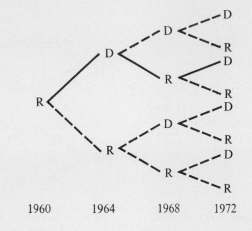

Figure 3.2   1960   1964   1968   1972

the (conditional[1]) probability that the outcome of the experiment
at time $t + 1$ will be j when the outcome at time t was i. For example,
the probability $p_{DR}^{(1)}$ is the probability that a voter will vote Republican
at time $t = 2$ if, at time $t = 1$, he voted Democratic. The reason for
calling $p_{ij}^{(t)}$ the "transition" probabilities is perhaps clear now: In
our example, they describe the probability of change (or no change)
in voting preference from one election to the next.

Our tree of logical possibilities can be used to represent a stochastic
process if we assign a probability $p_{ij}^{(t)}$ to each branch of the tree.
Using arbitrary numbers for the sake of illustration, we obtain the
diagram shown in Figure 3.3. Notice that the two branches originating from each outcome always add up to 1: $.20 + .80 = 1.00$,
$.60 + .40 = 1.00$, $.10 + .90 = 1.00$. This is in agreement with our
stipulation that the sum of $p_{ij}^{(t)}$ for a given experiment be 1.

One useful means of visualizing the process represented by the
above graph is to imagine a large number of voters, each of whom
is exposed to random forces of a very special kind: The net result
of these random forces is that about 20% of the voters who were

[1] For a distinction between unconditional and conditional probability, see, for
example, Kemeny et al. (1957), Chapter 4. Most generally, this distinction has to do
with how much the probability is assumed to depend on the occurrence of a prior
event: If certain probability holds true only if a certain prior event has occurred,
then the probability is conditional. The probabilities p_{ij} in Figure 3.3 are conditional
because they depend on the past history. For example, the probability of voting
Democratic in 1968 is .60 if the voter was a Democrat in 1964, .10 if he was a Republican
in 1964. The prior event upon which the probabilities of 1968 depend is thus the
casting of the ballot in 1964.

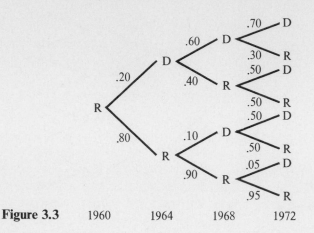

Figure 3.3   1960   1964   1968   1972

Republican in 1960 become Democrats, while 80% remain Re-publican. Between the 1964 and 1968 elections, the random forces are somewhat different: Now only about 10% of the 1964 Republi-cans become Democrats while 90% remain Republican—a pro-Republican four years, indeed. But, since we allowed some of the Republicans to become Democrats in 1964, the graph also shows what happens to them: About 60% remain Democrats, about 40% return to the Republican fold.

The stochastic process described here is rather complex and cannot be treated mathematically with ease. However, if we are willing to assume that $p_{RD}^{(t)}$ remains constant from year to year, and so does $p_{DR}^{(t)}$, then the process becomes a (finite) Markov chain that is amenable to mathematical analysis.

3.2   MARKOV CHAINS

In order to give a more exact form to the concepts discussed so far, let us represent graphically a Markov chain. Again using arbitrary numbers for $p_{ij}^{(t)}$, a Markov chains model of the voting process might look as illustrated in Figure 3.4. Note the difference between Figures 3.3 and 3.4. Figure 3.4 is simpler than Figure 3.3 in that the transition from i to j is the same for all t: $p_{RD} = .10$, $p_{RR} = .90$, $p_{DR} = .25$, $p_{DD} = .75$ without fail. This being the case, we can

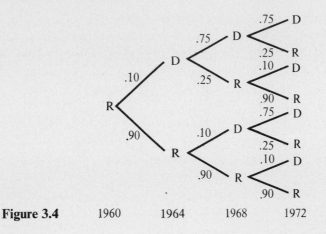

Figure 3.4   1960   1964   1968   1972

represent most of the information given graphically in Figure 3.4
through a matrix P:

$$\begin{array}{cc} & \begin{array}{cc} \mathbf{D} & \mathbf{R} \end{array} \end{array}$$

(3.1) $P = \begin{array}{c} \mathbf{D} \\ \mathbf{R} \end{array} \begin{bmatrix} .75 & .25 \\ .10 & .90 \end{bmatrix}$

This matrix describes essentially[2] the same process as does Figure 3.4
if we agree that the rows represent the possible outcomes i(D or R)
at time t, the columns the possible outcomes j at time $t + 1$, the
components of the matrix being the transition probabilities $p_{ij}^{(t)}$. We
now define matrices such as P above:

Definition. A square matrix is a *matrix of transition probabilities*
(a "transition matrix" for short), P, if all of its components are
non-negative and the sum of the components in a given row is 1.
   Notice that:

1. Only square matrices can serve as transition matrices.
2. It is not possible for P to have only zeros in a given row.
3. None of the components can be larger than 1 or smaller than 0.

   [2] One piece of information is missing when the process is represented by a matrix:
information about where it starts. As we shall see later, this missing information is
supplied by specifying a row vector such as in Example 1 below.

Let us inspect again the graphs in Figures 3.3 and 3.4. The difference between the two graphs can perhaps be described most succinctly by saying that the $p_{ij}^{(t)}$ of Figure 3.4 depend on (vary with) only the immediately preceding outcomes: If the outcome at time t was "vote Democratic," then $p_{ij}^{(t)}$ are given by the first row of P, by the vector $(.60, .40)$; if the outcome at time t was "vote Republican," then the $p_{ij}^{(t)}$ are the second row $(.20, .80)$. Contrast this with the graph of Figure 3.3 in which the probability of "voting Republican," for example, depends not only on the immediately preceding vote, but also upon the vote before that. To use a concrete example, compare two persons both of whom voted Republican in 1968, but only one voted Republican in 1964: The one who voted Republican in 1964 is assumed to be more likely to remain Republican in 1972 $(p_{RR}^{(1968)} = .95)$ than the person who voted Democratic in 1964 $(p_{RR}^{(1968)} = .50)$. In other words, in Figure 3.3 the probability of changing or keeping a political preference, $p_{ij}^{(t)}$, is assumed to be influenced not only by the previous election but also by the one before it. For this reason the graph of Figure 3.3 does not represent a Markov process.

Using Kemeny and Snell's (1960) terminology, we shall give a few more precise definitions. First of all, let us denote the sequence of actual outcomes of a series of experiments by $f_1, f_2, \ldots, f_t, \ldots$ where f_t is the outcome at time t; let the set of possible outcomes of a given experiment be $\{s_1, s_2, \ldots\}$. Then the expression $f_t = s_i$ stands for the statement "the outcome of the tth experiment is s_i." Second, let us distinguish between a Markov "process" and a Markov "chain."

Definition. A *Markov process* is stochastic process the transition probabilities of which depend at most on the immediately preceding outcome,[3] that is,

$$P(f_t = s_j \,|\, f_{t-1} = s_i, f_{t-2} = s_r, \ldots) = P(f_t = s_j \,|\, f_{t-1} = s_i) = p_{ij}^{(t)}$$

[3] When the transition probabilities do not depend even on the immediately preceding trial, the rows of P become identical and the Markov chains degenerate into the so-called independent trials process. See, for example, Kemeny et al. (1957), pp. 146–50.

where $P(f_t = s_j \,|\, f_{t-1} = s_i, f_{t-2} = s_r, \ldots)$ is the (conditional) probability that the outcome at time t is s_j if at time $t - 1$ the outcome was s_i, at time $t - 2$ it was s_r, and so on.

Definition. A *finite Markov chain* is a finite Markov process the transition probabilities of which do not depend on t.

Note that the difference between a Markov process and a Markov chain is that in a Markov chain the probabilities p_{ij} remain constant, $p_{ij}^{(t)} = p_{ij}$, while in a Markov process they may vary with time. Furthermore, it should be added that the term "stationary Markov process" is sometimes used instead of our "Markov chain."

It will be convenient for our purposes to restate the above definition as two separate assumptions. The reader should be able to see that the following two assumptions are implied by our discussion of the Markov chains:

Assumption 1. The corresponding row and column labels of the transition matrix P are identical, $s_i = s_j$ for all $i = j$. For example,

$$
\begin{array}{cc}
 & \text{1964 vote} \\
 & \text{Democrat} \quad \text{Republican} \\
\begin{array}{cc} \text{1960} & \text{Democrat} \\ \text{vote} & \text{Other} \end{array} &
\begin{bmatrix} p_{11} & p_{12} \\ p_{21} & p_{22} \end{bmatrix}
\end{array}
$$

does not represent a Markov chains process because the corresponding labels are not all identical: The second row is labeled "Other," the second column, "Republican."

Assumption 2. All transition probabilities $p_{ij}^{(t)}$ remain constant for all t (and hence the superscript t may be omitted). For example,

$$
\begin{array}{cc}
\text{1964 vote} & \text{1968 vote} \\
\begin{array}{c} \quad\; D \quad\;\; R \\ \begin{array}{c} \text{1960} \\ \text{vote} \end{array} \begin{array}{c} D \\ R \end{array} \begin{bmatrix} .75 & .25 \\ .10 & .90 \end{bmatrix} \end{array} &
\begin{array}{c} \quad\; D \quad\;\; R \\ \begin{array}{c} \text{1964} \\ \text{vote} \end{array} \begin{array}{c} D \\ R \end{array} \begin{bmatrix} .80 & .20 \\ .10 & .90 \end{bmatrix} \end{array}
\end{array}
$$

do not represent a Markov chains process, because $p_{11}^{(t)} = .75$ for the transition from 1960 to 1964, but $p_{11}^{(t)} = .80$ for the transition from 1964 to 1968.

The two assumptions on which the Markov chains process is based are deceptively simple. The reader might profit from a study of other "stochastic" (probability) processes to realize that these assumptions are by no means the only ones which can profitably be made.[4] A scientist may wonder how often one is empirically justified in assuming that the transition probabilities do not change with time; that is, he may question the second of the two assumptions. But even the first assumption, plausible as it may seem, is fairly strong. For example, behavioral scientists sometimes believe that one can distinguish as many or as few categories with respect to a given set of data as one wishes: that it makes no difference whether one distinguishes between "Democrats" and "Others" (two categories), or between "Democrats," "Republicans," and "Others" (three categories). Unfortunately, such an attitude is not always possible with respect to Markov chains: It can be shown that "collapsing" two categories into one may change substantially the nature of the process.[5] Hence the scientist who wishes to apply the Markov chains model to his data might wish to have each row in his matrix P correspond to a "real" category, as in this case "Democrat."

Terminology

It is customary in connection with Markov chains to use a somewhat different terminology from that used up to this point. The reader should familiarize himself thoroughly with this new terminology; it is surprising how many students are handicapped in their study of Markov chains by the simple fact that they have not learned the appropriate language.

The difficulty centers around the often-heard question: What is the probability that the process will be in a given state s_k at time t? Similarly, one often hears that "the process moves from state s_i to state s_j in one step." But the difficulty disappears when one realizes that the assertion "the process is in state s_k" has exactly the same meaning as "the outcome of the experiment is s_k"—where s_k is simply one of the possible outcomes from the set $\{s_1, s_2, \ldots, s_k, \ldots\}$.

[4] See, for example, *ibid.*, Chapter 4.
[5] For an example of the conditions under which several states may be lumped together, see Sec. 6.2, "Transition Matrix."

Hence the question "what is the probability that the process will be in a given state s_k at time t?" means the same as "what is the probability that the outcome of the experiment performed at time t is s_k?"

This identity of meaning should help the reader to master the new terminology. In our discussion, we shall be referring from now on to "states" rather than "outcomes." Notice, however, that we use three different indices when speaking of states:

1. Index i. To emphasize the transition from time t to time $t + 1$, the state *from* which the process moves is designated s_i.
2. Index j. In the same case, when the transition is emphasized, the state *into* which the process moves is designated s_j.
3. Index k. In discussing states without reference to the transition from t to $t + 1$—in other words merely the states at time t—that state is designated s_k.[6]

The conventions governing the indexing of states apply also to the indexing of probabilities. When one wishes to refer to the probability that the process *moves* from a certain state to another (possibly the same) state in one step, one designates this probability as p_{ij}, the already discussed transition probability. When one wishes to refer to the probability that the process *is* in a certain state at time t, one designates this probability as $p_k^{(t)}$. Note that while $p_k^{(t)}$ has the superscript t, p_{ij} does not: This is not necessary in dealing with Markov chains, since by Assumption 2 the transition probabilities remain constant. Thus, to simplify notation, the superscript t in p_{ij} is customarily omitted.

Fundamental Equation

It is possible to capture much of our discussion of Markov chains in one fundamental equation, fundamental in the sense that the theorems to be discussed in the next chapter are based upon it. This equation follows from Assumptions 1 and 2 and may be written as follows:

$$(3.2) \qquad\qquad p^{(t+1)} = p^{(t)}P$$

---

[6] We shall not always adhere to this notation in subsequent chapters. However, the distinctions on which this indexing is based will always have to be kept in mind.

where $p^{(t)}$ is the probability row vector with m components $p_k^{(t)}$, $p^{(t+1)}$ is the probability row vector with m components $p_k^{(t+1)}$, and P is an $m \times m$ transition matrix.

Example 1. Suppose we know that Jim voted Republican in 1960. Then the question is, what is the probability that he will vote Democratic in 1964, if the matrix of transition probabilities P is, as in (3.1),

$$P = \begin{array}{c} \\ D \\ R \end{array} \begin{array}{c} D \quad\quad R \\ \begin{bmatrix} .75 & .25 \\ .10 & .90 \end{bmatrix} \end{array}$$

To make it possible to apply eq. 3.2, we have to know the probability vector for 1960, $p^{(t)}$. But from the way the problem is phrased we know that Jim voted Republican in 1960—which means that the probability of his voting Republican in 1960 is 1. Hence we know that

$$p^{(1960)} = p^{(t)} = (0, \quad 1)$$

And we can apply eq. 3.2:

$$p^{(1964)} = p^{(t+1)} = (0, \quad 1) \begin{bmatrix} .75 & .25 \\ .10 & .90 \end{bmatrix} = (.10, .90)$$

Thus the answer to our question as to the probability that Jim will vote Democratic in 1964 is .10. But, by applying eq. 3.2, we receive also the answer to a question we did not ask, but might have: What is the probability that Jim will vote Republican in 1964? The answer is .90.

Example 2. Suppose we do not know for certain how Jim voted in the 1960 election, that we know only the probability of his voting in a certain way. Suppose we know that the probability that he voted Democratic in 1960 is .80, the probability that he voted Republican is .20, i.e., that

$$p^{(t)} = (.80, .20)$$

Suppose, furthermore, that the same transition matrix applies as did in Example 1. Then, using eq. 3.2 we write

$$p^{(t+1)} = (.80, .20) \begin{bmatrix} .75 & .25 \\ .10 & .90 \end{bmatrix} = (.62, .38)$$

In this case the probability that Jim will vote Democratic in 1964 is only .62, the probability of his voting Republican is .38.

Two Ways of Viewing Markov Chains

It is important that the reader acquire an intuitive understanding of the Markov chains processes. We already suggested that he might usefully interpret a voting process, represented by eq. 3.1, as involving a large number of voters who, at time t, vote either Republican or Democratic. The matrix P of eq. 3.1 represents random forces struggling to defeat as well as to reinforce each voter's political preferences: the various mass media, his friends, his own personality. The net result of these forces is that about 25% of the Democrats leave their party to vote Republican, while only about 10% of the Republicans become Democrats.

Given this interpretation, it is perhaps clear that the probability vector $p^{(t)}$ can be viewed primarily as representing the *proportion* of voters who vote Democratic or Republican. Mathematically, however, $p^{(t)}$ specifies the *probability* that an individual voter chooses one or the other political party. This view needs interpretation also, and the best interpretation is through the process of simulation.

Imagine a researcher who has at his disposal a *random device*[7] that can be adjusted to select a given outcome (such as "votes Democratic") with any probability he may wish to assign to it. The researcher now can use this device and the probabilities of eq. 3.1 to simulate the voting behavior of an individual voter. Specifically, he can simulate the situation of Example 2, where $p^{(t)} = (.80, .20)$. He does this by adjusting his device so that it chooses D with probability of .80 and R with probability .20, and then operates the device.[8] If the device selects "Democratic," the simulated voter is assumed to have chosen the Democratic candidate in the 1960 election; if it selects "Republican," the simulated voter is assumed to have voted Republican.

Now the researcher has a simulated voter whose 1960 vote is known. For the sake of simplicity, let us assume that the simulated vote for 1960 was Democratic. Then the individual's vote in the

[7] For an example of such a device, see Fig. 9.1.

[8] If he uses a device such as given in Fig. 9.1, he spins the pointer and observes where it stops.

1964 election can be simulated by adjusting the random device to the probabilities given in the *first row* of matrix (eq. 3.1)—first row because, by definition, this row specifies the transition probabilities of those who were Democrats at time t. Using these probabilities, (.75, .25), the random device selects an outcome for the 1964 elections, again either "Democratic" or "Republican." And again, depending on which outcome was chosen by the random device for the previous election, the first or the second row of eq. 3.1 is "fed" into it. In this fashion a specific vote is identified for every election.

Thus, in conjunction with a random device, the transition matrix of a Markov chains process can be used to simulate the behavior of an individual voter. Will the simulated sequence of votes be identical with that of any one actual voter? If by that question is meant whether, using the above procedure, one can predict how a specific individual will vote, the answer is no: It is very unlikely that the simulated sequence of votes will match the sequence characteristic of an actual voter. However, if we consider a large number of actual voters and a large number of simulated voters, then the proportion of those who vote Democratic in a given election will be about the same, whether we compute it from actual votes or from simulated votes. Let us hasten to explain, however, that this will be the case only if the transition matrix such as eq. 7.1 is a faithful representation of the voting process.[9]

[9] For some of the problems that arise when one wishes to determine whether a model is a faithful representation of the actual group process, see Sec. 7.4.

EXERCISES

1. Consider the following voting process:

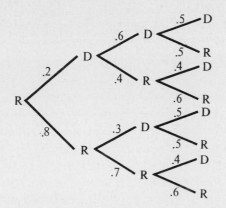

Determine whether this process is: (a) stochastic; (b) a Markov process (*Ans.*: Yes); (c) a Markov chain. Explain your answers.

2. Suppose that a Markov chain is represented by the matrix

$$P = \begin{bmatrix} .1 & .9 \\ .6 & .4 \end{bmatrix}$$

Represent this chain by a tree of logical possibilities, starting in state 1, and lasting for three steps.

3. Using the matrix of exercise 2, what is the probability that the process will be in state 2 at time $t = 3$ if, at time $t = 0$, (a) the process was in state 1? (b) the probability of being in state 1 was .4?

4. Suppose that a Markov process is given for three transitions:

$$P^{(1)} = \begin{bmatrix} .3 & .7 \\ .7 & .3 \end{bmatrix} \qquad P^{(2)} = \begin{bmatrix} .1 & .9 \\ .6 & .4 \end{bmatrix} \qquad P^{(3)} = \begin{bmatrix} .5 & .5 \\ .8 & .2 \end{bmatrix}$$

Represent this process by a tree of logical possibilities, assuming that it starts in state 1 and lasts until $t = 3$. Is this process a Markov chain?

5. Assuming that the process of exercise 4 starts in state 1, what is the probability that it will be in state 2 at time $t = 3$?

CHAPTER 4

Markov Chains: Some Important Theorems

Several important implications, actually theorems, follow from the definition of the Markov chains. These theorems are important to a behavioral scientist who wishes to use the Markov chains as a model for studying a social process, for these theorems can be viewed as specific predictions which can be tested empirically. These theorems provide answers to the following questions:

1. What is the probability that the process will be in a given state after n steps?
2. Can the process ever be in equilibrium?
3. Is the process approaching equilibrium?

Of these questions, the last two are perhaps of greatest interest to behavioral theory, for the concept of equilibrium plays an important part in most behavioral sciences.[1] Question 1 is of primary importance to the scientist who wishes to establish whether he is justified in using Markov chains as a model, although answers to all three questions can be used for that purpose.

---

[1] For some additional questions, see, for example, Kemeny et al. (1957), pp. 322–24 and p. 327.

4.1   PROBABILITY AFTER n STEPS

Suppose that we know the probability vector $p^{(t)}$ at a given time t, and that we know the transition matrix P as well; what is the probability vector after n additional steps, at time $t + n$?

Theorem 1.   The probability vector $p^{(t+n)}$ is given by

(4.1) $$p^{(t+n)} = p^{(t)}P^n$$

In other words, the probability vector at time $t + n$, $p^{(t+n)}$, is given by the product between $p^{(t)}$ and the nth power of the transition matrix P.

We shall not prove Theorem 1; instead, the reader can easily see that eq. 4.1 follows from eq. 3.2 in any specific case. For example, let $n = 2$. We can compute $p^{(t+2)}$ by repeated application of eq. 3.2; first, we apply eq. 3.2 to $p^{(t)}$ and thus obtain $p^{(t+1)}$:

(i) $$p^{(t+1)} = p^{(t)}P$$

However, eq. 3.2 implies that for any $p^{(t)}$ we can obtain $p^{(t+1)}$ by multiplying with P. Hence we can obtain $p^{(t+2)}$ from $p^{(t+1)}$ by multiplying $p^{(t+1)}$ by P:

(ii) $$p^{(t+2)} = p^{(t+1)}P$$

Now we substitute $p^{(t+1)}$ from (i) into (ii):

(iii) $$p^{(t+2)} = (p^{(t)}P)P = p^{(t)}P^2$$

And we see that the result, eq. iii, is in agreement with eq. 4.1, although we need eq. 3.2 to obtain iii. Hence, in this special case, the result due to eq. 4.1 is identical with the result obtained through the repeated application of eq. 3.2. Theorem 1 asserts that this will be true in all cases, for all n.

Example 2.   Find the probability that Jim, who voted Democratic in the 1960 election, will vote Democratic after six presidential elections, i.e., in 1984, if the transition matrix, as given in Example 3 of Chapter 3, is

$$P = \begin{bmatrix} .75 & .25 \\ .10 & .90 \end{bmatrix}$$

To solve this problem, we note first that Jim voted Democratic in 1960, which means that

$$p^{(t)} = (1, 0)$$

Since we are interested in the probability after six steps (elections), it follows from eq. 4.1 that

$$p^{(t+6)} = p^{(t)}P^6$$

We determine P^6 by repeated multiplication, i.e., $P^6 = PPPPPP$,

$$P^6 = \begin{bmatrix} .34 & .66 \\ .26 & .74 \end{bmatrix}$$

Hence

$$p^{(t+6)} = (1, 0)\begin{bmatrix} .34 & .66 \\ .26 & .74 \end{bmatrix} = (.34, .66)$$

In other words, the probability that Jim will vote Democratic in the 1984 election is .34.

4.2   EXISTENCE OF AN EQUILIBRIUM

The concept of an *equilibrium* plays an important role both in mathematics and in the various behavioral sciences. It is therefore of some interest to offer a definition that will satisfy both the mathematician's quest for precision and the behavioral scientist's desire to have the concept defined so that it is useful to him.

As a good starting point, let us observe that basic to the concept of an equilibrium is the notion of "no change" : a process is said to be in equilibrium at time t if it remains, in some way, the same at time t and thereafter. When we speak about Markov chains, the "sameness" is defined with respect to the probabilities of remaining in a given state : A Markov chain is in equilibrium, or, alternately, is a *stationary process*, if the probability of being in a given state k, $p_k^{(t)}$, remains constant, that is, if

$$(4.2) \qquad p_k^{(t+n)} = p_k^{(t)} \qquad \text{for all } k, n = 1, 2, 3, \ldots$$

Several comments are in order. First of all, the reader may be accustomed to the phrase "a process is in *a state* of equilibrium" instead of ours "a process is in equilibrium." We use the simpler terminology because in the theory of Markov chains the terms "state" has a very distinct meaning; to use the term in a dual sense would be confusing. Second, it should be noted that it is customary to ask not only whether a state of equilibrium exists, as we shall do in this section, but also whether or not it is stable, that is, whether the process always tends to reach it. We shall deal with this question in the next section.

Finally, a few words about terminology. We shall speak about the so-called *fixed probability vector p**, to refer to a probability vector $p^{(t)}$ that is stationary in the sense of eq. 4.2. Clearly, p^* is nothing else than a label given to a vector $p^{(t)}$ that satisfies eq. 4.2. When we say that a process (a Markov chain) approaches equilibrium, we mean that the probability vector $p^{(t)}$ that obeys the basic equation $p^{(t+1)} = p^{(t)}P^t$ approaches p^* so that the difference between every $p_k^{(t)}$ and the corresponding p_k^* grows progressively smaller. Later on, we shall even say that "a voter's behavior approaches equilibrium." By that we shall mean that the probability of his voting in a certain way, $p_k^{(t)}$, (which is, in our discussion, identical with the probability of his being in a certain state k) approaches p_k^*. Finally, we shall often say that "a process starts at $p^{(0)}$"; by that we shall mean that the probability of being in state k at time $t = 0$ is $p_k^{(0)}$.

Given this terminology, let us proceed to investigate whether we can determine the nature of the equilibrium if we know the transition matrix P. Specifically, can we determine the fixed probability vector p^* from the knowledge of P alone? We note that any vector $p^{(t)}$ must satisfy eq. 3.2, i.e., that

$$p^{(t+1)} = p^{(t)}P$$

and that p^* must, in addition, also satisfy eq. 4.2. It is not difficult to see that we can therefore write that

$$(4.3) \qquad p^* = p^*P$$

i.e., that the process will be in equilibrium if and only if p^* is a vector such that the transformation of p^* through P "sends p^* into itself," such that multiplying p^* by P yields again the very same vector p^*.

So far we have defined a process in equilibrium (eq. 4.2) and specified the conditions such a process must satisfy (eq. 4.3). However, we have not shown that a given process can satisfy these conditions, i.e., we have not as yet shown that vector p^* exists. In order to state the important existence theorem, it is necessary first to define the so-called regular Markov chains.

Definition. A transition matrix P is said to be *regular* if at least one power of P has only positive components.

To understand the reason behind this definition, recall that the product $p^{(t)}P^n$ yields a probability vector the components of which, $p_k^{(t+n)}$, represent the probability of being in state k after n steps. No matter what the components of $p^{(t)}$ are, of course, the vector $p^{(t+n)}$ must have only nonzero components if P^n has only nonzero components, i.e., if P is a regular matrix. But the fact that $p^{(t+n)}$ has only nonzero components means that every one of the states k can be reached by the process at time $t + n$. Thus the above definition of regular chains enables us to distinguish an important class of Markov chains processes—those that "move freely" from state to state. Such processes are quite different from the so-called absorbing chains—those processes which can be "captured" by a state in the sense that once the process reaches a certain state, it cannot leave it. The absorbing Markov chains will be discussed in Chapter 7.

In some instances it is quite clear whether matrix P is regular, for example,

$$P = \begin{bmatrix} .75 & .25 \\ .10 & .90 \end{bmatrix}$$

This matrix is obviously regular, since it contains no 0 components. On the other hand,

$$P = \begin{bmatrix} \frac{3}{4} & \frac{1}{4} \\ 1 & 0 \end{bmatrix}$$

may seem not to be regular, since it does contain 0. However, the above definition refers to any power of P—and therefore we consider P^2:

$$P^2 = \begin{bmatrix} \frac{13}{16} & \frac{3}{16} \\ \frac{3}{4} & \frac{1}{4} \end{bmatrix}$$

Since the second power of P is without zeros, we conclude that this matrix is also regular.

Theorem 2. If P is a regular transition matrix, then there exists one and only one fixed probability vector p^* as given by eq. 4.3.[2]

Notice that Theorem 2 applies only to regular matrices. The consideration of what happens when the matrix is not regular is beyond the scope of the present discussion.[3]

Example 2. Under what conditions is the voting process of Example 3 of Chapter 3 in equilibrium? In other words, under what conditions does the probability that Jim will vote Democratic remain the same in all subsequent elections?

Since we are referring to the voting process of Example 3, we are dealing with the transition matrix

(4.4) $$P = \begin{bmatrix} .75 & .25 \\ .10 & .90 \end{bmatrix}$$

And the problem is that of finding the fixed probability vector p^*, i.e., a vector p^* which satisfies eq. 4.3

$$p^* = p^*P$$

We note first that the matrix P is a *regular* matrix, since it contains no zeros. Therefore Theorem 2 applies and we know that one and only one p^* exists, and we proceed to find it. We can write eq. 4.3 as

$$(p_1^*, p_2^*) = (p_1^*, p_2^*)\begin{bmatrix} .75 & .25 \\ .10 & .90 \end{bmatrix}$$

which becomes

$$(p_1^*, p_2^*) = (.75p_1^* + .10p_2^*, .25p_1^* + .90p_2^*)$$

---

[2] For a proof, see Kemeny et al. (1957), p. 221.
[3] Chapter 7 discusses what happens when the matrix represents an absorbing chain.

It will be recalled that the expression $A = B$, where A and B are $n \times m$ matrices, can always be written as a set of $n \times m$ equations of the form $a_{ij} = b_{ij}$. Thus we write our result as

(i) $$p_1{}^* = .75p_1{}^* + .10p_2{}^*$$

(ii) $$p_2{}^* = .25p_1{}^* + .90p_2{}^*$$

Remembering that all probability vectors, by definition, must add up to 1, we add a third equation

(iii) $$p_1{}^* + p_2{}^* = 1$$

This system of three equations with two unknowns can be solved by using either (i) and (iii), or (ii) and (iii). Using (i) and (iii) we write

$$p_1{}^* = .75p_1{}^* + .10(1 - p_1{}^*)$$

and the solution is

$$p_1{}^* = \tfrac{10}{35} \approx .29$$

$$p^* = \tfrac{25}{35} \approx .71$$

This solution can be verified by substituting it into eq. 4.3: If the solution is correct, it must hold that

$$(\tfrac{10}{35}, \tfrac{25}{35}) = (\tfrac{10}{35}, \tfrac{25}{35}) \begin{bmatrix} .75 & .25 \\ .10 & .90 \end{bmatrix}$$

Performing the computations indicated on the right-hand side of the equation, we find that the identity does indeed hold. Hence $(\tfrac{10}{35}, \tfrac{25}{35})$ is the fixed-point probability vector for the given transition matrix P.

How do we interpret the stationary vector p^*? As indicated earlier, any probability vector $p^{(t+n)}$ can be given dual interpretation. Viewed as describing group behavior, this vector specifies the proportion of voters who vote in a given way (D or R) after n elections. The stationary vector p^* has an added significance: It is that vector which remains unchanged from election to election. Our example, then, can be interpreted as follows: If all voters were subject to the same random forces as given by the transition matrix of eq. 4.4, then the percentage of Democrats would remain unchanged from election to election if, and only if, this percentage were approximately 29%.

The second interpretation deals with individuals. Applied to our voter, Jim, $p_D{}^*$ describes the unchanging probabilities of his voting Democratic. In other words, given eq. 4.4, the specific combination of random forces impinging upon Jim, the probability that he will vote Democratic will remain constant only if it is about .29. Let us repeat, however, that this does not mean that Jim does not change his vote from election to election; indeed, even if his probability of voting Democratic is, in fact, .29, *he will vote Republican in about 71% of elections!* Thus it is only the probability that remains constant, not his vote.

4.3 APPROACHING AN EQUILIBRIUM

We have just demonstrated that a regular Markov chains process has one and only one equilibrium p^* but we have not shown as yet that all Markov chains reach p^*. As the reader familiar with other types of processes knows, it is perfectly possible for an equilibrium to exist even though a given process may never reach it, or may even fail to approach it.[4] In view of this fact, it is rather surprising that the following theorem holds for all regular Markov chains:

Theorem 3. If P is a regular transition matrix, and p^* is the fixed probability vector as defined by eq. 4.3, then for any $p^{(t)}, p^{(t+n)}$ approaches p^* as n grows large.[5]

The surprising thing about Theorem 3 is that it holds for "any $p^{(t)}$." This means that a given regular Markov chain always approaches the equilibrium p^* no matter where the chain starts. Notice that:

1. As a result of Theorems 2 and 3 we do not need to know $p^{(t)}$ to determine what equilibrium a given regular Markov chain is approaching; we need only to know P.
2. Unless the process starts in equilibrium, i.e., unless $p^{(t)} = p^*$, the regular Markov chain will never "quite reach" equilibrium.[6]

---

[4] When a model is fairly complex, more than one state of equilibrium may exist. For an example, see Kemeny and Snell (1962), Chapter 3.

[5] For a proof, see Kemeny et al. (1957), p. 22.

[6] If $p^{(0)} \neq p^*$, then $p^{(t)} \neq p^*$ for any finite t. See Figure 4.1.

Example 3.   Suppose that the same transition matrix applies to all of Jim's voting behavior and that this matrix P is the same as in eq. 4.4, i.e.,

$$P = \begin{bmatrix} .75 & .25 \\ .10 & .90 \end{bmatrix}$$

Show how Jim's voting behavior approaches an equilibrium on subsequent elections, if it is known that in 1960 Jim voted Democratic.

Since P is a regular matrix, we know by Theorem 3 that Jim's voting behavior will approach a fixed probability vector p^*. We have already found that for the matrix of eq. 4.4 equilibrium is given by

$$p^* = (\tfrac{10}{35}, \tfrac{25}{35})$$

and hence we know that the above vector will be approached by the process. To show, however, how Jim's behavior approaches this equilibrium, we shall use Theorem 1 to compute $p^{(t+n)}$ for several n, for $n = 0, 1, 2, 3, 4, 5, 6$.

First we note that because Jim voted Democratic in 1960, $p^{(t)}$ in this case is

$$p^{(1960)} = p^{(t)} = (1, 0)$$

Since we are considering only two-party votes, it is sufficient for our purposes to consider only one voting preference, say the Democratic preference. Hence the following table gives only the probability $p_D^{(t)}$ that Jim will vote Democratic in the various Presidential elections. These probabilities have been obtained by means of eq. 4.1.

n	$p_D^{(t)}$
0	1.00
1	.75
2	.59
3	.48
4	.41
5	.37
6	.34
.	.
.	.
.	.
∞	.29

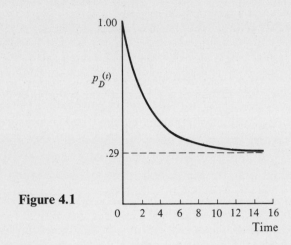

Figure 4.1

It may be useful to present the above results graphically, as shown in Figure 4.1. The graph shows the manner in which the probability $p_D^{(t)}$ approaches the fixed probability vector p^*: $p_D^{(t)}$ comes closer to p^* as time increases, but $p_D^{(t)} = p^*$ only after an infinite number of steps—in other words, for any finite number of steps, $p_D^{(t)} \neq p^*$.

EXERCISES

1. Consider a Markov chain defined by

$$P = \begin{bmatrix} .9 & .1 \\ .7 & .3 \end{bmatrix}$$

Assuming that the process starts in state 2, construct a graph analogous to Figure 4.1. Show the probability that the process will be in state 2 at time $t = 0, 1, 2, 3. \ldots$. What is p_2^*?

2. Suppose that in a given town the voting process is represented by the following matrix:

$$P = \begin{matrix} & \begin{matrix} D & R \end{matrix} \\ \begin{matrix} D \\ R \end{matrix} & \begin{bmatrix} .5 & .5 \\ 0 & 1 \end{bmatrix} \end{matrix}$$

Suppose, furthermore, that at time $t = 0$ there are 128 Republicans and 128 Democrats in that town. How many Republicans will there be at time $t = 1, 2, 3, 4, 5$? Can you guess what the ultimate number of Republicans will be if the total number of voters remains constant and P continues to apply? Is this process a regular Markov chain? (*Ans.*: No; it is an "absorbing" Markov chain).

3. Imagine that the voting process, of a very unlikely kind, is given by the following matrix:

$$P = \begin{array}{c} \\ D \\ R \end{array} \overset{\displaystyle D \quad R}{\begin{bmatrix} 0 & 1 \\ 1 & 0 \end{bmatrix}}$$

Suppose again that at time $t = 0$ there are 128 Republicans in this town and 128 Democrats. How many Republicans will there be in that town at time $t = 1, 2, 3, \ldots$? Do you see anything noteworthy about the difference between this process as it applies to the entire town and as it applies to individual voter? Is this process regular? (*Ans.*: No; it is a "cyclical" process.)

5. Now imagine that the voting process in a town is represented by the following matrix:

$$P = \begin{array}{c} \\ D \\ R \end{array} \overset{\displaystyle D \quad R}{\begin{bmatrix} .7 & .3 \\ .6 & .4 \end{bmatrix}}$$

Imagine, furthermore, that there are 90 Democrats and 90 Republicans at time $t = 0$. What will be the ultimate number of Republicans in that town (if the total number of voters remains constant)? Is this process regular?

PART TWO

MARKOV CHAINS MODELS

We turn now to the application of the theory of Markov chains to various group processes: social stratification, group conflict, and social mobility. It is our hope that, in discussing these various models, we shall be able to accomplish more than simply to acquaint the reader with these individual models; we hope also to touch upon some of the principles underlying the enterprise of model construction as well as upon some problems that remain unsolved.

For example, one of the problems which will have to be resolved before the theory of Markov chains can be applied is that of the relationship between the model and the data against which it is to be tested: Should this data be used both for estimating the transition probabilities p_{ij} and for testing the model? If one decides to use the data in this dual capacity, what procedures should one follow? Chapters 5 and 6, dealing with social stratification, illustrate some of the problems confronting the model builder who does not wish to use empirical data to define the p_{ij}'s of his model. Chapter 7 touches upon the problems typically encountered by the researcher who does want to use his data for both purposes: the problems of parameter estimation and of deriving implications that can be tested on the same set of data.

The last chapter of Part II, Chapter 8, considers still another question: What should one do if the model fails to fit the data? Should it be abandoned? Modified? We hope to shed some light on these questions by discussing some of the recent attempts at overcoming the shortcomings of regular Markov chains when applied to social mobility.

CHAPTER 5

Social Stratification: Structure

As any sociologist trained in sociometry is well aware, matrices can be used to describe various social structures such as those arising from the relationship of "liking." We shall apply matrix algebra to a relationship less commonly described by matrices, the relationship of "dominance." Not only shall we define quite precisely what is meant when we say that one person dominates another, but we shall lay foundations from which a great variety of results can be obtained. Matrix algebra will be used to define such crucial terms as "authority" and "concentration of authority," as well as to make distinctions parallel to those between, for example, the family "as a group" and the family "as an institution." There will be many implications which we shall not explore because they are not needed for our specific purpose, but which may be of considerable interest to some readers. For example, it is possible to use our concepts to define "power" and to derive some rather surprising theorems about indirect dominance.[1] Our discussion, then, can be viewed as a point of departure for a number of specific interests.

[1] See, for example, Kemeny et al. (1957), Chapter 7.

5.1 DOMINANCE RELATIONSHIP

As is well known, social stratification systems develop only if men tend to react to each other as if some were "better" than others. Fortunately for students of social stratification, this tendency is so wide-spread that most, perhaps all, known societies can be said to possess a stratification system. But it is equally well known that the value which serves as the main basis of the system differs from society to society, ranging from position in the kinship structure in some societies to possession of wealth in others.

Of particular interest to us will be stratification based on the fact that some individuals "dominate" others. Typically, when we say that "k dominates r" we shall refer to situations in which r does what k wants him to, in which k *influences* r. But the definition we shall actually be working with is more general and entirely formal. Formally, then, a *dominance relationship* is a relationship which is

1. antireflexive (a man cannot dominate himself),
2. nontransitive (it is possible that A may dominate B, B may dominate C and, at the same time, C may dominate A), and
3. antisymmetric (a man cannot dominate another man and be dominated by him in turn).

Of these three characteristics the third is perhaps the most important, since it distinguishes the relationship of dominance from another important social relationship—liking. While it is perfectly possible for two persons to have mutual liking for each other, it is by definition impossible to have mutual dominance. Furthermore, the reader perhaps will agree that antisymmetry is essential to the usual concepts of dominance. For example, an officer usually has the right to issue an order to an enlisted man but the enlisted man is not allowed to order him back.

5.2 DOMINANCE STRUCTURE

To arrive at the concept of a dominance structure, it is necessary to make some assumptions concerning the distribution of dominance relationships throughout a society. We shall assume that in the groups to be considered *a dominance relationship exists within every possible pair of members*, that is, that each member either dominates or is dominated by every other individual member. While this assumption is customarily made in the literature,[2] the reader may object to it as being utterly unrealistic, particularly in large societies. In a society with even a few thousand members, interaction between every two members is physically impossible; how then can one assume that a dominance relationship exists within every pair?

This objection is quite valid and it is undoubtedly true that a more realistic assumption would allow for pairs within which no dominance relationship exists. However, the resulting dominance process would be complicated and therefore unsuited for this introductory discussion. Furthermore, the present models can be applied to groups in which this assumption is justified: to preliterate tribes in which everybody knows everybody else, to groups of friends, to voluntary associations in a modern society such as political parties, and so on.

Another point should be clarified. Notice that by assuming that a member either dominates another or is dominated by him, we seem to be excluding the relationship of *equality*, a relationship which is clearly as important as dominance. But a moment's reflection reveals that we are doing nothing of the kind, that our conception of dominance actually helps us to define the relationship of equality. Equality can be viewed, first of all, as a "statistical" fact, as existing between two members if, over a period of time, each dominates the other about half of the time. Or, secondly, equality can be viewed as a matter involving the members' "authority," two individuals being equal if both dominate the same number of others.[3]

With these preliminary remarks out of the way, let us proceed to apply the assumption that dominance relationships exist between each and every pair of members. This assumption determines uniquely the number of distinct social structures that are possible in a society of a given size. To make this point clear, we shall consider in some detail the case of the smallest relevant group, the group with three members.

[2] See Rapport (1949a, 1949b, 1950).
[3] The second alternative will be adopted here. See the discussion of "authority index" in this chapter in Sec. 5.3.

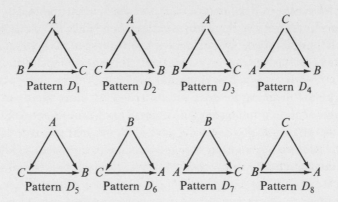

Figure 5.1. Distinct dominance patterns that are possible in a three-man group.

Let us use the following convention to represent the dominance relationships in a group. If member A dominates member B, we shall draw an arrow from A to B, $A \rightarrow B$. In a group with three members, A, B, and C, the eight graphs shown in Figure 5.1 can then be drawn, each graph corresponding to a distinct combination of dominance relationships.

The reader may question the somewhat unorthodox way in which the eight graphs are drawn. The labels A, B, and C are not attached to the same corners of the triangle; their positions change from graph to graph. But there is a reason behind this unorthodoxy, as becomes obvious when one observes the arrows rather than the labels. When the labels are ignored, the first two graphs become identical; similarly, the third through eighth graphs are identical. Thus the graphs in Figure 5.1 are drawn so as to emphasize an important distinction between a dominance "pattern" and a dominance "structure." We shall say that the distinct graphs that are possible in a group of size n when labeling is taken into account represent the dominance patterns, the distinct graphs that are possible when labeling is ignored represent the dominance structures. Thus in a three-man group there are only two distinct dominance structures, as shown in Figure 5.2.

Several points should be noted about these graphs:

1. The corners of the two triangles in Figure 5.2 are labeled 1, 2, 3, while the corners in the eight triangles in Figure 5.1 are labeled *A, B, C*. These distinctions in labeling correspond to the sociological distinction between an individual and his status: labels *A, B, C* refer to three specific individuals, labels 1, 2, 3 to three status positions. For example, in structure S_2 label 1 corresponds to the highest position (dominating two others), label 2 corresponds to the second-ranking position, label 3 to the lowest-ranking position.

2. There are eight distinct graphs involving individuals (Figure 5.1), but only two distinct graphs involving social positions (Figure 5.2). We shall, therefore, distinguish between dominance *patterns* (involving specific individuals *A, B, C*, ...) and dominance *structures* (involving "abstract" status positions 1, 2, 3, ...).

3. The labeling of the dominance structures is often arbitrary. For example, in structure S_1 of Figure 5.2 any one of the three corner points could be labeled "1." On the other hand, labeling of dominance patterns is not arbitrary, but is determined by the identity of the individuals who occupy the given status positions.

The reader may note that the above distinctions may serve to clarify distinctions often made in sociology, such as the distinction between the family "as a group" (pattern) and the family "as an institution" (structure).

The symbols of graph theory (labels and arrows) have considerable intuitive appeal since they represent the stratification system rather directly. But graph theory tends to lose this advantage when applied to larger groups. The graphs tend to become a complicated web of arrows with little intuitive appeal. Matrix algebra, although lacking the simple directness of a graph theory, can handle adequately

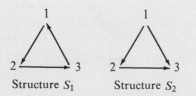

Structure S_1 Structure S_2

Figure 5.2. Distinct dominance structures that are possible in a three-man group.

$$\begin{array}{c}\begin{array}{ccc}A & B & C\end{array}\\\begin{array}{c}A\\B\\C\end{array}\begin{bmatrix}0 & 1 & 0\\0 & 0 & 1\\1 & 0 & 0\end{bmatrix}\end{array}\qquad\begin{array}{c}\begin{array}{ccc}A & B & C\end{array}\\\begin{array}{c}A\\B\\C\end{array}\begin{bmatrix}0 & 0 & 1\\1 & 0 & 0\\0 & 1 & 0\end{bmatrix}\end{array}\qquad\begin{array}{c}\begin{array}{ccc}A & B & C\end{array}\\\begin{array}{c}A\\B\\C\end{array}\begin{bmatrix}0 & 1 & 1\\0 & 0 & 1\\0 & 0 & 0\end{bmatrix}\end{array}\qquad\begin{array}{c}\begin{array}{ccc}A & B & C\end{array}\\\begin{array}{c}A\\B\\C\end{array}\begin{bmatrix}0 & 1 & 0\\0 & 0 & 0\\1 & 1 & 0\end{bmatrix}\end{array}$$

Pattern D_1 Pattern D_2 Pattern D_3 Pattern D_4

$$\begin{array}{c}\begin{array}{ccc}A & B & C\end{array}\\\begin{array}{c}A\\B\\C\end{array}\begin{bmatrix}0 & 1 & 1\\0 & 0 & 0\\0 & 1 & 0\end{bmatrix}\end{array}\qquad\begin{array}{c}\begin{array}{ccc}A & B & C\end{array}\\\begin{array}{c}A\\B\\C\end{array}\begin{bmatrix}0 & 0 & 0\\1 & 0 & 1\\1 & 0 & 0\end{bmatrix}\end{array}\qquad\begin{array}{c}\begin{array}{ccc}A & B & C\end{array}\\\begin{array}{c}A\\B\\C\end{array}\begin{bmatrix}0 & 0 & 1\\1 & 0 & 1\\0 & 0 & 0\end{bmatrix}\end{array}\qquad\begin{array}{c}\begin{array}{ccc}A & B & C\end{array}\\\begin{array}{c}A\\B\\C\end{array}\begin{bmatrix}0 & 0 & 0\\1 & 0 & 0\\1 & 1 & 0\end{bmatrix}\end{array}$$

Pattern D_5 Pattern D_6 Pattern D_7 Pattern D_8

Figure 5.3. Distinct dominance patterns that are possible in a three-man group.

even very large groups and, even more important, can be programmed easily on high-speed computers. Thus we shall "translate"
Figures 5.1 and 5.2 into the language of matrix algebra. Starting
with the eight dominance patterns of Figure 5.1, we obtain the
matrices of Figure 5.3. Figure 5.2, displaying two dominance
structures, is transformed into the two matrices illustrated in Figure
5.4.

Comparison of the matrices of Figures 5.3 and 5.4 with the arrows
of Figures 5.1 and 5.2 suggests the basic principle whereby matrix
algebra can be used to represent a dominance matrix: Whenever

$$\begin{array}{c}\begin{array}{ccc}1 & 2 & 3\end{array}\\\begin{array}{c}1\\2\\3\end{array}\begin{bmatrix}0 & 1 & 0\\0 & 0 & 1\\1 & 0 & 0\end{bmatrix}\end{array}\qquad\begin{array}{c}\begin{array}{ccc}1 & 2 & 3\end{array}\\\begin{array}{c}1\\2\\3\end{array}\begin{bmatrix}0 & 1 & 1\\0 & 0 & 1\\0 & 0 & 0\end{bmatrix}\end{array}$$

Structure S_1 Structure S_2

Figure 5.4. Distinct dominance structures that are possible in a three-man group.

individual k dominates individual r, we insert 1 in the kth row and rth column of the matrix; otherwise we insert 0.

What is gained by the matrix representation of the dominance patterns or structures? As already mentioned, by converting the empirically observable structures into matrices with numbers, we can arrive at a rapid and reliable decision with respect to a number of questions—by inspecting the matrices visually if they are small, by having a high speed computer do the inspection if they are large. It will be noted that all matrices in Figures 5.3 and 5.4 have (1a) a square shape; (2a) zeroes on the main diagonal; and (3a) "complementary" components (if the component in row k and column r is 1, then the entry in column k and row r is 0, and vice versa). It can be shown that these three conditions must be satisfied by any dominance matrix, i.e., any matrix which describes dominance relationships that (1b) exist between each pair of members and (2b) are defined as antireflexive, nontransitive, and antisymmetric.[4] As a result, it is always possible to prove that a given matrix is a dominance matrix by showing that it satisfied the easily demonstrable properties 1a–3a rather than the original (and rather difficult to demonstrate) properties 1b and 2b.

However, the advantages of matrix representation go even further. It is easy to determine by means of matrix algebra whether two societies have the same dominance structure, for if they do,

[4] It is not difficult to see that when only zeros are permitted on the main diagonal, then a member is not allowed to dominate himself; when the components must be "complementary," then mutual dominance is ruled out and a dominance relationship must exist within each pair of members. Furthermore, the fact that we do not require transitivity is reflected in the fact that we allow for groups having less than complete concentration of authority (see Sec. 5.3). Were we to define dominance as a transitive relationship (i.e., so that A dominating B and B dominating C implies that A dominates C), then only one dominance structure would be possible:

$$\begin{bmatrix} 0 & 1 & 1 & 1 & \cdots & 1 \\ 0 & 0 & 1 & 1 & \cdots & 1 \\ 0 & 0 & 0 & 1 & \cdots & 1 \\ 0 & 0 & 0 & 0 & \cdots & 1 \\ & & & \cdot & & \\ & & & \cdot & & \\ & & & \cdot & & \\ 0 & 0 & 0 & 0 & \cdots & 0 \end{bmatrix}$$

then it must be possible to obtain the dominance matrix characteristic of the first society by interchanging the rows and columns of the dominance matrix characteristic of the second society.[5] Without matrix representation, to make such distinctions is tedious for small groups, practically impossible for large societies.

5.3   CONCENTRATION OF AUTHORITY

While the concept of a dominance relationship is used to characterize the relationship between pairs of individuals, a related concept, variously labeled as "power" or "authority," is often used to characterize the relationship between one individual and the whole group. Following Homans' terminology,[6] we shall apply the term "authority

[5] To illustrate what is meant by "interchanging" the rows and columns, consider pattern D_1 of Figure 5.3:

$$\text{(i)} \qquad \begin{array}{c} \\ A \\ B \\ C \end{array} \begin{array}{ccc} A & B & C \\ \left[\begin{array}{ccc} 0 & 1 & 0 \\ 0 & 0 & 1 \\ 1 & 0 & 0 \end{array}\right] \end{array}$$

Now suppose that we wish to interchange the first and the second rows and columns, we proceed as follows. First, we relabel the rows and columns to correspond to the desired interchange:

$$\text{(ii)} \qquad \begin{array}{c} \\ B \\ A \\ C \end{array} \begin{array}{ccc} B & A & C \\ \left[\begin{array}{ccc} 0 & 1 & 0 \\ 0 & 0 & 1 \\ 1 & 0 & 0 \end{array}\right] \end{array}$$

Second, we change the components in (ii) so that each component in (ii) has the same labels as it had in (i):

$$\text{(iii)} \qquad \begin{array}{c} \\ B \\ A \\ C \end{array} \begin{array}{ccc} B & A & C \\ \left[\begin{array}{ccc} 0 & 0 & 1 \\ 1 & 0 & 0 \\ 0 & 1 & 0 \end{array}\right] \end{array}$$

Third, we note that (iii) is identical, except for the labels, with pattern D_2 of Figure 5.3. Since D_2 thus has been shown to be obtainable from D_1 by interchanging rows and columns, we conclude that D_1 and D_2 represent the same dominance structure.

[6] Homans (1961) says, "Let us define *authority* as follows: The larger the number of other members a single member is regularly able to influence, the higher is his authority in the group" (p. 286).

index" to the number of other persons dominated by one individual, reserving the term "power" for a more complicated relationship between an individual and his group.[7] Given the conventions accepted in the construction of dominance matrices, it is clear that a given member's authority index is determined by summing the row assigned to him in the dominance matrix. For example, consider the following four-man group:

$$D = \begin{array}{c} \\ A \\ B \\ C \\ D \end{array} \begin{array}{cccc} A & B & C & D \\ \begin{bmatrix} 0 & 1 & 0 & 1 \\ 0 & 0 & 1 & 0 \\ 1 & 0 & 0 & 1 \\ 0 & 1 & 0 & 0 \end{bmatrix} \end{array}$$

In this group, member A's authority index is 2, B's index is 1, C's is 2 and D's is 1. Thus it is possible to define for any $n \times n$ dominance matrix an *authority vector* V and a column vector with n components v_k, each v_k representing the authority index of a member k. Thus for the above four-man group the authority vector is

$$V = \begin{bmatrix} 2 \\ 1 \\ 2 \\ 1 \end{bmatrix}$$

One question of interest to the student of social stratification is the degree to which a system is "authoritarian," that is, the extent to which authority is concentrated in the hands of a very few individuals. Even more important is often the question concerning what conditions lead to such a concentration of authority, a point which we shall examine in Chapter 6. At this point we shall merely define an index which characterizes this concentration, the so-called hierarchy index.

First, however, note that our assumption that a dominance relationship exists between each pair of individuals puts a definite

[7] Power has been defined, for example, as the number of others a person can influence directly or through intermediaries. See Kemeny et al. (1957), p. 311.

limit on the maximum and minimum concentration of authority which can exist in a group of a given size. For example, the maximum and minimum concentration of authority in a six-man group is given by the following two authority structures:

$$V_1 = \begin{bmatrix} 5 \\ 4 \\ 3 \\ 2 \\ 1 \\ 0 \end{bmatrix} \qquad V_2 = \begin{bmatrix} 3 \\ 3 \\ 3 \\ 2 \\ 2 \\ 2 \end{bmatrix}$$

Notice that in the most authoritarian group (V_1) the top individual dominates five others; that in the most egalitarian group (V_2) each individual dominates either three or two others; and that an absolute equality in a six-man group is impossible.

We shall follow Landau (1951) in defining an index that describes a degree of concentration of authority. It is possible to think of such concentration as deviation from equality. The greater the number of members who are unequal and the larger their inequality, the greater is the concentration of authority in their group. It can be shown that in a group having n members (n being an odd number) complete equality prevails if each member dominates $(n - 1)/2$ others. The degree to which a member k deviates from this equalitarian ideal may be conveniently[8] measured by the expression

$$\left(v_k - \frac{n - 1}{2} \right)^2$$

where v_k is the actual number of others dominated by member k—his authority index. The extent to which the entire society deviates from the ideal of equality may be measured by summing the above expression for all individual members k. It can be shown that when a group in fact has as high a concentration of authority as possible,

[8] This expression is convenient in determining the probability that a certain concentration of authority will occur in a group. See Sec. 6.2, "Probability That Authority Is Concentrated."

this sum is

$$\sum_{k=1}^{n} \left(v_k - \frac{n-1}{2}\right)^2 = \frac{n(n^2-1)}{12}$$

Thus, if we wish our measure to be equal to 1 when the maximum concentration prevails, which again is a useful requirement, we should divide the left-hand side of the above equation by the right. The resulting measure is Landau's *hierarchy index h*:

$$(5.1) \qquad h = \frac{12}{n(n^2-1)} \sum_{k=1}^{n} \left(v_k - \frac{n-1}{2}\right)^2$$

where n is the size of the group, v_k is the kth component of the authority structure vector V (i.e., v_k is the number of others dominated by the kth individual). Notice that this index has the property of varying between 0 and 1, $h = 1$ characterizing societies with a maximum concentration of authority and $h = 0$ characterizing societies with an absolute equality of authority. As indicated above, however, in some groups equality is not possible and hence sometimes the most egalitarian group has a hierarchy index above 0. For example, in a six-man group the maximum possible equality, as given by V_2, is

$$h_2 - \frac{12}{6 \times 35}\left[\left(3 - \frac{5}{2}\right)^2 + \left(3 - \frac{5}{2}\right)^2 + \left(3 - \frac{5}{2}\right)^2\right.$$

$$\left. + \left(2 - \frac{5}{2}\right)^2 + \left(2 - \frac{5}{2}\right)^2 + \left(2 - \frac{5}{2}\right)^2\right] = \frac{3}{35}$$

The hierarchy index, because of its relative simplicity, will be an important tool in determining the impact of various social processes on the social stratification of a society. In particular, while it is often difficult to determine exactly what dominance structure is likely to arise, it is usually relatively simple to determine the expected value of the hierarchy index, and thus the "usual" degree of concentration of authority.

For the student interested in measuring the concentration of authority in a group, it should be added that Landau's index h is by no means the only measure possible, nor is it always the best. For example, it is possible to use the information theory to define an index that relates concentration of authority to the "amount of uncertainty" in the group. Starting from the basic assumption that a system which allows for a choice among a number of alternatives is in the state of greatest uncertainty when each alternative is equally likely to be chosen, Coleman (1960) defines a measure of the uncertainty for a dominance structure H such that

$$H = -\sum_k p_k \ln p_k$$

where p_k is the proportion of others that are dominated by member k and $\ln p_k$ is the natural logarithm of p_k. Index H may be used as a measure of concentration of authority because it varies with it: The greater the concentration, the smaller the degree of uncertainty in the structure and hence the smaller the value of H. Perhaps it should be added that high concentration of authority indeed corresponds to low uncertainty. When authority is concentrated, then the probability that a member k will dominate another member is *not* the same for all members k.

Some readers may feel that H is a better measure of concentration than h because it is less ad hoc. H is based on the information theory, a theory which has been applied with success to a number of highly diverse fields, while h has no such basis. Other measures may be offered on similar grounds. For example, it is possible to define measure g as

$$g = \frac{\prod_{k=1}^{n} v_k}{\left(\prod_{k=1}^{n} v_k/n\right)^n}$$

where v_k is the number of others dominated by member k, $\prod_{k=1}^{n} v_k$ is the product $v_1 v_2 \cdots v_k \cdots v_n$. Some statisticians might prefer g to the hierarchy index h on the grounds that g is often found to be more sensitive to differences between individual v_k than is h.[9]

In spite of the availability of other, possibly superior, measures of concentration of authority, we shall use Landau's hierarchy index h. The reason for our choice is simple. As we shall show in the next chapter, Landau has used h to arrive at some interesting

[9] We are indebted for this point to Professor Gleser of John Hopkins University.

conclusions about the conditions under which a society is likely
to have a high concentration of authority.

1. The authority vectors that are possible in a four-man group (which
satisfies the assumptions of Chapter 5) and the corresponding number of
distinct dominance structures and patterns are as follows:

Number of Corresponding

Vectors	Dominance Structures	Dominance Patterns
(3, 2, 1, 0)	1	24
(2, 2, 2, 0)	2	8
(2, 2, 1, 1)	4	24
(3, 1, 1, 1)	2	8
Total	9	64

What is the largest and the lowest hierarchy index possible in a four-man
group?

2. Represent graphically the eight dominance patterns that are possible
in a group with the authority vector (3, 1, 1, 1).

3. Represent graphically and in matrix form the two dominance structures
that correspond to the dominance vector (3, 1, 1, 1).

4. Choose either one of the two dominance structures of exercise 3. Show
that it is possible to obtain the four dominance pattern matrices associated
with that structure by interchanging the rows and columns of the dominance
structure matrix.

CHAPTER 6

Social Stratification:
Process

The structural-functional school, perhaps the most prominent school of sociological thought today, explains the existence of social stratification by emphasizing its beneficial aspects. For example, Davis and Moore (1945) argue that social stratification is necessary because the most essential and the most demanding jobs attract personnel with the needed qualifications only if high rewards are attached to such jobs. Granting the plausibility of this argument—which not all sociologists are willing to do—we are still faced with the fact that this explanation is not complete, for it explains only why stratification systems tend to be maintained, not why they tend to emerge. In order to use the functional argument to explain the origin of social stratification one would have to assume that men have always known the benefits of stratification, even before it actually existed in their society, even before they had any experience with it. Few sociologists are willing to make this assumption today; most would probably maintain that social stratification develops accidentally, in a trial-and-error fashion. Only after it has come into being do men experience the alleged benefits associated with it, and social stratification is then supported by additional social mechanisms.

Implicit in this concept is the assumption that the trial-and-error process leads to concentration of authority in a sufficiently large number of cases to make the benefits of such concentration obvious to all. Is this assumption justified? Does a random process really lead to a concentration of authority? We shall attempt to answer these questions by considering a Markov chains process that arises when we make some reasonably realistic assumptions about dominance encounters between men. In our discussion we shall be guided by the pioneering work of Rapoport (1949a, 1949b, 1950) and Landau (1951a, 1951b, 1953).

6.1 ASSUMPTIONS

"Nothing succeeds like success" is a popular version of a proposition which appears to be firmly rooted in contemporary psychological theory. Stated in more technical language, this proposition asserts that winning in a struggle for power has a "halo effect," that a person who wins once will be expected to win again and therefore in fact often does. The social-psychological theory of expectation and the learning theory both support this proposition. According to the expectation theory, the person who succeeds tends to expect success; the one who fails tends to expect failure.[1] And, a person's actual performance tends to be influenced by his expectations, so that he who expects success usually succeeds, he who expects failure usually fails.

The expectation theory alone would be sufficient to account for the halo effect of success. But to the extent to which the winners surround themselves with visible signs of success, with status symbols, this tendency will be even more pronounced, for now the man who has failed often has not only his own failure to take into account but also the obvious success of his "opponent." As the learning theory suggests, stimulus generalization is likely to occur and the man will see his opponent as similar to those who have defeated him in the past, and will lower even further his own level of expectation.

Probability of Dominance

Let us translate some of these considerations into mathematical language. To say that men surround themselves with status symbols

[1] See, for example, Thibault and Kelley (1959) pp. 82–83.

is to say, in effect, that the authority of a person, that is, the number of others dominated by him, is made plain for all to see. Thus we can consider the "halo effect" to be dependent on the actual authority of member k: The higher his authority index v_k, the more likely he is to emerge victorious from future struggles. But of course this probability of victory has to depend not only on his own authority, but also on the authority of his opponent; if the authority of his opponent is higher than his own, then he is likely to lose the fight. Thus it seems reasonable to postulate that the probability of winning depends on the *difference* between the authority indices of the two combatants. The higher is person k's authority relative to person r's authority, the more likely is k to win over r:

$$P_{kr} = f\,(v_k - v_r)$$

where P_{kr} is the probability that k wins a specific encounter ("fight") with r, f is a function that causes P_{kr} to grow when $v_k - v_r$ grows.

Just what kind of a function should f be? At this point we have no a priori grounds for postulating any one of a number of possible functions; thus we shall choose one of the simplest alternatives, a linear function: P_{kr} will be assumed to be linear with the difference $v_k - v_r$.

We know that P_{kr} is a probability measure; thus its values will have to remain between 0 and 1. Furthermore, it is reasonable to require that an encounter between individuals of equal authority will end in a draw, that is, that both have the same chance of victory. The function which can satisfy all these requirements is

(6.1) $$P_{kr} = \tfrac{1}{2}[1 + w(v_k - v_r)]$$

It is perhaps clear that eq. 6.1 states the following assumption about the outcome of a dominance encounter:

Assumption 1.   The probability that k dominates r (after k and r meet in a dominance encounter) is linear with the difference between k's and r's authorities: the higher is k's authority than r's before the encounter, the more likely it is that k dominates r immediately after the encounter.

Note that function of eq. 6.1 indeed satisfies our requirements. To start with, it is easy to see that when $v_k - v_r = 0$, then $P_{kr} = \tfrac{1}{2}$.

In other words, when the two individuals have equal authority, each is equally likely to be victorious. In order that we satisfy the requirement that P_{kr} remain between 0 and 1, we have to set the limits to the coefficient w as follows:

$$(6.2) \qquad\qquad 0 \leq w \leq \frac{1}{n-1}$$

When $w = 0$ the probability $P_{kr} = \frac{1}{2}$. But what happens when $w = 1/(n-1)$? It is obvious that in a group with n members, an individual can dominate at most $n-1$ others; thus the highest possible authority index is $n-1$. And the lowest number of others an individual can dominate is zero. Thus the largest difference $v_k - v_r$ that can occur in a group with n members is $v_k - v_r = n-1$. If coefficient w remains within the limits of eq. 6.2, it follows that the absolute value of $w(v_k - v_r)$ can be at most 1.

Of course $v_k - v_r$ can be either positive or negative. When k is the top man, the difference is positive; when r is the top man, the difference is negative. Hence, given eq. 6.2, $w(v_k - v_r)$ can be at most $+1$ or -1. If it is $+1$, $P_{kr} = 1$; if it is -1, $P_{kr} = 0$. Thus we have shown that eqs. 6.1 and 6.2 guarantee that P_{kr} will remain between 0 and 1.

Finally, it is easy to prove that eq. 6.1 specifies a linear relationship: Any equation that can be written as $Y = BX + A$ specifies a linear relationship between X and Y—and we can write eq. 6.1 as $P_{kr} = \frac{1}{2}w(v_k - v_r) + \frac{1}{2}$. Identifying P_{kr} as Y, $v_k - v_r$ as X, $\frac{1}{2}w$ as B and $\frac{1}{2}$ as A, we can write eq. 6.1 as $Y = BX + A$, thus showing it to describe a linear relationship.

For these reasons, eqs. 6.1 and 6.2 represent a reasonable translation into a mathematical theory of our verbal theories about dominance encounters. This translation, however, discloses one consideration that remained hidden in our verbal theorizing: The degree to which difference in authority predetermines the outcome of a "fight," w, may itself vary. In some cases this difference may be of considerable importance [when w is close to $1/(n-1)$], in others it may be of little importance (when w is close to 0). We can hypothesize, if we wish, that the impact of the difference in authority is in itself culturally determined: In some societies it is virtually impossible for the superior to be wrong; in others, the ideas of a superior receive almost as much criticism as do the ideas of a subordinate. We like to think of the United States as a country in which everybody is open to criticism (w is close to 0); on the other hand, Nazi Germany and prewar Japan could conceivably be viewed as representing the other extreme, since blind obedience of superiors was required.

One additional function of coefficient w should be mentioned. Consider the situation when k has a higher authority than r, and k and r get into a "fight." Equation 6.1 specifies that (unless $w = 0$) k is likely to win this fight, the larger is w, the more likely it is that k will win. Now the fact that k had a higher *authority* than r tells us nothing about the *dominance relationship* of the two before the fight, for even though k's authority is higher, it is possible that k was dominated by r before the encounter.[2] Now if in fact k was dominated by r before the fight, the very fact that the fight occurred makes it likely that k's authority will increase. Since k will probably win the encounter, it is likely that he will add a new name to the list of those he already dominates, thus increasing his authority index. Inversely, r is likely to lose the fight, and will therefore have to subtract one person from the list he dominates; hence his authority index will decrease.

Now suppose that before the fight k already dominates r. In this case, the encounter is not likely to change the situation, k still will dominate r; consequently, the relative authority of the two men will probably remain unchanged. It is clear, therefore, that w plays the following important role: The larger is w, the more likely it is that the authority differences will be maintained. For this reason, we shall call w the *bias against equalization of authority*.

Probability of Encounter

So far we have considered the dominance relationship which emerges between k and r if the two men happen to meet. We shall now propose several assumptions specifying the conditions under which k and r actually do meet. We shall again idealize reality. The main distortion will be the assumption that two encounters cannot occur simultaneously—for example, that in a four-man group it is

---

[2] In other words, it is possible for k to dominate more individuals than does r (k has higher authority) and yet for k to be dominated by r.

impossible for an encounter between A and B to take place at the same time that an encounter between C and D takes place. This is a distortion, although not as serious a one as it may seem at first. Suppose that we look at the ongoing interaction in the following way: We observe all the encounters that start at the beginning of the interval we refer to as "time $t = 1$." As soon as any one encounter terminates (when a dominance relationship has been established) we rule that the period $t = 1$ has terminated. As soon as the next encounter terminates, we rule that the interval $t = 2$ has terminated, and so on. Through this procedure we assume merely that two encounters do not terminate at the same time—a much less offensive assumption. These considerations are expressed in the following formal assumption:

Assumption 2. Exactly one dominance encounter occurs between time t and $t + 1$ (for all $t = 1, 2, \ldots$).

The second assumption we wish to make at this time is:

Assumption 3. All possible encounters are equally likely to occur, i.e.,

$$(6.3) \qquad e_{kr} = \frac{1}{N}$$

where e_{kr} is the *probability of encounter* at time t between members k and r, N is the number of possible pairs in a group with n members, i.e.,

$$N = \frac{n(n - 1)}{2}$$

Are we justified in making Assumption 3? We do not know. While in very large societies this assumption is patently false, in smaller groups it may be fairly plausible. To be sure, there is a considerable amount of evidence suggesting that "sociable" interaction tends to occur primarily among social equals, but we are not considering such interaction alone. As Homans (1961) states, "... a man's social behavior displays two tendencies: a tendency to interact with, and respect, persons who are in some sense 'better' than himself and a tendency to interact with, and like, persons in some sense similar to himself."[3] This being the case, it may be that Assumption 3 is the best possible first approximation to reality.

[3] Homans (1961), p. 334.

6.2   THE PROCESS

We shall now show that the above assumptions concerning the probability of dominance, P_{kr}, and the probability of encounter, e_{kr}, are sufficient to determine a Markov chains process. Let us warn the reader, however. To say that the above assumptions are sufficient is not to say that the job of defining the Markov chains process is an easy one. As will become obvious in a moment, the procedure is lengthy and laborious. But it is essential that the reader follow it step by step, since failure to do so will seriously hamper his understanding of the resulting process.

Transition Matrix

The first important point concerns the *states* of the Markov chains process. Contrary to what the reader may expect, the states of the process will not be individual members, but rather entire groups or, more precisely, the specific dominance patterns that are possible in a group of size n. For example, in a three-man group the resulting Markov chains process will have eight states since there are eight distinct dominance patterns in a three-man group (see Figure 5.1). The corresponding *transition probabilities* p_{ij} will thus be the probabilities that a group which has (at time t) the dominance pattern i will change into a group which has (at time $t + 1$) the dominance pattern j.

To illustrate how the individual components of the matrix p_{ij} are found, consider probability p_{32}—the probability that a group having dominance pattern D_3 changes (as a result of an encounter at time $t + 1$) into a group with dominance pattern D_2. The numbering of the dominance patterns having been given in Figure 5.3, our job now is to determine the probability of the following transformation:

$$D_3 = \begin{array}{c} \\ A \\ B \\ C \end{array}\begin{array}{ccc} A & B & C \\ \left[\begin{array}{ccc} 0 & 1 & 1 \\ 0 & 0 & 1 \\ 0 & 0 & 0 \end{array}\right] \end{array} \rightarrow D_2 = \begin{array}{c} \\ A \\ B \\ C \end{array}\begin{array}{ccc} A & B & C \\ \left[\begin{array}{ccc} 0 & 0 & 1 \\ 1 & 0 & 0 \\ 0 & 1 & 0 \end{array}\right] \end{array}$$

We note first that this transformation presupposes that two dominance relationships be reversed: the relationships between A and B
and between B and C. But clearly two dominance relationships
can be reversed only if two dominance encounters occur at time
$t + 1$—and this is forbidden by Assumption 2. Hence this transformation is impossible and

$$p_{32} = 0$$

Note that the same considerations apply to one-half of the 64
possible transformations; that is, one-half of the possible transformations involve at least two encounters and hence are not permitted
by Assumption 2. Hence one-half of the components p_{ij} will be zero.

Let us turn our attention to the transformations that are not
eliminated by Assumption 2. Of particular interest is the transformation which sends a dominance pattern into itself, that is, which
keeps the pattern unchanged. Consider, for example, the probability
of the transformation of D_3 into D_3—the probability of

$$D_3 = \begin{bmatrix} 0 & 1 & 1 \\ 0 & 0 & 1 \\ 0 & 0 & 0 \end{bmatrix} \rightarrow D_3 = \begin{bmatrix} 0 & 1 & 1 \\ 0 & 0 & 1 \\ 0 & 0 & 0 \end{bmatrix}$$

Notice that this transformation is not "screened out" by Assumption
2, because it does not presuppose that more than one encounter
has taken place. However, there is nothing about this transformation
to indicate which encounter actually took place; any one of the
three could have occurred. Hence the probability of the above
transformation is the probability that A met B and A won over B,
or that A met C and A won over C, or that B met C and B won
over C. What is the probability that A met B? According to eq. 6.3
this probability is

$$e_{AB} = \frac{1}{N} = \frac{2}{n(n-1)} = \frac{2}{3 \times 2} = \frac{1}{3}$$

What is the probability that A won over B? We know that the
probability that A won over B *if A and B met* is given by eq. 6.1;
implicit in our discussion is the notion that, if A and B did not meet,

the probability of A winning over B is 0 (A obviously could not win a fight that did not occur). Thus the conditional probability[4] that A won over B is

$$
P_{AB} = \begin{cases} \frac{1}{2}[1 + w(v_A - v_B)] = \frac{1}{2}[1 + w(2 - 1)] = \frac{1}{2}(1 + w) \\ \qquad\qquad\qquad\qquad\qquad\qquad\quad \text{if } A \text{ and } B \text{ met} \\ 0 \qquad\qquad\qquad\qquad\qquad\qquad\quad \text{if } A \text{ and } B \text{ did not meet} \end{cases}
$$

Since the knowledge that A and B met gives us no information whatsoever about who won the fight, the event "A and B met" and the event "A won over B" are said to be independent[5] of each other, and we can write the (unconditional) probability that A won over B as

$$
P(A \text{ won over } B) = P_{AB}e_{AB} + 0(1 - e_{AB}) = P_{AB}e_{AB} =
$$

$$
= \tfrac{1}{3} \times \tfrac{1}{2}(1 + w) = \tfrac{1}{6}(1 + w)
$$

The reason for writing the above equation is perhaps clear. The fact that "winning" is independent of "meeting" means, by definition, that the probability that A and B met and A won over B is given by the product $P_{AB}e_{AB}$. And the (unconditional) probability that A won over B is the probability that A and B met and A won over B or that A and B did not meet ($1 - e_{AB}$ being this probability) and A won over B. Since $P_{AB} = 0$ when A and B did not meet, we obtain the above results.

In a similar fashion it is possible to compute the probability that A met C and A won over C

$$
e_{AC}P_{AC} = \tfrac{1}{3} \times \tfrac{1}{2}[1 + w(2 - 0)] = \tfrac{1}{6}(1 + 2w)
$$

[4] This probability is conditional because the occurrence of the "desired" event (A wins over B) is contingent upon the occurrence of another event (A and B meet). For a discussion of conditional probabilities, see, for example, Kemeny et al. (1957), pp. 129–31.

[5] Two events are said to be independent precisely when occurrence of one has no effect upon the probability that the second event will occur. The mathematical significance of having two such events, X and Y, is that the probability that X occurs and that Y occurs is the product $P_X P_Y$.

and the probability that B met C and B won over C

$$e_{BC}P_{BC} = \tfrac{1}{3} \times \tfrac{1}{2}[1 + w(1 - 0)] = \tfrac{1}{6}(1 + w)$$

But of course this still does not give us the transition probability p_{33}. As stated above, this probability is equivalent to the probability "A meets B and A wins over B, *or* A meets C and A wins over C, *or* B meets C and B wins over C." Since the three main events comprising the statement in the quotes (k meets r and k wins over r) are assumed to be mutually exclusive, the connective "or" corresponds to the operation of summation.[6] Hence p_{33} is given by

$$p_{33} = e_{AB}P_{AB} + e_{AC}P_{AC} + e_{AC}P_{BC}$$
$$= \tfrac{1}{6}[(1 + w) + (1 + 2w) + (1 + w)] = \tfrac{1}{6}(3 + 4w)$$

Our final illustration concerns the transition probability that is neither 0 nor one involving the transformation of a pattern into itself. Consider, for example, the transition probability p_{35}—the probability that the following transformation takes place:

$$D_3 = \begin{bmatrix} 0 & 1 & 1 \\ 0 & 0 & 1 \\ 0 & 0 & 0 \end{bmatrix} \rightarrow D_5 = \begin{bmatrix} 0 & 1 & 1 \\ 0 & 0 & 0 \\ 0 & 1 & 0 \end{bmatrix}$$

First we determine, by comparing D_3 and D_5, which encounter must have taken place. Clearly, since the relationship between B and C is reversed (B dominates C in D_3, C dominates B in D_5), the one encounter that occurred must have been between B and C. Hence the probability p_{35} is simply the probability that B and C met and that C won over B:

$$p_{35} = e_{BC}P_{CB} = \tfrac{1}{3} \times \tfrac{1}{2}[1 + w(0 - 1)] = \tfrac{1}{6}(1 - w)$$

It makes no difference, of course, whether we write e_{BC} or e_{CB}, the probability that B meets C being identical with the probability

---

[6] Two events are said to be mutually exclusive if they have no elements in common. Since, by definition, only one encounter can occur at a given time, the events "A meets B," "A meets C," and "B meets C" are mutually exclusive. And, if events X and Y are mutually exclusive, then $P(X$ or $Y) = P(X) + P(Y)$.

that C meets B. Furthermore, note that the probability of dominance, P_{CB}, depends on the authority B and C have *before* the transformation takes place. Hence the authority of B, v_B, is $v_B = 1$ and the authority of C is $v_C = 0$, both authority indices being computed from dominance pattern D_3.

Proceeding in the manner indicated by these examples, one can compute all 64 transition probabilities characteristic of a three-man group. The resulting matrix of transition probabilities P is shown in Table 6.1. It is possible, however, to represent the same

Table 6.1. Transition Probabilities among the Dominance Patterns

Dominance Patterns	010 001 100	001 100 010	011 001 000	010 000 110	011 000 010	000 101 100	001 101 000	000 100 110
010 001 100	$\frac{1}{2}$	0	$\frac{1}{6}$	$\frac{1}{6}$	0	$\frac{1}{6}$	0	0
001 100 010	0	$\frac{1}{2}$	0	0	$\frac{1}{6}$	0	$\frac{1}{6}$	$\frac{1}{6}$
011 001 000	$\frac{1-2w}{6}$	0	$\frac{3+4w}{6}$	0	$\frac{1-w}{6}$	0	$\frac{1-w}{6}$	0
010 000 110	$\frac{1-2w}{6}$	0	0	$\frac{3+4w}{6}$	$\frac{1-w}{6}$	0	0	$\frac{1-w}{6}$
011 000 010	0	$\frac{1-2w}{6}$	$\frac{1-w}{6}$	$\frac{1-w}{6}$	$\frac{3+4w}{6}$	0	0	0
000 101 100	$\frac{1-2w}{6}$	0	0	0	0	$\frac{3+4w}{6}$	$\frac{1-w}{6}$	$\frac{1-w}{6}$
001 101 000	0	$\frac{1-2w}{6}$	$\frac{1-w}{6}$	0	0	$\frac{1-w}{6}$	$\frac{3+4w}{6}$	0
000 100 110	0	$\frac{1-2w}{6}$	0	$\frac{1-w}{6}$	0	$\frac{1-w}{6}$	0	$\frac{3+4w}{6}$

matrix in a more compact form, as follows:

$$(6.4) \qquad P = \begin{bmatrix} \frac{1}{2} & 0 & \frac{1}{6} & \frac{1}{6} & 0 & \frac{1}{6} & 0 & 0 \\ 0 & \frac{1}{2} & 0 & 0 & \frac{1}{6} & 0 & \frac{1}{6} & \frac{1}{6} \\ a & 0 & b & 0 & c & 0 & c & 0 \\ a & 0 & 0 & b & c & 0 & 0 & c \\ 0. & a & c & c & b & 0 & 0 & 0 \\ a & 0 & 0 & 0 & 0 & b & c & c \\ 0 & a & c & 0 & 0 & c & b & 0 \\ 0 & a & 0 & c & 0 & c & 0 & b \end{bmatrix}$$

where $a = \frac{1}{6}(1 - 2w)$, $b = \frac{1}{6}(3 + 4w)$, and $c = \frac{1}{6}(1 - w)$. Notice that the matrix shown in eq. 6.4 is a true matrix of transition probabilities in the sense that each row sums up to one.

Equilibrium Vector

We could use matrix P to compute the equilibrium vector p^*. But this would be a lengthy procedure, and an unnecessary one, since we are really not interested in all eight dominance patterns, but only in the two dominance structures that are possible in a three-man group—structures S_1 and S_2:

$$S_1 = \begin{bmatrix} 0 & 1 & 0 \\ 0 & 0 & 1 \\ 1 & 0 & 0 \end{bmatrix} \qquad S_2 = \begin{bmatrix} 0 & 1 & 1 \\ 0 & 0 & 1 \\ 0 & 0 & 0 \end{bmatrix}$$

Fortunately we can transform the above 8×8 matrix P with dominance *patterns* for states into a 2×2 matrix with dominance *structures* for states. We recall (see Figures 5.1 and 5.2) that dominance structure S_1 can be obtained from either D_1 or D_2, while dominance structure S_2 can be obtained from any one of the patterns $D_3, \ldots, D_8$. It turns out that we can "lump" together states 1 and 2 into one state, states 3 to 8 into another, obtaining a 2×2 matrix P,

$$(6.5) \qquad P = \begin{bmatrix} \frac{1}{2} & \frac{1}{2} \\ a & b + 2c \end{bmatrix}$$

the states of which are the dominance structures S_1 and S_2.

Since we warned in Chapter 3 against "collapsing" matrices, let us consider a method whereby one can determine whether such collapsing is permissible. To see whether we can lump together states 1 and 2 on one hand, and states 3 through 8 on the other, we first write an 8 × 2 matrix obtained from (6.4) by lumping together only the columns:

$$
\begin{array}{c@{\quad}c}
\{1, 2\} & \{3, 4, 5, 6, 7, 8\} \\
\end{array}
$$

$$
\begin{array}{c}
1 \\ 2 \\ 3 \\ 4 \\ 5 \\ 6 \\ 7 \\ 8
\end{array}
\left[
\begin{array}{cc}
\frac{1}{2} & \frac{1}{2} \\
\frac{1}{2} & \frac{1}{2} \\
a & b + 2c \\
a & b + 2c \\
a & b + 2c \\
a & b + 2c \\
a & b + 2c \\
a & b + 2c
\end{array}
\right]
$$

We now observe that in this partially lumped matrix the rows corresponding to the lumped states are identical: the first and second rows are identical; rows 3 through 8 are identical. Not all transition matrices have this property, but in those which do the rows can be lumped together in the same partition as their columns, and thus we obtain the matrix of eq. 6.5. A theorem[7] states that the equilibrium vector p^* obtained from the lumped matrix is the same as the vector we would have obtained had we computed p^* (with eight components) from the original 8 × 8 matrix P of eq. 6.4 and then lumped the states to obtain a two-component vector p^*. Thus we proceed to compute p^* from eq. 6.5. Recalling that equilibrium vector p^* has to satisfy $p^* = p^*P$, we write

$$
(p_1{}^*, p_2{}^*) = (p_1{}^*, p_2{}^*)
\begin{bmatrix}
\frac{1}{2} & \frac{1}{2} \\
a & b + 2c
\end{bmatrix}
$$

[7] See Kemeny and Snell (1960).

Solving this equation we obtain

$$p^* = \left(\frac{2a}{1 + 2a}, \frac{1}{1 + 2a} \right)$$

Substituting $a = \frac{1}{6}(1 - 2w)$, we obtain

(6.6)
$$p^* = \left(\frac{1 - 2w}{4 - 2w}, \frac{3}{4 - 2w} \right)$$

Beginning of the Process

So far we have dealt with the problem of what happens to the process once it is on its way. But we have completely ignored its nature at the beginning. What kind of society are we assuming to exist at the very beginning of the process—a society with complete equality, or one with complete concentration of authority?

Two answers are possible. The first, although mathematically impeccable, will probably leave the reader somewhat dissatisfied: This answer is that it does not matter where the process starts. Recall our earlier statement (Chapter 4, Theorem 3) that the fixed probability vector p^* is independent of the point of origin, that the process inevitably approaches it, no matter where it starts. In terms of our three-man group example, therefore, it makes no difference whether the group was, to start with, completely equalitarian (dominance structure S_1) or completely authoritarian (dominance structure S_2); the process will approach p^* of eq. 6.6 in either case.

It is easy to see why this answer may leave some readers uneasy. To say that it does not matter what dominance structure exists at the very beginning of the process implies that some dominance structure must exist to start with. And it may seem logical that, if the dominance process ever had a beginning, this beginning must have been characterized by a total absence of dominance relationships. At the "beginning," some may argue, man was free from domination by others.

For our purposes, however, this argument is immaterial. We shall show that even if man did start from a condition of complete freedom, the fixed probability vector p^* still would characterize our societies, provided that the assumptions we have made concerning the dominance process are correct.

We have assumed earlier that a dominance relationship exists between each and every two members of a society. Let us now change this assumption, and assume instead that, at time $t = 0$, there were absolutely no dominance relationships within any group. But we will assume that dominance relationships are established between each two members who meet after time $t = 0$. As before (see eq. 6.3) we assume that the probability of dominance encounters between any two members k and r, e_{kr}, is the same for all possible pairs;

$$e_{kr} = \frac{1}{N}$$

where N is the number of possible pairs. Since we are not interested in the *kind* of dominance structure that is likely to arise, merely in the question as to whether a dominance relationship will ultimately emerge between every two members, we can assume that the probability of k dominating r when the two meet is any probability P_{kr}. If the reader wishes, he may assume that until dominance relationships are established between every two members, $P_{kr} = \frac{1}{2}$, that is, that k is just as likely to win as r.

Will a dominance relationship be established ultimately for every possible pair? It is convenient mathematically to consider a somewhat different question, which is, what is the probability that a given pair k and r do *not* meet after n encounters have taken place in a group? When there are N pairs in a group and each pair is equally likely to meet, the probability that a given pair does not meet on any one trial is $(N - 1)/N$. After n trials, the probability that k and r have not as yet met is $[(N - 1)/N]^n$. Now the number $(N - 1)/N$ is a number larger than zero but smaller than one; it can be shown that as such a number is raised to the nth power and as n increases, the power of the number approaches zero. In other words, as the number of encounters increases, the probability that k and r have not met as yet approaches zero. Since this is true for every pair k and r, it follows that, as time goes by, the probability that a pair remains without a dominance relationship also approaches zero. Hence, as time passes, the probability that the group will have *some* dominance structure approaches 1.

Of course we have not shown what kind of structure will emerge as a result of this "structure-creating" process. But this is not necessary; as already stated, no matter what structure this original process leads to, if bias against equalization of authority w begins to operate as soon as a structure is completed, then the transition matrix such as in eq. 6.4 applies and the process tends to reach the one and only equilibrium p^*.

The process just described, although in some ways a gross over-simplification, does make sense in certain respects. It seems reasonable to assume that the bias against equalization w is a cultural phenomenon, and as such starts operating only in well-established societies. Our tentative assumption that $P_{kr} = \frac{1}{2}$ until all dominance relations are established allows such an interpretation. However, let us repeat: We are not committed to the assumption that $P_{kr} = \frac{1}{2}$ until all dominance relations are established; any P_{kr} for the pre-structure process will do.

Probability That Authority Is Concentrated

By computing the equilibrium vector p^* we have answered some of the questions asked at the beginning of the chapter, at least for three-men groups. We argued that the functional explanation of social stratification is insufficient unless we can determine the likelihood that the "original" trial and error process itself leads to concentration of authority. Our point was that men can hardly be assumed to know the value of concentration of authority until they have had experience with it. We can now express the likelihood that concentration of authority occurs in a three-man group. Since concentration of authority is found only in groups having dominance structure S_2,

$$S_2 = \begin{bmatrix} 0 & 1 & 1 \\ 0 & 0 & 1 \\ 0 & 0 & 0 \end{bmatrix}$$

the probability that authority is concentrated in a three-man group corresponds to the probability that S_2 occurs. But it is obvious that the best estimate of this probability is p_2^*, the probability approached by all three-man groups that satisfy our assumptions. Hence the probability that authority is concentrated in a three-man group is

$$p_2^* = \frac{3}{4 - 2w}$$

Let us take a good look at this probability. First of all, it may be useful to realize that one interpretation of $p_2{}^*$ is that, if we were to investigate a random sample of all the three-man groups which obey our assumptions, the proportion of groups with dominance structure S_2 would be about $3/(4 - 2w)$. Second, let us note how $p_2{}^*$ depends on the bias w. If the bias is nonexistent, $w = 0$, then

$$p_2{}^* = \frac{3}{4}$$

If the bias is maximum $w = \frac{1}{2}$, then

$$p_2{}^* = 1$$

that is, concentration of authority is certain to occur. Hence we conclude that in a three-man group concentration of authority is the rule rather than the exception, and that men certainly can be assumed to have had sufficient opportunity to experience concentration of authority in such three-man groups.

But what about groups having more than three members? Is a concentration of authority the rule in those groups as well? The reader perhaps has had a sufficient taste of the labor involved in computing p^* even when $n = 3$ to recognize that the work required for larger groups may be prohibitive. Fortunately, it is relatively easy to compute a quantity that is related to p^*, the so-called expected hierarchy index $E(h)$. It will be recalled (see eq. 5.1) that the hierarchy index for structure S is defined as

$$h_s = \frac{12}{n(n^2 - 1)} \sum_{k=1}^{n} \left(v_k - \frac{n - 1}{2} \right)^2$$

where n is the number of members in the group and v_k the authority index of the kth member. For the three-man group, the hierarchy index h_1 associated with S_1 can be shown to be 0 (i.e., complete equality prevails in S_1), while the index h_2 associated with S_2 can be shown to be 1 (i.e., maximum concentration of power prevails). We can write the two hierarchy indices connected with the two structures, h_1 and h_2, as a column vector h':

$$h' = \begin{bmatrix} h_1 \\ h_2 \end{bmatrix} = \begin{bmatrix} 0 \\ 1 \end{bmatrix}$$

Now, following the standard definition of an "expected value,"[8] we can define the *expected hierarchy index at equilibrium, E(h)*, as

(6.7) $$E(h) = p^*h'$$

where p^* is the equilibrium (row) vector. Applying eq. 6.7 to the three-man group, we obtain

$$E(h) = \left(\frac{1 - 2w}{4 - 2w}, \frac{3}{4 - 2w} \right) \begin{bmatrix} 0 \\ 1 \end{bmatrix} = \frac{3}{4 - 2w}$$

What is the meaning of $E(h)$? While p^* can be interpreted as the proportion of groups having dominance structure S, $E(h)$ can be interpreted as the average (mean) hierarchy index one would obtain from a random sample of all groups of size n. In other words, if one took a random sample of all groups of size n and computed the hierarchy index h for each group in the sample, the mean h for the whole sample would be close to $E(h)$.

In a three-man group, $E(h_2)$ and p_2^* are identical, but this is just a coincidence, due to the fact that in a three-man group only two distinct dominance structures are possible and the two corresponding hierarchy indices are 0 and 1. In groups larger than $n = 3$ the index $E(h)$ has quite clearly the properties of a summary measure— one which does not correspond to any p_k^*. Landau (1951b) shows that the expected hierarchy index for a group of any size n (provided that the group satisfies our assumptions) is

(6.8) $$E(h) = \frac{3}{(n + 1)[1 - \frac{1}{2}w(n - 2)]}$$

Since the proof of eq. 6.8 is somewhat involved, we shall not give it here. Instead, let us gain some intuitive understanding of this result, again by considering the extreme values of w. If no bias exists ($w = 0$), then eq. 6.8 simplifies to

(6.9) $$E(h) = \frac{3}{n + 1}$$

---

[8] Kemeny et al. (1957) give the following definition: "If in an experiment the possible outcomes are numbers, $a_1, a_2, \ldots, a_k$, occurring with probability $p_1, p_2, \ldots, p_k$, then the *expected* value is defined to be $E = a_1p_1 + a_2p_2 + \cdots + a_kp_k$" (p. 166). Using this definition and the definition of the "inner product" of two vectors, the definition of eq. 6.7 follows.

If the bias is as large as possible, i.e., if $w = 1/(n - 1)$ (see eq. 6.2), then

$$E(h) = \frac{3}{(n + 1)[1 - (n - 2)/2(n - 1)]}$$

It can be seen that when $n = 3$, the expected hierarchy index for the maximum bias ($w = \frac{1}{2}$) is $E(h) = 1$ while for a large group, say $n = 1,000$, we obtain for the maximum bias ($w = 1/999$):

$$E(h) = \frac{3}{1001(1 - 499/999)} = .006$$

Stated simply, even if the bias is maximum, the expected hierarchy index in large groups is close to 0; that is, large groups are likely to be equalitarian. In fact, the expected hierarchy index for the maximum bias in large groups is approximately

(6.10) $$E(h) \approx \frac{6}{n}$$

6.3   DISCUSSION

When we began our discussion of the social stratification process we posed the following question: If social stratification results from a purely random process, does inequality arise often enough for a man to learn the benefits of stratification? We posed this problem because some proponents of the functional theory of social stratification maintain that inequality is found in all societies because inequality is functional, because it provides the necessary motivation to man the important jobs.

Closer examination reveals that this problem consists of two distinct subproblems. The first is whether a random (trial-and-error) process, free from sanctions that preserve inequality, *leads* to inequality in enough cases to give man an opportunity to learn its benefits. The second problem is whether, once he learns about these benefits, man can introduce sanctions that will *preserve* inequality in his society.

Emergence of Inequality

In this chapter, we have considered a dominance process in which a bias w was operating against equalization. Such a bias is a cultural phenomenon—cultural because it presupposes a rather elaborate system of status symbols identifying certain individuals as persons of high authority. Thus, if we wish to consider the "original," pre-cultural process, we should focus upon the random process that results when the bias $w = 0$. How likely is it that such a process leads to inequality?

Equation 6.9 provides an answer: The expected hierarchy index in a society with n members is $3/(n + 1)$. Thus, for example, if no bias is operating and the dominance encounters occurred just as we have assumed, we could expect many cases of inequality in three-man groups, since the expected hierarchy index is close to 1 (i.e., $\frac{3}{4}$). In fact, as long as we consider small groups, inequality is a frequent result of the random process: the expected hierarchy index is $\frac{3}{5}$, $\frac{3}{6}$, $\frac{3}{7}$, ... for groups with 4, 5, 6, ... members. But when we start considering large groups, the low expected hierarchy index suggests that the random process leads only rarely to inequality. In a group with 1000 members, for example, the expected hierarchy index is only $3/1001 \approx .003$, which is close to 0.

The answer we give to our first question, then, is a qualified yes, for even if the "original" process was a random, trial-and-error one, men must have had some opportunity, perhaps enough, to experience complete inequality. However, they had this experience as members of small groups.

This conclusion opens a Pandora's box of possibilities. One is reminded, for example, of the fact that preliterate societies are organized around the institution of the family, their kinship system being merely its natural extension. Furthermore, some sociologists tell us that absolute monarchy historically developed from and conceptually is reminiscent of the institution of the family.[9] The point, of course, is that a nuclear family is a small group—a man, a woman, and children. Would it be too far-fetched to argue that the inequality found in preliterate societies and in absolute monarchies is a result of man's experience as a member of his family,

[9] See, for example, Weber (1947) and his concept of "traditional dominance."

that these social organizations *had* to emphasize inequality because they used a small group, a family, as their blueprint?

There is an argument which should be considered at this point. One could maintain that the process we have postulated is not realistic because it does not take into account the inborn differences between men. It is not necessary to postulate cultural differences to account for social stratification even in large societies, one may argue, since there may be biological differences between men leading to inequality even in large societies. According to this argument the more intelligent, the healthier, the stronger individuals will inevitably find their way to the top even without cultural sanctions, thus establishing inequality even in large societies.

Unfortunately for this argument, Landau (1951a) showed that when some reasonable assumptions are made about the distribution of superiority among men, and when one assumes that an inherently "superior" man is more likely to win than an inherently "inferior" individual, equality is still the rule rather than the exception in large societies. Similarly, Landau (1951b) has shown that the psychological factors mentioned previously—the "halo effect" of success[10]—do not lead to inequality in large societies, either.[11]

It should be clear that it has not been proven that a random dominance process will lead inevitably to equality in large societies; perhaps it is possible to define noncultural biases that do so. But since to date all such attempts have failed, a critical reappraisal of some of our theoretical notions is justified.

Maintenance of Inequality

It might seem, at first, that it is just as difficult to maintain inequality in large societies as it is to arrive at it through a random process. According to eq. 6.10, even if the bias against equalization is as large as possible, the expected hierarchy index for a large society of size n is about $6/n$. Since without the bias the expected index is $3/n + 1$, the introduction of the bias at best about doubles

[10] Expressed as an assertion that a person who won a previous battle is more likely to win in the future than is a person who lost a previous battle.

[11] More precisely, Landau showed that large societies will tend to be equalitarian even if there exists a bias "against reversal of dominance," that is, even if the fact that k won over r in a previous fight makes future victory of k over r more likely than the future victory of r over k.

the expected hierarchy index. For a society of, say, 1000 men the largest bias leads to the expected hierarchy index of only about .006, thus showing that almost complete equality is a rule in societies of that size.

But closer examination reveals that this result is something of an artifact. Remember that we had to set an upper limit to the bias w, the limit being $1/(n-1)$. This limit itself is a function of the size of the group. For example, the largest bias in a three-man group is $\frac{1}{2}$, while in a 1000-man group it is only $1/999$. Thus the bias against equalization fails to preserve inequality in large groups, for the reason that in large groups only a small bias is possible.

Landau (1951b) has shown that a bias exists which is certain to preserve any inequality. Should a society adopt the rule that a subordinate can win over his superior only if the two have almost equal authority (specifically, only if $v_k - v_r \leq 1$), then a complete hierarchy is certain to emerge and be preserved. This result offers an interesting insight into modern bureaucracies—the army, hospitals, and even universities and churches. Nearly complete hierarchy, in which an order descends down the line of command but never the reverse, is one of the fundamental organizational principles of bureaucracies,[12] a principle that is maintained in spite of all the forces that mitigate against inequality in modern industrial societies. Could it be that Landau's condition for the maintenance of a hierarchy is not only a sufficient condition, but also a necessary one, that a hierarchy can be preserved in no other way than by such stringent rules?

The results to date are only fragmentary and hence merely suggestive. But the reader who questions the value of building simple models of group behavior, should be happy to see the wealth of nonmathematical implications found in our results.

Let us add one more thought. If it is true that equality is the result of the random dominance process in large societies, if it is true that hierarchial organization is the most efficient form of organization for some purposes of a modern industrial society, and if it is true that modern industrial societies tend to be very large, then it is reasonable to expect that modern societies will have conflicting norms concerning equality. The very size of the society will foster

[12] See, for example, Weber (1946).

de facto equality; the need for efficiency will foster norms of inequality.

That this dilemma should exist comes hardly as a surprise to the student of modern societies. However, let us emphasize that we offer a different explanation for this dilemma than is normally given. Usually one thinks that industrialization, with its economy based on money, is the factor which fosters equalitarian values; we suggest that the bigness of modern societies should be considered an additional factor.

Word of Caution

In our attempt to show how simple models such as our model of social stratification can be helpful to the student of group behavior, we may be criticized for having overplayed our hand. It is one thing to show that a particular model implies that equality is the rule rather than the exception in large societies, it is quite another to show that inequality could not have arisen through the trial-and-error process. The catch, of course, is the definition of the term "trial-and-error process": If our definition is accepted, we have proved our point; if it is not, then we have failed to do so.

Several objections can be raised against our definition. One can object that our model does not apply to large societies because there, as we have stated earlier, the assumption that every member is equally likely to meet another member is patently false. Or one can point out that trial-and-error usually involves learning, that the probability of dominance as well as the probability of encounter may change as a result of experience. Finally, one may object to our working with Landau's hierarchy index h, a measure which may not be the best index of concentration of authority. Had we used a different index, we might have obtained different results.

These are thoughtful criticisms of the model discussed in this chapter, and there may be others. However, let us look at the other side of the picture. To show that other, possibly better, definitions of the trial-and-error process could be offered is not the same thing as to show that the results obtained with our model are invalid. It is perfectly possible that the same results would be obtained even if we altered the assumption that the probability of meeting is the same for everybody, and even if we used one of the better measures of concentration of authority. And Landau (1951b) has shown that a certain type of learning does not alter the results: If one assumes that a person who has once lost to another member is more likely than before to lose to him in future encounters, even then inequality is rare in large societies.

It seems to us that the implications of a model should be evaluated in the same way as the implications of any theory: the more evidence one can gather in its support, the more justified one feels in working with it. Furthermore, a theory with all its implications should be given serious consideration until it has been demonstrated that it is contradicted either by the data or by an equally plausible theory.

EXERCISES

1. Using the table of exercise 1 of Chapter 5, consider the number of distinct dominance patterns in which the maximum concentration of authority occurs. If each dominance pattern is equally likely to occur, what is the probability that a four-man group will have a maximum concentration of authority?

2. As was shown in Chapter 5, in a three-man group there are eight distinct dominance patterns, six of them exhibiting maximum concentration of authority. Hence the probability that a three-man group has a maximum concentration of authority (if each pattern is equally likely to occur) is $\frac{6}{8} = \frac{3}{4}$. Using the results of exercise 1, compare three-man and four-man groups. In which group is it more likely that the authority will be fully concentrated? Does your answer support the conclusion of Chapter 6 that as group size increases the probability of concentration decreases?

3. Use the table of exercise 1 of Chapter 5 to define a hierarchy index for all authority indices possible in a four-man group. Define a column vector h' such as given in eq. 6.7.

4. Use the table of exercise 1 of Chapter 5 to define a probability (row) vector p which associates a probability p_j with the occurrence of authority vector j. Using the column vector h' defined in exercise 3 above, compute the expected hierarchy index $E(h) = ph'$. Is the resulting expected index the same as that obtained from eq. 6.9? Why?

CHAPTER 7

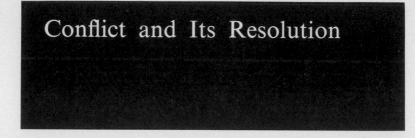

Conflict and Its Resolution

Conflict has always held a special fascination for men. Not only is much of recorded history an account of wars and popular uprisings, but also the greater part of serious literature deals with man's inner or social conflicts. Recently, the ever increasing price exacted from the participants in a conflict is causing a change from this original fascination to apprehension and even horror. And our concern now is not only with winning wars but also with how to avoid them.

In this chapter we shall consider conflict as a stochastic process of a special kind, as an *absorbing* Markov chains process. The model of conflict to be discussed can be applied to any two-sided social conflict, an electoral conflict between Democrats and Republicans as well as to a war between two nations. Our main interest, however, will be the conflict between the (wrong) opinion of a group majority and the (correct) opinion of an isolated group member. The experimental version of this conflict is that of Asch (1952); the mathematical model designed to describe the resolution of this conflict is from Cohen (1958, 1963).

7.1   ABSORBING MARKOV CHAINS

Before turning to the conflict between a group majority and an isolated group member, we shall augment our knowledge of Markov chains to include the so-called absorbing chains. So far we have discussed only the "regular" chains, chains with matrices P such that some power of P has only nonzero entries. A matrix of transition probabilities P is said to represent an *absorbing Markov chain* if (1) it has at least one "absorbing state," and (2) from every state of the matrix it is possible (not necessarily in one step) to reach an absorbing state.

As the name suggests, an *absorbing state* is a state which, once entered, cannot be left. For example, the matrix

(7.1)
$$P = \begin{bmatrix} 1 & 0 & 0 & 0 \\ p_{21} & p_{22} & p_{23} & 0 \\ 0 & p_{32} & p_{33} & p_{34} \\ 0 & 0 & 0 & 1 \end{bmatrix}$$

is an example of an absorbing Markov chain (chosen here because it happens to be the matrix that fits conflict situations). The features that make eq. 7.1 an absorbing chain are:

1. At least one row has 1 on the major diagonal, that row corresponding to the absorbing state. Matrix eq. 7.1 has two absorbing states, s_1 and s_4.

2. It is possible to reach an absorbing state, s_1 or s_4, from each state: When the process is in s_1, it remains there with probability $p_{11} = 1$; if it is in state s_2, it reaches s_1 (in one step) with probability p_{21}; if it is in s_3, it reaches s_4 (in one step) with probability p_{34}; finally, if it is in s_4, it remains there with probability $p_{44} = 1$.

We shall now give, without proof,[1] the main results of the theory of absorbing Markov chains. First, *Theorem 1* states that such chains are certain to end (although not necessarily in a finite number of steps) in an absorbing state. For example, when the process is

---

[1] For proofs see, for example, Kemeny and Snell (1960), Chapter 3.

defined by matrix 7.1, it is certain to end in either state s_1 or state s_4.

The second and third theorems deal with the mean number of times a process is in a given state as well as with the probability that the process will end in a given absorbing state. In order to state these theorems for eq. 7.1 let us rewrite P in the *canonical form*, by shifting its rows and columns so that the two rows with absorbing states form the first two rows of the new matrix:

$$(7.2) \qquad P = \begin{array}{c} \\ 1 \\ 4 \\ 2 \\ 3 \end{array} \begin{array}{cccc} 1 & 4 & 2 & 3 \\ \left[\begin{array}{cc|cc} 1 & 0 & 0 & 0 \\ 0 & 1 & 0 & 0 \\ \hline p_{21} & 0 & p_{22} & p_{23} \\ 0 & p_{34} & p_{32} & p_{33} \end{array} \right] \end{array}$$

Note the two broken lines dividing the matrix into four segments. Let us label the four segments as follows:

$$(7.3) \qquad P = \left[\begin{array}{c|c} I & 0 \\ \hline R & Q \end{array} \right]$$

Note that the left upper segment is an identity matrix I; the upper right segment is a zero matrix 0; Q and R are matrices containing the transition probabilities *from* nonabsorbing states—R into absorbing states (p_{21}, p_{34}), Q into nonabsorbing states ($p_{22}, p_{23}, p_{32}, p_{33}$).[2]

Theorem 2. The mean number of times the process will be in state j if it starts in state i (if the process goes on until it is absorbed), n_{ij}, is a component of the so-called fundamental matrix N, where

$$(7.4) \qquad N = (I - Q)^{-1}$$

and I and Q are as defined in eq. 7.3, $(I - Q)^{-1}$ being the inverse[3] of the difference $I - Q$.

In order to understand this theorem, note that, after one step, the expected number of times the process will be in state j, if (before

---

[2] A zero matrix 0 is a matrix with zero components.
[3] For a definition of A^{-1}, the inverse of a matrix A, see Chapter 2.

the step) it was in state i, is p_{ij}. The expected number of times in state j after two steps will be the sum $p_{ij} + p_{ij}^{(2)}$, where $p_{ij}^{(2)}$ is the probability that the process is in state j after two steps if it starts in process i.[4] Since we are dealing with *non*absorbing states p_{ij}, and since matrix Q deals with transition from and to nonabsorbing states, we can write that the expected number of times the process will be in state j after two steps if it starts in state i, $n_{ij}^{(2)}$, is a component of matrix $N^{(2)}$ where

$$N^{(2)} = Q + Q^2$$

(We substitute Q^2 for $Q^{(2)}$ because the probability of being in state j after t steps is given by Q^t.) It is easy to see that the expected number in state j if the process starts in i *after t steps* is $N^{(t)} = Q + Q^2 + \cdots + Q^t$. However, the fundamental matrix N deals with the total number of times the process will be in state j—which means that we have to include time $t = 0$, too. At time $t = 0$, the process either was in state j, or it was not. After a moment's thought, it becomes clear that the (expected) number of times the process is in state j at time $t = 0$ if it starts in state i is given by the identity matrix I, and we write that

$$N = I + Q + Q^2 + \cdots = \sum_{t=0}^{\infty} Q^t$$

since $Q^0 = I$. And, it can be shown that

$$\sum_{t=0}^{\infty} Q^t = (I - Q)^{-1}$$

hence eq. 7.4 follows directly.

Theorem 3. If the process starts in a nonabsorbing state s_i, it will end in the absorbing state s_k with probability b_{ik}, where b_{ik} is a component of the matrix B such that

(7.5) $$B = NR$$

N being the fundamental matrix defined by eq. 7.4, R the submatrix defined by eq. 7.3.

[4] The two probabilities are added because the trials are assumed to be mutually exclusive: a trial starts only after the previous one has ended.

Let us apply these two theorems to matrix eq. 7.1. We find that applying eq. 7.4 yields

$$(7.6) \qquad N = \begin{array}{c} \\ 2 \\ \\ 3 \end{array} \begin{bmatrix} \dfrac{1 - p_{33}}{\Delta} & \dfrac{p_{23}}{\Delta} \\[2ex] \dfrac{p_{32}}{\Delta} & \dfrac{1 - p_{22}}{\Delta} \end{bmatrix}$$

where $\Delta = (1 - p_{22})(1 - p_{33}) - p_{23}p_{32}$. Note that the labeling of matrix N corresponds to that of matrix Q in eq. 7.2: the matrix represents the transitions from and to states 2 and 3. Thus, for example, the upper left component is n_{22} (instead of n_{11} as one might expect), representing the mean number of times the process will be in state 2 if it starts in state 2 and continues until absorbed. As eq. 7.6 suggests, this number will be

$$n_{22} = \frac{1 - p_{33}}{(1 - p_{22})(1 - p_{33}) - p_{23}p_{32}}$$

Let us make sure that we understand the meaning of n_{22}. Imagine that we simulate the process by using matrix 7.1 and a random device which, on each trial, determines which one of the four states is reached on that trial.[5] Imagine that (1) each simulation run starts in state 2, (2) each simulation run goes on until it reaches an absorbing state, and (3) a large number of identical simulation runs (i.e., using the same matrix 7.1 is generated. We record the number of times each simulation run was in s_2, call it m_{22}, add all m_{22} (for all runs), Σm_{22}, and divide by the total number of separate simulation runs M. Then, clearly, the mean $\Sigma m_{11}/M$ is the number of times the simulation runs were in state 2 "on the average"—and this number will be close to n_{22}.[6]

[5] One can imagine an electronic computer using (1) the probability matrix P of eq. 7.1, and (2) a table of random numbers. For each time t, the simulated subject is in state s_i. The computer determines the state into which the simulated subject moves at time $t + 1, s_j$, by selecting a number from the table of random numbers and "fitting" it with the probability b_{ij}. For example, let $p_{21} = .03$, $p_{22} = .85$, and $p_{23} = .12$. Then the range 000 to 029 corresponds to the transition from s_2 to s_1, the range 030 to 879 to transition from s_2 to s_2, and the range from 881 to 999 to transition from s_2 to s_3. Thus, if at time t the subject is in state s_2 and the computer draws number 703 from the table, the simulated subject moves into (remains in) state s_2.

[6] More precisely, as the number of simulation runs, M, increases, the mean m_{22}/M approaches the expected number n_{22}.

Applying the second theorem (eq. 7.5) to eq. 7.1 we find that

$$
(7.7) \qquad B = \begin{matrix} 2 \\ \\ 3 \end{matrix} \begin{bmatrix} \dfrac{p_{21}(1-p_{33})}{\Delta} & \dfrac{p_{23}p_{34}}{\Delta} \\[2em] \dfrac{p_{32}p_{21}}{\Delta} & \dfrac{p_{34}(1-p_{22})}{\Delta} \end{bmatrix}
$$

where Δ is defined as in eq. 7.6. Note again the labeling. It is identical with that of submatrix R. The component b_{31}, for example, gives the probability that the process will end in the absorbing state s_1 if it starts in state s_3. Returning to our simulation example, imagine that we again run a large number of simulations, this time each starting in state 3. The proportion of runs ending in s_1 will be close to b_{31}.

7.2   EXPERIMENTS

Asch's (1952) experiments with group pressure are by now a classic in the field of social psychology. Their objective was to study some of the conditions which "induce individuals to remain independent or to yield to group pressures *when these are contrary to fact.*"[7]

Perhaps the most startling finding was that approximately one-third of the subjects went along with the group majority, reporting as true something that clearly was false, only because the majority was unanimous in its (wrong) opinion. It was shocking to discover that many men—college students at that—value social approval so much they are willing to lie rather than risk the disfavor of the majority by telling the truth.

Main Design

In experiments fashioned after those of Asch but conducted by Cohen (1958, 1963), a naive subject was placed in a group together with several (usually six or seven) "confederates," the confederates having been secretly coached by the experimenter to hold unanimously to a wrong opinion. And they were always asked to express this opinion before the naive subject was called on.

[7] Cohen (1963), p. 15.

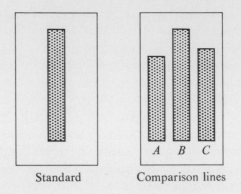

Standard   Comparison lines

Figure 7.1. Examples of experimental stimuli.

The experiment started by presenting to the group a set of two cards as shown in Fig. 7.1. The cards were large and made of white cardboard; the left card bore a single heavy black "standard" line, the right card three "comparison" lines A, B, and C, one of which was always of the same length as the standard line (line B in Figure 7.1). The purported task was for each participant to state simply which one of the comparison lines was the same length as the standard. But, of course, the confederates had been instructed to name unanimously the wrong line. Thus, when it was the naive subject's turn to speak, he was confronted with six or seven unanimous wrong judgments. In most cases, the naive subject knew quite clearly that the preceding judgments were wrong since the differences between the comparison lines were large enough to make a mistake very unlikely.[8] The crucial question was, of course, whether the naive subject would go along with the majority anyway, or whether he would report truthfully what he saw.

After all the participants had rendered their judgment, a new set of two cards identical with the first pair was presented, and the participants were again asked to name the equal-length comparison line. The confederates again rendered a unanimous and wrong judgment; the naive subject was again faced with the same dilemma. In each experiment 36 "critical" sets of cards were presented.[9] To

[8] Separate experiments have shown that subjects make almost no mistakes when they view the very same lines in private (without group pressure).

[9] Each experiment consisted of 38 trials, but only 36 trials, $t = 2, 3, \ldots, 38$, were critical in the sense of involving conflicting group pressures.

allay any possible suspicion on the part of the naive subject, the confederates were instructed to render a correct judgment on the first two trials of every experiment.

Cohen decided to vary systematically the obviousness of the majority's mistakes. In some experiments the difference between the correct line and the line chosen by the majority was small, $1\frac{1}{4}$ in.; in others it was rather large, $1\frac{3}{4}$ in. Cohen ran 33 experiments under "moderate" conflict conditions (in which the majority was only $1\frac{1}{4}$ in. off) and 27 experiments under the "extreme" conflict conditions (in which the majority was $1\frac{3}{4}$ in. off). The two types of experiments were as follows:

Critical Trials

Trial:	1, 2, 3, 4,	...,	38
Moderate:	$N, N, M, M,$	...,	M
Extreme:	$N, N, E, E,$	...,	E

where N stands for "neutral" trials (a trial on which the majority guessed correctly), M for moderate conflict condition, E for extreme conflict condition.

Cohen focused his attention on this variation because he felt that when the majority is obviously wrong (extreme conflict), it will exercise much greater pressure upon the naive subject than when its mistake is relatively minor. Consequently, he expected to find that naive subjects would behave differently when the testimony of their eyes is in extreme conflict with the judgment of the majority than when the conflict is moderate.

Main Findings

Cohen's data indicate that he was correct in expecting that the obviousness of a majority's error would make a difference. He found that when the conflict was extreme, the naive subjects were more inclined to defy the majority and told the truth more often than when the conflict was moderate. More specifically, when the majority's error was blatant, progressively more defying (correct) answers were given as the experiment was repeated; when the majority's mistake was only moderate, no significant tendency was observed for the nonconforming responses either to increase or decrease with time. Figure 7.2 shows the main time trends.

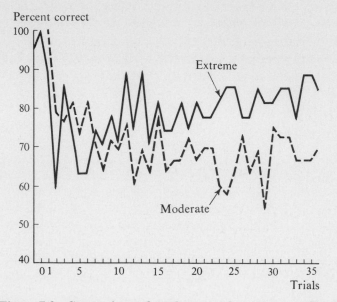

Figure 7.2. Comparison of moderate and extreme conflict conditions.

Furthermore, Cohen found that a subject was much more likely to switch his responses, from independence to conformity and vice versa, in the early trials than in the later trials. Since a subject can be in an absorbed state only if he repeats the same response,[10] this finding supports the decision to view the behavior of naive subjects as an absorbing Markov chain process.

Open-end interviews with the naive subjects following the experiment confirm the view that Asch's design created a conflict situation. Subjects were seriously concerned over their disagreement with the majority and most of those who conformed confessed readily that they had known the correct response. But many clearly were

[10] By definition, he is in state s_1 at time t only if he gives a T response at time t and thereafter. To be in state s_4 at time t, he has to respond F at time t and thereafter.

confused about what was going on. A subject who went along with the majority nine times said: "I was not sure of my answers, but I wasn't sure the others were right either. I just did not have the strength of my convictions. I felt bad when I made choices going with the group; I didn't think I was right then, but I got tired of bucking them."[11]

7.3 THE MODEL OF CONFLICT

Cohen notes that matrix 7.1 may be used to describe the behavior of the naive subjects in Asch's experiments. Such a subject, argues Cohen, either is undecided whether or not to go along with the group and deny the evidence of his own eyes, or he has made a decision. If he is undecided, he will still, at a given time, either be overtly conforming or overtly nonconforming. In this way, four "mental" states may be defined as (1) s_1, absorbed nonconformity, (2) s_2, temporary nonconformity, (3) s_3, temporary conformity, and (4) s_4, absorbed conformity.

Each of these states is given an operational as well as a theoretical definition. The *operational* definition utilizes observable behavior, the conforming or nonconforming response of a subject. The operational definitions of the four states are as follows:

1. s_1: If the subject is in this state, he will respond correctly (not conform) on trial t and on every subsequent trial.
2. s_2: If subject is in this state, he will respond correctly (not conform) on trial t and may or may not respond correctly on subsequent trials.
3. s_3: If subject is in this state, he will give an incorrect (conforming) response on trial t, and may or may not respond correctly on subsequent trials.
4. s_4: If the subject is in this state, he will respond incorrectly (will conform) on trial t and on every subsequent trial.

The *theoretical* definitions utilize unobservable mental processes. States s_2 and s_3 correspond to being undecided or uncertain,

[11] Cohen (1963), p. 26.

states s_1 and s_4 to being decided or sure of himself. We shall see later that this dual definition complicates estimation of the matrix P from the data gathered in actual experiments.

The application to conflicts of matrix of eq. 7.1 necessitates several assumptions. First of all, note that $p_{24} = 0$, $p_{13} = 0$ in eq. 7.1, which corresponds to the following assumption:

Assumption 1. A temporary conformist cannot become an absorbed nonconformist in one step, nor can a temporary nonconformist become an absorbed conformist in one step.

This assumption is really a definition of the terms "absorbed nonconformity" and "absorbed conformity": One can enter into these states only through the "empirically close" nonabsorbed state, i.e., s_1 through s_2, s_4 through s_3.

The second assumption simplifies mathematical computations and seems to be eminently plausible. Essentially, it is assumed that without a distracting group pressure, the subject reports correctly what he sees, and hence one may say the following:

Assumption 2. At time $t = 0$ (just before the experiment begins), all subjects are temporary nonconformists, i.e.,

$$p^{(0)} = (0, 1, 0, 0)$$

The third assumption, strictly speaking, violates the theory of absorbing Markov chains. Although this theory holds that an absorbing state is certain to be reached but not necessarily in a finite number of steps, we shall say the following:

Assumption 3. All subjects made up their minds (i.e., reached an absorbing state) on or before the last trial.

This assumption will be necessary for some of the mathematical computations to be discussed later.[12] At this point, let us note that, although this assumption does violate the Markov chains theory, it seems to be a good enough approximation for all practical purposes.[13]

---

[12] This assumption is not made explicitly by Cohen. Kemeny and Snell (1962) make this assumption (p. 57) in order to be able to estimate p_{ij} mathematically. See the Appendix.

[13] It can be shown that only a very small proportion of subjects may be expected to take longer than 36 trials before absorption.

One of the reasons why model construction often goes hand in hand with experimentation is that experiments can be designed to yield data necessary for testing the model. But even when the data are as needed for the test, the task of testing the model may be far from simple. Cohen's work reveals some of the possible difficulties.

Two major steps may be distinguished in testing a model. The first involves using the data to estimate the free parameters of the model,[14] in our case, the transition probabilities p_{ij} of matrix eq. 7.1. The second step involves the derivation of implications from the model which can be tested by a different set of data than that used for estimation purposes, and comparing these implications with the data to see whether the fit is close enough.

Estimation of the Matrix

Suppose for a moment that it were possible to cross-tabulate the data from Asch's experiment as follows:

$$
\begin{bmatrix}
N_{11} & 0 & 0 & 0 \\
N_{21} & N_{22} & N_{23} & 0 \\
0 & N_{32} & N_{33} & N_{34} \\
0 & 0 & 0 & N_{44}
\end{bmatrix}
\begin{matrix}
N_1 \\
N_2 \\
N_3 \\
N_4
\end{matrix}
$$

where N_{ij} stands for the number of time subjects switched from state s_i to state s_j, N_i for the total number of times the subjects were in state s_i. If we had such data, the estimates of the probabilities would be simple indeed. The best estimate of p_{ij} would be

$$(7.8) \qquad\qquad p_{ij} \approx \frac{N_{ij}}{N_i}$$

where "$\approx$" stands for "is close to."

Unfortunately, we cannot observe directly which (mental) state the subject is in at time t, we can merely observe which response he gives at that time—a correct ("defying") response T, or an incorrect (conforming) response F. As a result, we do not know most of the N_{ij} and none of the N_i. To see why this is so, consider a sequence

[14] The free parameters of a model are the quantities that are expressed by non-numerical symbols in the model (such as p_{ij}). Until specific numbers are substituted for these quantities, the model cannot generate specific predictions [such as $p^{(t)}$].

of responses that actually occurred in Cohen's experiments:

$$\underbrace{\text{(T)TTTTTTTFTTTTTFTTF}}_{\text{initial segment}}\underbrace{\text{TTTTTTTTTTTTTTTTTTTTT}}_{\text{final segment}}$$

The (T) response at the beginning of the sequence did not actually occur; it is inferred as the subject's "tendency" at the time $t = 0$, just as stated by Assumption 2 of the model. Furthermore, note that we have divided the sequence into the initial and the final segments. The final segment consists of (1) the terminal (last) response, and (2) the entire uninterrupted sequence (of T-responses in the above example) that ends in the terminal response.

Now let us use the operational definitions of the four states and try to determine in which state the subject was at each trial. Note that we have no difficulty in the initial segment, for all responses there have to correspond to nonabsorbed states.[15] Hence, in the initial segment, T always indicates that the subject was "temporary nonconformist" (state s_2), F is always a sign that he is a "temporary conformist" (state s_3). But we do have a problem when it comes to the final segment. We have no way of telling at which point of the final segment the subject actually became absorbed, when he decided to be a nonconformist. We do know, or rather, we assume, that the subject in our example was an absorbed nonconformist *on the very last trial*, but prior to that time, any T-response may be counted either as "temporary" or "absorbed" nonconformity.[16] As a result, we cannot know the total (initial plus final segment) number of trials in which a subject was in state s_1, s_2, s_3, or s_4; nor can we know most of the transitions from one state to another. As already indicated, the only quantity we can observe directly is the number of transitions from s_2 to s_3 and back: all such transitions occur, by definition, in the initial segment and correspond to switches from response T to F and vice versa. In short, we know none of the N_{ij}/N_i of eq. 7.8 and hence we cannot estimate directly any one of the p_{ij}.

[15] Because the final segment includes, by definition, the entire uninterrupted sequence of a given response, a response in the initial segment will always be followed (sooner or later) by an opposite response. Hence all responses in the initial segment are unabsorbed.

[16] Any response within the terminal segment could be the turning point at which the subject made up his mind (became absorbed). Note, for example, that a T response can be counted as a *temporary* nonconformity even if it lies in the middle of the final segment: The definition of temporary nonconformity allows for the subsequent responses to be (all) T.

This difficulty can be circumvented in either of two ways: (1) by defining quantities that can be directly estimated from the data and that lead to the definition of the p_{ij}, or (2) by searching for a matrix P that yields the best fit (smallest chi-square) between the predicted and the observed vector $p^{(t)}$. Cohen used the second approach: He programmed a high-speed computer to consider a large number of distinct matrices P that satisfy eq. 7.1, and [using the equation $p^{(t)} = p^{(0)}P$] to compute $p^{(t)}$ for each $t = 1, 2, \ldots, 36$, and for each matrix P. He selected as *the* matrix P that matrix which showed the smallest differences between the probability of giving a conforming response at time t, $p_1^{(t)} + p_2^{(t)}$, and the proportion of subjects actually giving the correct response at that time.

The first, more mathematically oriented, approach was applied to Cohen's data by Kemeny and Snell (1962). The procedure needed to derive quantities which can be used to estimate P directly is somewhat involved, and hence we relegate it to the Appendix, and give here only the end result of that procedure, the two matrices that define the Markov chains under moderate and extreme conditions:

$$
\begin{array}{cc}
\text{Moderate conflict} & \text{Extreme conflict} \\[4pt]
(7.9) \quad P = \begin{bmatrix} 1 & 0 & 0 & 0 \\ .05 & .66 & .29 & 0 \\ 0 & .46 & .49 & .05 \\ 0 & 0 & 0 & 1 \end{bmatrix} & P = \begin{bmatrix} 1 & 0 & 0 & 0 \\ .07 & .74 & .19 & 0 \\ 0 & .42 & .55 & .03 \\ 0 & 0 & 0 & 1 \end{bmatrix}
\end{array}
$$

The two matrices estimated by Kemeny and Snell are different from those arrived at by Cohen, although the data were the same in both cases. This suggests that using "brute force" (a computer that considers many, but not all, possibilities) is not always a good substitute for mathematical reasoning. Since the approach applied by Kemeny and Snell is superior to the brute force approach,[17] we shall henceforth consider only the transition matrices of eq. 7.9.

[17] Usually, when the "brute force" approach to a problem is used, many possibilities are excluded from consideration. For example, Cohen (1963) in estimating the probabilities p_{ij} considered only p_{ij} that differed by an increment of .10, thus omitting all p_{ij} that differed by a smaller increment. Hence it is always possible that the brute force approach misses an important possibility. Mathematical reasoning, on the other hand, will always strive for (and, if successful, will achieve) taking *all* the possibilities into account. For example, Kemeny and Snell can *prove* that the matrices of (7.9) contain the best estimates of the probabilities p_{ij}.

7.4   GOODNESS OF FIT

It would seem that the best way to determine whether the matrices of (7.9) fit the data is to use the equation $p^{(t)} = p^{(0)}P$ to define $p^{(t)}$ for $t = 1, \ldots, 36$, and to compare these predictions against observations. However, this procedure is neither the only one available, nor necessarily the best one. We shall consider, therefore, another method as well.

The Probability of a Correct Response

As was indicated earlier, the data gathered in Cohen's experiments allow us to determine the proportion of correct responses (i.e., the proportion of subjects who were nonconformist, temporary or absorbed) for each time t. Given the transition matrices of (7.9) and Assumption 2 concerning the probability vector at time $t = 0$, we can compute $p^{(t)}$ for each time t from $p^{(t)} = p^{(0)}P$. Since the sum $p_1^{(t)} + p_2^{(t)} = p_T^{(t)}$ is the probability that a subject gives a correct (T) answer at time t, we can compare that sum with the proportion of actually observed correct responses. Figures 7.3 and 7.4 give the comparison in graphic form.

Even a cursory inspection of the two figures reveals that the predicted and the observed paths look different. The predicted curves are smooth; the observed curves oscillate up and down. But this difference cannot be construed as evidence against the validity of the model. The predicted curves are smooth because, conceptually, they are based on an infinite number of cases; thus the ups and downs due to random disturbances (when the number of cases is small) have been eliminated. It follows that, if we increased the number of subjects, the observed time path would become smoother, resembling more nearly the predicted path.

We could compute chi-square between the predicted probabilities and the observed proportions, hoping thus to ascertain whether the apparent disturbances are indeed due to random disturbances occasioned by the small number of subjects. However, we shall not do so, because the computation of chi-square would, in this case, utilize quantities whose estimates are highly correlated with the estimates of the transition matrices P.

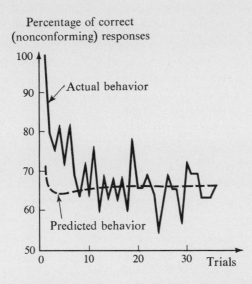

Figure 7.3. Predicted and actual behavior under moderate conflict conditions.

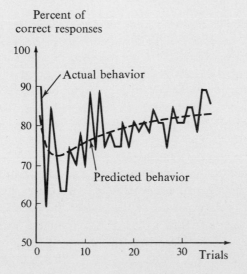

Figure 7.4. Predicted and actual behavior under extreme conflict conditions.

To show why the two estimates are correlated, let us use a simple illustration: Consider a case involving only three subjects whose responses in the 36 critical trials are as shown in Table 7.1. Note that each subject i has associated with him a transcript that starts with (T), his (assumed) response tendency at time $t = 0$. The quantities in the last two columns refer to the number of *response switches*: N_{iTF} represents the number of times subject i switched from T (the correct response) to the F (the incorrect response), N_{iFT} the number of times he switched from F to T.

Table 7.1.

Subject i	Sequence of Responses	N_{iTF}	N_{iFT}
1	(T)TTTTTTFTTTTFTTTFTTTTTFFFTTTTFTTTTTTT	5	5
2	(T)TTTFFTTTTTFTTTTFFFTFFFFTTTTTTTTFTTTTT	5	5
3	(T)TTFFFFTTTTTTTTTTFTTTTTTTTTFFFFFFFFFFF	3	2
Total		13	12

The procedure described in the Appendix deals with quantities such as N_{TF} and N_{FT}. These are computed by adding the individual items, which for Table 7.1, are $N_{TF} = \sum_i N_{iTF} = 13$, and $N_{FT} = \sum_i N_{iFT} = 12$. The resulting sums are used to estimate the transition probabilities p_{ij}. For example,

$$p_{33} \approx \frac{N_{FF}}{N_{FT} + N_{FF}}$$

where N_{FF} is the total number of times F is followed by F in the initial segment of the response sequence.

The crucial point is that the quantities N_{TF} and N_{FT} are used not only in estimating the transition matrices p_{ij} but also, implicitly, in computing the *observed* proportion of T-responses. Let us consider the number of F-responses at the end of the experiment, at time $t = 36$. We see in Table 7.1 that only one subject (in our example) gave an F-response. Note that the difference $N_{TF} - N_{FT} = 1$, is also one. This is no coincidence. The difference $N_{TF} - N_{FT}$ is always equal to the number of F-responses at time $t = 36$. As a result, we can arrive at the proportion of F-responses at time

$t = 36$, $P_{\text{F}}^{(36)}$, from

$$P_{\text{F}}^{(36)} = \frac{N_{\text{TF}} - N_{\text{FT}}}{N}$$

where N is the number of subjects.

Now consider how one arrives at the predicted proportion of F-responses at time $t = 36$. This proportion is obtained from the probability vector $p^{(36)} = p^{(0)}P^{36}$, by adding

$$p_{\text{F}}^{(36)} = p_3^{(36)} + p_4^{(36)}$$

Thus $p_{\text{F}}^{(36)}$ is derived from matrix P, the estimates of which are based on N_{TF} and N_{FT}; $P_{\text{F}}^{(36)}$ depends directly on these quantities. Consequently, the prediction and the observation must be related; we cannot assume that they are independent and apply standard statistical tests such as chi-square.

It is true that the a priori correlation between the observed and predicted proportion of F-responses (and, therefore, of T-responses as well) is less pronounced for $t < 36$ than for $t = 36$. But it is not difficult to see that *some* such correlation will always exist. Thus we shall not attempt to ascertain whether the discrepancies shown in Figures 7.3 and 7.4 are due to chance; we merely note that they seem to be none too large. We reserve a more rigorous test for the next section in which we shall consider a measure which does not suffer from the deficiency just described.

Probability of Exactly k Switches

Let us consider again the example of Table 7.1. It is possible to use the individual response sequences to identify not only switches of a given kind but also switches of any kind. Let us denote the total number of switches by subject i (whether these switches be from T to F or from F to T) by k such that

$$k = N_{i\text{TF}} + N_{i\text{FT}}$$

In the example of Table 7.1, $k = 10$ for subjects 1 and 2, $k = 5$ for subject 3. We could add the individual quantities k and arrive at the total number of switches observed in the experiments (for all subjects), but the resulting measure would be correlated with N_{TF} and N_{FT} just as closely as the measure considered in the previous section. For this reason, we shall use k to define a different measure, *the number of subjects who have the same k*. Turning to our example, we observe that two of our three subjects have $k = 10$, one of the three has $k = 5$. And we say that the proportion of exactly ten switches is $\frac{2}{3}$; the proportion of exactly five switches is $\frac{1}{3}$. Our task now is to use our model to predict such proportions, to derive the *probability* of exactly k switches. We shall refer to such a probability as r_k.

The manner in which r_k is derived is again rather involved and we refer the reader to the more advanced treatment given in Kemeny and Snell (1962).[18] Here we shall merely outline the method by considering the derivation of r_0, the probability of exactly zero switches.

It follows from our discussion that the basic datum for determining the *number* of switches, k_i, is the sequence of responses of an individual subject. It is clear, furthermore, that the transcript with *no* switches has to look as follows:

$$(T)TTTTTTTTTTTTTTTTTTTTTTTTTTTTTTTTTTTTT$$

We wish to express in terms of the p_{ij} of our model the probability that such a transcript will occur—this is what we mean by "deriving r_0 from our model." But here we encounter a problem: the transcript deals with the observable responses T; the transition probabilities p_{ij} deal with the unobservable states i and j. Specifically, we know that the above T-responses correspond to state 1 or 2. But we do not know where the "turning point" is located, since the transition from state 2 to state 1 could have occurred at any point of the sequence. (Note that only one such transition between states 2 and 1 is possible: Once the subject is in state 1, he remains there.)

Since we do not know where the turning point is, we will have to consider all of its possible locations. Let us start by considering an arbitrary location,

$$\underbrace{(s_2)s_2s_2s_2\cdots s_2s_1\cdots s_1}_{i+1}$$

where s_2 means that the subject was in state 2, s_1 that he was in state 1, and $i + 1$ is the number of trials during which the subject

---

[18] Kemeny and Snell do not derive r_k explicitly, but they present the reader with sufficient background to allow him to derive r_k by himself.

was in state 1. To say that we do not know the location of the turning point means that we have to assume that $i + 1$ can vary from zero to infinity.[19]

Now consider the situation when $i + 1 = 1$, that is, when the subject becomes an absorbed conformist (moves into state 1) on the very first trial. Since we are assuming that, at time $t = 0$, the subject was in state 2, we can derive the probability of his moving from state 2 into state 1 in *one step* directly from the transition matrix: this probability is p_{21}. Now suppose the subject moves from state 2 to state 1 in *two* steps ($i + 1 = 2$). We know that there is only one way in which such a transition could have been accomplished. The subject had to be in state 2 on the first trial (this transition occurring with probability p_{22}), moving into state 1 on the second trial (this transition occurring with probability p_{21}). Since the two events are independent, it follows that the probability of being in state 2 on the first trial *and* being in state 1 on the second trial is given by the product $p_{22}p_{21}$.

We proceed in similar fashion for any number of steps. For example, for $i + 1 = 3$ (reaching state 1 in three steps) it is necessary that the subject be in state 2 on the first two trials (which occurs with probability $p_{22}p_{22} = p_{22}^2$), and then move into state 1 (with probability p_{21}). Thus the probability of reaching state 1 in three steps is $p_{22}^2 p_{21}$. To generalize, the probability that state 1 is reached in $i + 1$ steps, P_{i+1}, is

$$P_{i+1} = p_{22}^i p_{21}$$

So far we have obtained the probability that state 1 is reached in $i + 1$ steps. But this is not the answer we are after. We wish to know the probability of exactly zero switches, r_0. A moment's reflection shows that P_{i+1} and r_0 are related, that the sequence with exactly zero switches can be obtained either when $i + 1 = 1$ (in one step) or when $i + 1 = 2$ (in two steps) and so on, until one can say, "or when $i + 1 = \infty$ (in an infinite number of steps)." Since the event $i + 1 = 1$ (state 1 reached in one step) can happen only if the remaining events ($i + 1 = 2, 3, \ldots$) do not occur—in other words,

[19] By assuming that the point of absorption need not lie within the 36 critical trials of an experiment we are in effect contradicting Assumption 3. However, as we noted, that assumption is actually a violation of the theory of Markov chains. Hence, by allowing $i + 1$ to vary from zero to infinity, we are removing that violation.

since the events "reaching state 1 in $i + 1$ steps" are mutually exclusive events—it follows that the probability that $i + 1 = 1$ or $i + 1 = 2 \ldots$ or $i + 1 = \infty$ is given by the sum of the individual probabilities P_{i+1}. Since, as we have just shown, the statement "there are no switches in the sequence" is equivalent to the statement "state 1 was reached in 1 step or 2 steps . . . or an infinite number of steps," it follows that

$$r_0 = P_1 + P_2 + \cdots = \sum_{i=0}^{\infty} P_{i+1} = p_{21} \sum_{i=0}^{\infty} p_{22}^i$$

It can be shown[20] that

$$\sum_{i=0}^{\infty} p_{22}^i = \frac{1}{1 - p_{22}}$$

and hence

$$r_0 = \frac{p_{21}}{1 - p_{22}}$$

Thus we have achieved our objective; we have derived r_0 from our model. We could proceed in similar fashion to arrive at $r_1, r_2, \ldots,$ and thereby discover the general relationship between p_{ij} and r_k. We would discover that the relationship is quite different when k is odd than when k is even. For this reason, we define variable m such that k can equal either $2m$ (when k is even) or $2m + 1$ (when k is odd):

	Even	Odd
m	$k = 2m$	$k = 2m + 1$
0	0	1
1	2	3
2	4	5
.	.	.
.	.	.
.	.	.

Instead of pursuing the analysis further, we use Kemeny and Snell's results (1962), and write

$$(7.10) \quad r_k = \begin{cases} \dfrac{p_{21}C^m}{1 - p_{22}} & \text{when } k \text{ is even } (k = 2m) \\[3ex] \dfrac{p_{23}p_{34}C^m}{(1 - p_{22})(1 - p_{33})} & \text{when } k \text{ is odd } (k = 2m + 1) \end{cases}$$

[20] See, for example, Cohen (1963).

where

$$C = \frac{p_{23}p_{32}}{(1 - p_{22})(1 - p_{33})}$$

Thus, for example, to determine the probability of exactly 5 switches (r_5) we note that 5 is an odd number and hence the equation $k = 2m + .1$ is applicable. Solving this equation for $k = 5$, we obtain $m = 2$; using eq. 7.10 we write

$$r_5 = \frac{p_{23}p_{34}}{(1 - p_{22})(1 - p_{33})}\left[\frac{p_{23}p_{32}}{(1 - p_{22})(1 - p_{33})}\right]^2$$

Let us now consider whether there is an a priori correlation between the predicted and the observed values of r_k. Since (7.10) shows r_k to depend on the transition probabilities p_{ij} and since these are estimated from quantities such as N_{TF} and N_{FT}, it follows that r_k, N_{TF}, and N_{FT} are correlated. However, the *observed proportion* of exactly k switches, R_k, does not depend on these quantities. To be sure, it does depend on N_{iTF} and N_{iFT} since $k = N_{iTF} + N_{iFT}$; but the knowledge of the total frequencies N_{TF} and N_{FT} gives us no clue to the number of subjects with exactly k switches. Hence we can use standard statistical tests to evaluate the differences between the observed and predicted proportions of exactly k switches.

Although we could compare proportions, we shall follow Kemeny and Snell and compare frequencies—the observed number of subjects with exactly k switches and the predicted number of such subjects. The observed number of such subjects is derived directly from the transcripts of the experiments; the predicted number is given by the product Nr_k, where N is the total number of subjects. Table 7.2 shows the comparisons for moderate conflict, Table 7.3 for the extreme conflict condition. Note that not every value of k was considered separately in the tables. In order to keep the predicted number of cases above the minimum required for the computation of chi-square, it was necessary to combine categories.

Each table has two columns of predicted frequencies. We shall explain the significance of the second columns shortly; for the moment, let us consider only the first columns, for these represent the predictions based on the models of eq. 7.9. We note that chi-square for moderate conflict is 13.06, for the extreme condition,

Table 7.2. Fit of the Model to Moderate Conflict

k	Number of Subjects Who Switched Responses Exactly k Times:		
		Predicted by:	
	Observed	Eq. 7.9	Eq. 7.11
0	10	5.22	9.95
1	1	2.61	2.17
2 or 4	5	7.02	4.28
3 or 5	4	3.51	3.14
6, 8, or 10	2	5.43	3.74
7, 9, or 11	1	2.71	2.75
Larger than 10, even	5	4.33	4.02
Larger than 11, odd	5	2.17	2.95
χ^2	—	13.06	4.58

0.21. Any standard chi-square table reveals that the probability that the discrepancy of Table 7.2 is due to pure chance is very small, less than .10, but also reveals that this probability is large for Table 7.3, more than .99. Thus, we find strong support for a conclusion which might have been suggested by the graphical representation shown in Figures 7.1 and 7.2: The model for extreme conflict fits the data much better than does the model for moderate conflict.

Table 7.3. Fit of the Model to Extreme Conflict

k	Number of Subjects Who Switched Responses Exactly k Times:		
		Predicted by:	
	Observed	Eq. 7.9	Eq. 7.12
0	6	6.83	9.61
2 or 4	9	8.18	5.98
6, 8, or 10	5	5.22	4.36
Larger than 10, even	3	2.78	3.06
Odd	4	4.00	3.99
χ^2	—	.21	2.98

Rather than speculating about the reasons for this difference in fit, we shall follow Kemeny and Snell in attempting to improve the fit of the model for the moderate conflict. To start with, we note from Table 7.2 that the model is not uniformly bad. Its lack of fit is due primarily to underestimating the frequency of exactly *zero* switches. This fact led Kemeny and Snell to investigate what would happen if Assumption 2 were changed to postulate that some subjects entered the experiments as absorbed nonconformists. This possibility is of interest because a subject who is in state 1 (an absorbed nonconformist) at time $t = 0$ will always have a transcript with no switches. Adding such subjects amounts to increasing the number of sequences with no switches, thereby improving the fit of the model.

A total of 33 subjects participated in the moderate experiments; therefore, 33 different assumptions can be made about the number of subjects who started the experiments in state 1. We can assume that this number was $0, 1, 2, \ldots, 33$. The systematic approach would be to consider all 33 possibilities, and to determine the fit for every case. However, Kemeny and Snell discuss only the case when about 20% of the subjects (i.e., 7 subjects out of 33) start as absorbed nonconformists, and make the following assumption:

Assumption 2'. At time $t = 0$, 20% of the subjects were absorbed nonconformists, the rest were temporary nonconformists,

$$p^{(0)} = (.20, .80, 0, 0)$$

At first glance it would seem that all one needs to arrive at a modified model is to use the new starting vector $p^{(0)}$ with the old matrix of eq. 7.9. However, a moment's reflection suggests that this is not so, that a new transition matrix must be computed. As shown in the Appendix, the number of transitions from T to T, N_{TT}, plays an important role in estimating the transition probabilities p_{ij}. But there will be 7 uninterrupted sequences of T-responses that cannot play this role: those sequences of 36 T-responses associated with the 7 subjects assumed to start in the absorbing state 1. Since we know (by assumption) that these subjects *start* in an absorbing state, we need not (and cannot) guess at which point these subjects *became* absorbed. As shown in the Appendix, such guessing is a part of the procedure used in estimating p_{ij}. Hence we cannot apply this procedure to the 7 uninterrupted sequences of T-responses, and therefore we must decrease N_{TT} from the original $N_{TT} = 228$ to $N_{TT} = 221$.

This is the only modification that is necessary, however. With it we can apply the procedure described in the Appendix, and we obtain:

$$(7.11) \quad P' = \begin{bmatrix} 1 & 0 & 0 & 0 \\ .04 & .65 & .31 & 0 \\ 0 & .46 & .49 & .05 \\ 0 & 0 & 0 & 1 \end{bmatrix} \quad \text{for moderate conflict}$$

We now use (7.11) and (7.10) to compute the values of r_k for $k = 0$, $1, \ldots$. The product Nr_k again yields the predicted number of subjects who switched exactly k times. These predictions are shown in the last column of Table 7.2. And we see that the new model fits the data much better than did the old—the chi-square has been reduced from 13.06 to 4.58. The probability that the discrepancy is due to pure chance is still not as high as one might wish (only about .70), but this does represent a considerable improvement, since this probability for the original model was only about .10.

So far, so good. However, we encounter a problem which Kemeny and Snell did not have to face since they did not consider the case of extreme conflict. The problem is of the "having your cake and eating it too" variety: We cannot assume that 20% of the subjects were absorbed nonconformists in the moderate conflict *and* that none of them were absorbed nonconformists in the extreme conflict. After all, the difference between the moderate and extreme conditions involved only the experimental conditions, trials $t = 1, 2, \ldots$; it had nothing to do with the selection of the subjects—with $t = 0$. Thus, if we make Assumption 2' for moderate conflict, we should make it for extreme conflict also.

The problem arises, of course, from the fact that shifting to Assumption 2' means altering the goodness of fit. However, in the case of extreme conflict the fit is already excellent and to alter it is likely to make it worse. And this prediction is supported by the results, for when we make adjustments in N_{TT} for the extreme case (changing it to $N_{TT} = 68$), we obtain the following matrix:

$$(7.12) \quad P' = \begin{bmatrix} 1 & 0 & 0 & 0 \\ .06 & .73 & .21 & 0 \\ 0 & .42 & .55 & .03 \\ 0 & 0 & 0 & 1 \end{bmatrix} \quad \text{for extreme conflict}$$

Using (7.12) and (7.10), we obtain the various r_k and the predicted frequencies Nr_k, as shown in the last column of Table 7.3. Note that the chi-square has indeed increased, from .21 to 2.98; the corresponding decrease of the probability that the discrepancy is due to chance is from .99 to about .60. Thus the switch from Assumption 2 to Assumption 2' decreases the goodness of fit of our model to the extreme conflict.

We see that modification of a model to increase its fit to the data at hand is not always a step in the right direction. Additional evidence may show that a different modification would have been better, and perhaps none at all would be best. In the present case, we could resolve our difficulties by searching for a starting vector $p^{(0)}$ that minimizes the difference for both conditions. For example, we could search for $p^{(0)}$ such that the probability of the discrepancy being due to pure chance is the same for both extreme and moderate conditions and is as high as possible. It is quite likely that this program would yield a unique definition of $p^{(0)}$.

Such an approach would be desirable if we were interested in evaluating our model on the basis of all the data available up to now. We note that the modified model has roughly the property of equalizing the level of significance for both conditions: the probability that the revised model's deviation from observed behavior is due to chance is approximately the same for both conditions—about .70 for moderate conflict, about .60 for extreme conflict. It would be possible to examine systematically whether there exists another starting vector $p^{(0)}$ which yields an even higher probability for both models. For our purposes, however, we are satisfied with our results and conclude that the fit of the model is fairly good.

This conclusion raises almost as many questions as it answers. In the first place, one may wonder why we consider the fit to be "fairly good" when it is customary to require that findings be significant at the .05 level or better, i.e., that the observed differences be attributable to chance in at least 95% of cases. Our results certainly do not meet these standards. We shall deal with this question in some detail in the next chapter. At this point let us simply note that the problems involved in testing a model are somewhat different from those arising when one wishes to determine whether two means or two proportions are significantly different, to cite typical examples of statistical approach. When we compare a model's predictions we expect the model to be different from that which it represents, particularly when we are dealing with simple models which almost by definition cannot describe the subject matter with complete accuracy. Hence our standards for what constitutes a "good enough fit" have to be less stringent than those traditionally applied in statistical analysis.

The second question concerns the finality of our results. If it was possible for new data to raise doubts about the switch from Assumption 2 to Assumption 2′, is it not possible that future data may discredit *any* model supported by presently available data? The answer can only be yes. It is indeed possible that this may happen. However, the more data that are available to test a model and the more diverse the conditions from which the data come, the less likely it is that future research will lead to such surprises. Furthermore, lack of finality is not unique to mathematical models. All scientific theories are subject to future refutation.

Lastly, it should be noted that our test of the model has not made exhaustive use even of the data at hand. True, we have shown that the incidence of exactly k switches is about as we would expect it to be; but we have not shown that the data support the model with respect to other possible implications. The point is that many models have a number of distinct implications, some of which may be supported by the data while others are contradicted by it. We have not searched for implications other than r_k and thus we are open to the criticism that we have not shown conclusively that our data support our model.

However, these considerations should be viewed in proper perspective. It seems unreasonable to expect a model-builder to test his model exhaustively; indeed, we shall argue later that to spend

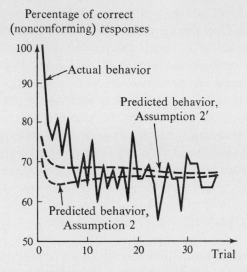

Figure 7.5. Predicted and actual behavior under moderate conflict conditions.

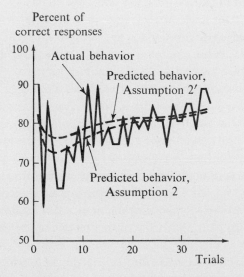

Figure 7.6. Predicted and actual behavior under extreme conflict conditions.

too much time on any one model may be poor strategy. On the other hand, one should be aware that there may be implications of the model which do not fit the data, and that someone might take the trouble to point it out. Indeed, the history of science suggests that this happens at times—discovery of a flaw in an old theory may be the starting point of a new theory.

We shall spend no more time testing the model. But it is interesting to note that visual inspection of the time-path of p_T supports our conclusions based on r_k, for, as is shown in Figures 7.5 and 7.6, the revised model does seem to fit the data better for moderate conflict, more poorly for extreme conflict.

7.5   USEFULNESS OF THE MODEL

Figures 7.3 to 7.6 show our model's capacity to predict the behavior of an "average" subject in Asch's experiments. This capacity in itself is a considerable accomplishment. A small number of estimates—the 4 free parameters p_{ij}—are sufficient to generate an infinite number of predictions, one for each $t = 0, 1, 2, \ldots$. A theory which can do so much is, by most scientists' standards, a rather good one. But a truly great theory not only predicts, it also explains something we could not understand without it.

It is implicit in the manner in which Cohen's model is constructed that it does not have as much explanatory power as do some other comparable models. As Berger et al. (1962) point out, some models are *theoretical-construct* models while others are *descriptive*. A descriptive Markov chains model, for example, arrives at the definition of the probability matrix P directly from the empirical data, while a theoretical-construct model derives P from certain theoretical considerations. For instance, the model of stratification, described in Chapters 5 and 6, is a theoretical-construct model since the probability matrix P was derived from some assumptions about the probability of dominance. Cohen's model, on the other hand, is a descriptive model, since the P was estimated directly from the data.

This distinction between the two types of models is useful in evaluating the explanatory power of a model. A theoretical-construct model will always have a greater explanatory power than the descriptive type, precisely because the "built-in" theory allows one to tell why some of the implications of the model hold true. Thus we can say, for example, that the reason why the concentration of authority is greater in some small groups than in others may be the existence of bias against the reversal of dominance. We have shown that the larger such a bias, the greater will be the concentration of authority in a small group.

Explanations of this kind cannot be offered by using Cohen's model, but we still can provide some explanations. The difference is that now the explanation will be in terms of some unique features *of the matrix P*, not in terms of some independent theory. To illustrate, let us try to explain the difference between the observed time paths of responses in moderate and extreme conflicts. As shown in Figure 7.1, the responses during moderate conflict tend to stabilize at about 65% of the T-responses, while the responses during extreme conflict, after an early "dip," tend to increase. Note that Cohen's model predicts this difference. The predictions shown in Figure 7.6 increase (at $t = 36$) faster than in Figure 7.5. Why?

In order to answer this question, let us note that it is possible, at time t, to divide the subjects into two "camps," the conformists (giving F-responses) and the nonconformists (giving T-responses). Note, furthermore, that the proportion of T-responses, $p_T^{(t)}$, may be viewed as a measure of the size of the nonconformist camp: the larger is $p_T^{(t)}$, the larger is that camp.

A moment's reflection shows that the only time the nonconformist camp can decrease in size is when the proportion leaving that camp is larger than the proportion entering it. Since the proportion leaving the nonconformist camp at time t is $p_2^{(t)}p_{23}$ and the proportion entering it is $p_3^{(t)}p_{32}$, it follows that the nonconformist camp will be decreasing—that is, the proportion $p_T^{(t)}$ will be decreasing—if and only if

$$p_2^{(t)}p_{23} > p_3^{(t)}p_{32}$$

Now both Assumption 2 and Assumption 2' imply that $p_T^{(0)} = 1$; provided that it is possible to leave the nonconformist camp (that $p_{23} \neq 0$), it follows that the above inequality is satisfied for time $t = 0$, and that *the early trend will be for $p_T^{(t)}$ to decrease.*

How long will this trend continue? As long as the proportion leaving the nonconformist camp is larger than the proportion entering it, that is, as long as this inequality holds. It is obvious also that the trend will be reversed if the inequality is reversed, that is, if it should ever happen that the proportion leaving the nonconformist camp is smaller than that entering it. Can these conditions for reversal be spelled out more definitely?

We start by observing that, before the decrease in $p_T^{(t)}$ is reversed, it has to be true for a moment, no matter how short this moment and no matter whether it corresponds to any one trial t, that the decrease is stopped, that the inequality becomes an equality.[21] The proportion leaving the nonconformist camp (during this moment) has to be the *same* as the proportion entering it:

$$p_2^{(2)}p_{23} = p_3^{(3)}p_{32}$$

Let us investigate the conditions under which this *equal exchange equilibrium*[22] will be stable, so that once it is reached it cannot be left.

We reason as follows: If the movement across the boundary of the two camps is equal, as the above condition stipulates, then the only way in which this equal exchange can be disturbed is through an unequal rate of "attrition." One of the camps must be more successful in removing subjects from across-the-boundary circulation than is the other. Since the rate at which a camp takes its members out of circulation is given by the probability of becoming absorbed, it follows that the equal exchange equilibrium will be disturbed only if the absorption probabilities of the two camps are unequal, that is, only if $p_{21} \neq p_{34}$. Inversely, we observe that the equal exchange equilibrium will be *stable* only if the two rates of absorption are equal, $p_{21} = p_{34}$.

Thus we arrive at the conclusion that the difference between the extreme and moderate conditions must be due to the difference between the absorption probabilities. Since the observations suggest that the proportion of T-responses, $p_T^{(t)}$, tends to stabilize at a certain level, it must be true that p_{34} and p_{21} for the moderate conflict are almost equal. Since we see no such stabilization for the extreme

---

[21] It can happen that the reversal occurs "in between" two time periods t and $t + 1$ in the sense that the proportion is decreasing at time t and increasing at time $t + 1$.

[22] "Equal exchange equilibrium" is an important concept in the theory of *regular* Markov chains (see, for example, Berger and Snell, 1957). Our use of the term in connection with absorbing Markov chains is in many respects similar.

conflict, it must be true that, for the model applicable to the extreme conflict, $p_{34} \neq p_{21}$. Using the matrices of the original models as given i (7.9), we see that

$$p_{34} = .05, p_{21} = .05 \qquad \text{for the moderate model}$$
$$p_{34} = .03, p_{21} = .07 \qquad \text{for the extreme model}$$

that is, both expectations are confirmed. Furthermore, our discussion suggests that the equal exchange equilibrium will be disturbed in the "upward" direction—that is, the nonconformist camp will start increasing after the original decrease—only if its absorption rate is larger than the absorption rate for the conformist camp, $p_{34} < p_{21}$. And we see that this condition is also satisfied for the extreme conflict.

In this way we account for the "dip" observed in the extreme conflict and the lack of such a dip in the moderate conflict in terms of the absorption probabilities p_{21} and p_{34}. We conclude that the important consequence of making the discrepancy of the majority's error more obvious (changing from the moderate to the extreme conflict) is that a subject will be less likely to become an absorbed conformist than an absorbed nonconformist. The more obvious the discrepancy, the greater the excess of those who decide to defy the group over those who decide to conform.

EXERCISES

1. An Asch conformity experiment with 40 subjects yielded the following matrix:

$$P = \begin{bmatrix} 1 & 0 & 0 & 0 \\ \frac{7}{136} & \frac{10}{17} & \frac{49}{136} & 0 \\ 0 & \frac{24}{49} & \frac{3}{7} & \frac{4}{49} \\ 0 & 0 & 0 & 1 \end{bmatrix}$$

If a subject starts as a "temporary nonconformist" (state 2), how long will it take him, on the average, before he reaches state 1 or 4? In other words, how many trials will he "usually" go through before he makes up his mind either to be a conformist or a nonconformist?

2. Using the matrix of exercise 1, compute the probability that the process is absorbed in state 1 if it starts in state 3.

3. Imagine that you had only three subjects in an Asch-type experiment, but that (for practice's sake) you wished to estimate from this meager data the probability p_{33} in matrix of eq. 7.1. Let the transcripts of the three subjects be

Subject 1   (T)TTTFFTFTFTTTFTTTTFTTTTTFFFTTFTTTTTT
Subject 2   (T)FFFTFFTTTFTFTFFFFTFTFTTTTTTFFFFTTTT
Subject 3   (T)FFFTFTFFTTTTTTTTFTTTTTTTFFFTTTTTTTT

Estimate p_{21} and p_{22} using the formulae in the Appendix:

$$p_{21} \approx \frac{N_{TF}(N - N_{TF} + N_{FT})}{(N_{TT} + N_{TF})(N + N_{FT})} \qquad p_{22} \approx \frac{N_{TT}}{N_{TT} + N_{TF}}$$

4. Using the results of exercise 3, compute the probability that there will be a subject who does not switch his responses at all (the probability of exactly 0 switches). What will the transcript of such a subject look like?

5. Consider the following two transition matrices:

$$P = \begin{bmatrix} 1 & 0 & 0 & 0 \\ .7 & .2 & .1 & 0 \\ 0 & .6 & .2 & .2 \\ 0 & 0 & 0 & 1 \end{bmatrix} \qquad P' = \begin{bmatrix} 1 & 0 & 0 & 0 \\ .1 & .7 & .2 & 0 \\ 0 & .4 & .5 & .1 \\ 0 & 0 & 0 & 1 \end{bmatrix}$$

Suppose that the starting vector is $p^{(0)} = (0, \frac{1}{2}, \frac{1}{2}, 0)$ and let $r^{(t)} = p_1^{(t)} + p_2^{(t)}$; what will be the starting trend for $r^{(t)}$? Will it increase or decrease at first (is $r^{(1)} > r^{(0)}$)? Determine the trend for each matrix.

6. Using P and P' of exercise 5, determine (a) whether either one of the two processes has a stable equal exchange equilibrium, and (b) whether the early trend of $r^{(t)}$ will ever be reversed.

CHAPTER 8

Social Mobility

Of the topics studied by social scientists, few are better suited for the application of Markov chains than social mobility. There are several reasons for this. In the first place, in the study of social mobility one is dealing with *easily observable* states, for whether the study concerns occupational mobility, social class mobility, or migration, the researcher experiences relatively little difficulty in determining whether a person is or is not in a given state (an occupation, a social class, a geographic area). Second, these processes typically involve *large numbers of people*. As a result, not only is it easy to arrive at reliable estimates of the transition matrices, but also the very assumption that the process is stochastic makes better sense when it involves large numbers than when the numbers are small. Finally, the data needed to estimate the transition matrices are usually *available* in ready-made form in the publications of various governmental agencies, notably the U. S. Bureau of Census. Thus it is easy to obtain the data needed for applying the theory of Markov chains.

It is not surprising, therefore, to find that the area of social mobility abounds with attempts at applying the Markov chains theory. We shall consider here two main examples of such application, to occupational mobility and to migration.

8.1   OCCUPATIONAL MOBILITY

A process of considerable practical interest is the flow of workers
through the industrial structure of a given nation. Is there a tendency
for the workers to desert a particular occupational category in
favor of another? Is it likely that in the future some important jobs
will lack manpower? Answers to such questions may be important
to those in government or industry charged with the responsibility
of keeping the economy sound, for they may suggest that remedial
action is needed.

Blumen et al. (1955) addressed themselves to such a problem.
Using the BOASI (Bureau of Old Age and Survivors Insurance)
one percent sample of all workers in the United States who have
been covered by social security since 1937, the authors developed
various models of occupational mobility. Of interest to us will be
their Markov chains model.

The Model

Before attempting to formulate a model of occupational mobility,
Blumen et al. subjected the data of the BOASI sample to a preliminary analysis. One fact emerging from this analysis was that mobility
differs with respect to age and sex: Men were more likely to move
to new jobs than women, young workers more than old ones. For
this reason, the authors decided to divide the sample into several
sets, each containing workers of the same sex and approximately
the same age. We shall report here only the results pertaining to
males aged 20 to 24; the chief results for other workers are similar,
even though each set of workers is characterized by different
parameters p_{ij}.

The BOASI sample utilizes a very detailed classification of
occupations, recognizing no less than 77 distinct industries. Blumen
et al. decided to combine many of these categories into broader
ones. Table 8.1 shows their classification system involving ten
"industry code groups," $A, B, \ldots, K$.

Given the ten industry code groups, and the fact that we are
interested in the movement of workers to and from these groups,
the simplest way of defining a Markov chains model is obvious.

Table 8.1. Description of the Ten Industry Code Groups

Industry Code Groups	Code Groups and the Two-Digit Industries They Include[b]
A (Agr.)	01, 07, 08, 09—Farms, Agricultural Service, Forestry, and Fisheries
B (Const.)[a]	10–17—Mining and Construction
C (20–26)	Food and Kindred Products, Tobacco, Textile Mills, Apparel, Lumber, Furniture and Fixtures, Paper and Allied Products
D (27–32)	Printing and Publishing, Chemical Products, Petroleum Products, Rubber Products, Leather Products, Stone and Clay Products
E (Metal)	19 and 33–39—Ordnance, Primary Metals, Fabricated Metals, Machinery, Electrical Equipment, Transportation Equipment, Professional and Scientific Equipment, Miscellaneous Manufacturing
F (Tr., Co., Ut.)	40–49—Transportation, Communication, and Utilities
G (Trade)	50–59—Wholesale and Retail Trade
H (Bus.)	60–67—Banks, Insurance, and Real Estate
J (Serv.)	70–90—Service, Amusement, and Professions
K (Gov., Un.)	94, 95, 99, 100—Government and Unclassified

[a] Although this group includes Mining, the great majority of the workers in it are associated with the Construction Industries. For example, Table A300 (Workers, by Last Industry and Age, 1947) of the 1947 *Handbook of Old-Age and Survivors Insurance Statistics* shows that 73.7 percent of the workers in Mining and Contract Construction were in Contract Construction.

[b] The numbers preceding the industries are the codes assigned to the various industries in the two-digit classification of the BOASI sample.

REPRINTED from Blumen, Kogan, and McCarthy (1955), by permission of the New York State School of Industrial and Labor Relations and the Cornell University Press.

The ten industry code groups may serve as the states of the transition matrix P. However, these ten states do not cover all the cases of the BOASI sample: at a given time, a worker could be classified not only as belonging to one of the ten industry code groups, but also as "not being on the social security payrolls." Since such a classification was usually not permanent, many workers gaining or losing social security coverage as time went by, it will be necessary to add an eleventh state U ("uncovered"), to the list of states of the Markov chain.

Once the states of the process are defined, the nature of the data is such that estimation of the transition probabilities is very simple. Probability p_{ij} is estimated by the ratio N_{ij}/N_i, where N_{ij} is the total number of workers who moved, between two quarters,[1] from state i to state j; N_i is the total number of workers who, during quarter t $(t = 1, 2, \ldots)$, were in state i. Table 8.2 gives the resulting matrix P.

The authors tested this model in a way that is different from anything we have discussed so far. Using the fact that the probability

Table 8.2. One-Quarter Transition Matrix P

(based on the sum of all one-quarter observations)

Code Group of Origin	Code Group of Destination										
	A	B	C	D	E	F	G	H	J	K	U
A	.407	.035	.081	.012	.046	.023	.081	.000	.035	.000	.279
B	.001	.727	.021	.009	.022	.012	.036	.004	.011	.002	.155
C	.001	.016	.761	.008	.022	.009	.038	.003	.010	.002	.129
D	.000	.014	.019	.815	.021	.011	.027	.003	.011	.001	.077
E	.000	.016	.015	.010	.827	.011	.032	.002	.008	.002	.078
F	.001	.021	.012	.008	.018	.777	.030	.004	.011	.002	.116
G	.001	.020	.020	.008	.019	.012	.788	.004	.016	.002	.112
H	.000	.019	.016	.006	.015	.012	.048	.787	.015	.003	.079
J	.001	.024	.018	.007	.023	.012	.054	.005	.704	.002	.151
K	.000	.052	.052	.022	.073	.009	.082	.017	.030	.468	.197
U	.002	.039	.037	.012	.033	.017	.065	.006	.028	.002	.760

$P =$

REPRINTED from Blumen, Kogan, and McCarthy (1955), by permission of the New York State School of Industrial and Labor Relations and the Cornell University Press.

vector at time t, $p^{(t)}$, is given by

$$p^{(t)} = p^{(0)}P^t$$

Blumen et al. focus their attention on the powers of matrix P, P^t, rather than on the probability vector $p^{(t)}$. This approach has the advantage of allowing for a larger number of comparisons between the prediction and observation [each P^t yields, when there are eleven states, $11^2 = 121$ probabilities p_{ij} but only eleven probabilities $p_k^{(t)}$]. Its disadvantage, however, is that each comparison may be based on a relatively small number of cases and hence the differences between observation and prediction may be subject to considerable chance fluctuations.

[1] Since an employer has to make quarterly reports, the data in the BOASI sample were organized on a quarterly basis as well. It was therefore natural to use quarters as the periods t of the Markov chains process.

Table 8.3. Comparison of Predicted and Observed Fourth-Order Matrices

Code Group of Origin		Code Group of Destination											Number of Observations
		B	C	D	E	F	G	H	J	K	U	
A	Exp.	.029	.076	.117	.031	.098	.047	.162	.009	.058	.003	.372	
	Obs.	.125	.062	.031	.062	.125	.094	.156	.000	.062	.000	.281	(32)
B	Exp.	.002	.311	.064	.028	.071	.036	.115	.013	.038	.004	.318	
	Obs.	.001	.530	.037	.021	.043	.020	.067	.010	.014	.002	.256	(1,575)
C	Exp.	.001	.054	.363	.026	.070	.030	.117	.011	.035	.004	.287	
	Obs.	.001	.025	.568	.013	.052	.016	.074	.006	.016	.003	.225	(2,019)
D	Exp.	.001	.047	.057	.450	.066	.032	.092	.009	.033	.002	.210	
	Obs.	.002	.036	.033	.610	.061	.024	.066	.006	.024	.001	.135	(1,068)
E	Exp.	.001	.049	.050	.028	.488	.033	.100	.007	.029	.003	.210	
	Obs.	.002	.033	.037	.021	.619	.023	.064	.006	.021	.002	.170	(2,897)
F	Exp.	.002	.061	.048	.025	.063	.378	.102	.012	.036	.004	.270	
	Obs.	.001	.037	.019	.023	.048	.574	.074	.008	.022	.005	.190	(1,047)
G	Exp.	.002	.059	.060	.026	.063	.036	.432	.011	.042	.003	.265	
	Obs.	.002	.036	.040	.022	.039	.024	.598	.010	.031	.002	.196	(3,456)
H	Exp.	.001	.056	.052	.022	.054	.034	.132	.388	.040	.005	.217	
	Obs.	.000	.047	.027	.013	.020	.034	.067	.574	.040	.003	.174	(298)
J	Exp.	.001	.067	.060	.024	.073	.036	.143	.014	.268	.003	.312	
	Obs.	.000	.039	.026	.009	.044	.026	.104	.013	.504	.001	.233	(1,068)
K	Exp.	.001	.088	.092	.042	.127	.032	.161	.026	.054	.051	.324	
	Obs.	.000	.110	.088	.033	.121	.022	.209	.022	.011	.088	.297	(91)
U	Exp.	.002	.083	.084	.032	.086	.042	.152	.015	.056	.004	.444	
	Obs.	.001	.063	.060	.023	.067	.032	.126	.014	.046	.003	.564	(7,377)

REPRINTED from Blumen, Kogan, and McCarthy (1955), by permission of the New York State School of Industrial and Labor Relations and the Cornell University Press.

The authors used matrix P of Table 8.2 and raised it to the fourth and to the eighth powers. The resulting matrices P^4 and P^8, as well as the corresponding observations, are displayed in Tables 8.3 and 8.4. The amount of data shown in the two tables is bewildering and, to some extent, defies attempts at conclusions. However, as the authors point out, one feature of these tables is conspicuous. *The model seriously underestimates the number of workers who stay in a given industry code group: Moreover, this discrepancy grows larger with time.* To see this, let us consider the main diagonal entries of the two matrices. As Table 8.5 shows, the percentage differences between predicted and observed values are consistently larger for P^8 than

Table 8.4. Comparison of Predicted and Observed Eighth-Order Matrices

Code Group of Origin		A	B	C	D	E	F	G	H	J	K	U	Number of Observations
A	Exp.	.002	.086	.105	.042	.116	.053	.181	.016	.058	.004	.337	
	Obs.	.000	.062	.062	.000	.125	.156	.312	.000	.000	.000	.281	(32)
B	Exp.	.002	.144	.087	.040	.104	.050	.163	.018	.052	.004	.336	
	Obs.	.003	.449	.039	.020	.048	.035	.079	.014	.023	.006	.284	(1,448)
C	Exp.	.002	.077	.176	.039	.103	.046	.163	.016	.050	.004	.324	
	Obs.	.002	.037	.461	.023	.046	.021	.101	.007	.022	.002	.278	(2,017)
D	Exp.	.001	.070	.080	.218	.099	.046	.141	.015	.047	.003	.279	
	Obs.	.000	.064	.044	.459	.083	.024	.091	.011	.030	.002	.192	(1,081)
E	Exp.	.001	.072	.075	.040	.276	.046	.147	.013	.044	.004	.279	
	Obs.	.002	.045	.042	.034	.489	.031	.094	.010	.023	.002	.227	(2,777)
F	Exp.	.002	.081	.076	.038	.097	.166	.152	.017	.050	.004	.316	
	Obs.	.003	.056	.033	.022	.054	.440	.090	.020	.026	.010	.245	(1,016)
G	Exp.	.002	.080	.084	.039	.098	.049	.261	.017	.053	.004	.314	
	Obs.	.002	.047	.051	.025	.046	.038	.491	.020	.044	.002	.235	(3,259)
H	Exp.	.001	.077	.077	.035	.090	.048	.170	.158	.052	.004	.287	
	Obs.	.000	.044	.007	.015	.026	.085	.096	.439	.074	.000	.214	(271)
J	Exp.	.002	.084	.085	.038	.105	.049	.178	.018	.105	.004	.333	
	Obs.	.002	.061	.033	.018	.054	.035	.145	.019	.339	.000	.294	(1,083)
K	Exp.	.002	.089	.096	.047	.130	.048	.179	.023	.056	.006	.325	
	Obs.	.000	.113	.097	.032	.121	.048	.137	.032	.024	.048	.347	(124)
U	Exp.	.002	.090	.095	.042	.112	.052	.179	.019	.058	.004	.346	
	Obs.	.001	.069	.068	.035	.077	.040	.153	.018	.055	.004	.482	(7,820)

for P^4. Furthermore, inspection of Tables 8.3 and 8.4 reveals that in all diagonal elements except one (the code group A in Table 8.4) the observed proportion is *higher* than the predicted probability p_{ij}. Thus, indeed, the proportion of those who stay in the same code group is underestimated by the model. The differences are so large that we do not have to compute a measure of goodness of fit to know that they cannot be due to chance.

The Equilibrium Process

It happens at times that a Markov chains model which does not fit the actual data when various implications of the model are

Table 8.5. Percentage Differences* between Expected and Observed Main Diagonal Entries for Fourth- and Eighth-Order Change Matrices

Code Group of Origin	Fourth Order	Eighth Order
B	70.4	211.8
C	56.5	161.9
D	35.6	110.6
E	26.8	77.2
F	51.9	165.1
G	38.4	88.1
H	47.9	177.8
J	88.0	222.8
U	27.0	39.3

* Entries are $100\left(\dfrac{\text{Obs.}-\text{Exp.}}{\text{Exp.}}\right)$.

REPRINTED from Blumen, Kogan, and McCarthy (1955), by permission of the New York State School of Industrial and Labor Relations and the Cornell University Press.

considered nevertheless does fit it with respect to one particular implication, the fixed probability vector p^*. Let us, therefore, investigate the possibility that the process described by our model is in fact an equilibrium process.

We know that the fixed probability vector p^* can always be computed from the equation that describes the "no change" condition, $p^* = p^*P$. Therefore, we could use the matrix of Table 8.2 to compute p^*. However, Blumen et al. preferred to simplify their task by computing p^* from a smaller matrix than the 11×11 matrix of Table 8.2. They combined industry code groups with small numbers of workers into larger occupational categories, arriving at the five states listed in Table 8.6. Using the same method of estimation as before, the authors arrived at the following matrix of transition probabilities:

$$(8.1) \qquad P = \begin{bmatrix} .832 & .033 & .013 & .028 & .095 \\ .046 & .788 & .016 & .038 & .112 \\ .038 & .034 & .785 & .036 & .107 \\ .054 & .045 & .017 & .728 & .156 \\ .082 & .065 & .023 & .071 & .759 \end{bmatrix}$$

The fixed probability vector p^* for the above P is

(8.2) $p^* = (.270, .184, .076, .148, .322)$

Using the actual data, the authors arrived at the following overall proportions of workers actually in each of the five states:

$$\bar{p}^* = (.282, .170, .068, .137, .343)$$

The degree of discrepancy between p^* and $\bar{p}^*$ again may be ascertained by using the chi-square statistic. The total number of observations on which $\bar{p}^*$ is based is 20,928, thus yielding the chi-square of

Table 8.6.

		Included in the State
State	Code	Group
1	C, D, E	(20–32, Metal)
2	G	(*Trade*)
3	F, H	(Tr., Co., Ut., Bus.)
4	A, B, J, K	(Agr., Constr., Serv., Gov., Un.)
5	U	(*Uncovered*

96.27. The probability that a value of this size would occur by chance is considerably smaller than .001; that is, the difference between $\bar{p}^*$ and p^* is almost certainly "real"—not due to chance.

Criteria for Accepting a Model

Given this result, the reader steeped in the tradition of empirical research may feel that the model has been proven worthless. The discrepancy between predictions and observations is clearly not attributable to chance, hence the model should be discarded. We agree that it is not a very good model, but our grounds for rejecting it will be somewhat more diverse than those used in much of empirical research.

First of all, we are not bothered too much by the fact that p^* and $\bar{p}^*$ are significantly different. Consider the fact that the chi-square computed for the comparison is based on almost 30,000 observations, and that, for four degrees of freedom, the chi-square would have to be less than 9.488 to occur by pure chance (at .05 level). This means that the mean difference between p_k^* and $\bar{p}_k^*$ would have to be (with 30,000 observations) less than $9.488/(5 \times 30,000) = .00006$—a very small difference indeed. Would one not be justified in calling the model "good" even if the mean difference between predicted and observed proportions was as "large" as .00007? Even though such a difference would, with 30,000 observations, yield a significant chi-square? In fact, some theoreticians would consider even the difference between our p^* and $\bar{p}^*$ to be small enough to call the fit good,[2] although the mean difference in our case is .0132.

This suggests that, while the concern with the significance of the differences between prediction and observation is important, it should not be the only one. We need other criteria than the level of significance to evaluate mathematical models. But what should these additional criteria be?

The most honest answer to this question is that, at present time, there is no agreement on such criteria. While the enterprise of model construction has a fairly long and respectable tradition in some behavioral sciences (notably economics), the tradition of constructing models *and testing them against observations* is quite young. As a result, we shall have to wait until we have gained more experience in constructing and testing models before we can hope to formulate universally acceptable criteria.

There are some criteria, however, which seem reasonable even today. The most basic of these, in our opinion, is that *a model should fit the data as well as or better than a different but comparable model.*[3] In other words, if one can show that a particular model does a better job of predicting (even though the discrepancy between prediction and observation is too large to be due to chance) than does a different but comparable model, then one is justified in working with that model until a better one comes along. Clearly, this criterion is based on the assumption that science is a cumulative enterprise, the beginnings of which may be quite inauspicious.

We do not have a "different but comparable" model of occupational mobility to which our results could be compared, and thus

[2] For example, Kemeny and Snell (1960) typically consider that such differences are small enough, see especially pp. 191–200.

[3] One may view two different modes as "comparable" if the number of free parameters is the same in both. This definition is based on the distinction between theoretical-construct models and descriptive models discussed in Chapter 7. The fewer free parameters (which have to be estimated from the data) the model has, the closer is the model to the theoretical-construct end of the dichotomy. Since one can always construct a model that fits data perfectly if one is willing to leave a sufficiently large number of parameters free, it seems reasonable to compare the predictive power of only those models that leave the same number of parameters free.

we must look for additional criteria. And it seems reasonable to view the systematic and growing underestimation of the proportion of workers remaining in the same industry code group as grounds for rejecting the model. It appears that something is basically wrong with a model if it leads to such a *systematic* misrepresentation of reality. On the other hand, the closeness between p^* and $\bar{p}^*$ has led the authors to conclude that something "regular" is going on in the observed industrial movement. And they proceed to consider a modified version of the model.

Towards a Modified Model

We shall describe only the essentials of the so-called mover-stayer model that is the result of the attempt by Blumen et al. to make the model more realistic. Their main assumption is that the original model underestimated systematically the proportion of "stayers" (those who remain in a given industry code group) because the stayers are different from the "movers" (those who move into a different industry code group). The transition matrix that applies to the movers does *not* apply to the stayers.

More specifically, Blumen et al. assume that it is possible to divide all workers into two groups, the stayers and the movers, and that the stayers are workers who never move from one industry code group to another but remain in the same group quarter after quarter. This assumption can be utilized to define formally the modified model. Let the transition matrix that applies to the movers be M, and let S be a matrix (not a transition matrix) such that

$$
(8.3) \qquad S = \begin{array}{c}
\\
A \\
B \\
C \\
\cdot \\
\cdot \\
\cdot \\
U
\end{array}
\begin{array}{cccccc}
A & B & C & \ldots & U & \\
\left[\begin{array}{ccccc}
s_1 & 0 & 0 & \ldots & 0 \\
0 & s_2 & 0 & \ldots & 0 \\
0 & 0 & s_3 & \ldots & 0 \\
\cdot & \cdot & \cdot & & \cdot \\
\cdot & \cdot & \cdot & & \cdot \\
\cdot & \cdot & \cdot & & \cdot \\
0 & 0 & 0 & \cdots & s_{11}
\end{array}\right]
\end{array}
$$

s_k being the proportion of stayers in industry code group k. Then the transition matrix "applicable at time t," $P^{(t)}$, is given by

$$(8.4) \qquad\qquad P^{(t)} = S + (I - S)M^t$$

where I is an identity matrix. Matrix $P^{(t)}$ plays the same role in the new model as P^t did in the old. The distribution of the workers among the industry code groups at time t, $P^{(t)}$, is given by $p^{(t)} = p^{(0)}P^{(t)}$ rather than, as in the old model, by $p^{(t)} = p^{(0)}P^t$. To put it quite simply, in order to describe the time-path of the process, we raise to a tth power not matrix P but matrix M. The reason for this modification is obvious. Equation 8.6 is a guarantee that a worker who is classified as a stayer at time $t = 0$ will remain a stayer forever, just as we wished to assume that he would, since the only changes occur among the movers governed by matrix M.

Using (8.3) and performing the additions and multiplications indicated in (8.4), we note that it holds for each component *not* on the diagonal, $p_{ij} \neq p_{ii}$, that

$$p_{ij} = (1 - s_i)m_{ij}$$

Since the proportion of stayers in state i is normally larger than zero, $1 - s_i$ is normally smaller than 1. Thus (8.4) and (8.3) imply that the same type of operation will be performed on the movers' matrix at each time t. The nondiagonal elements of M^t are *decreased* every time, each row by a constant factor $1 - s_i$. Similarly, it is easy to see that (8.3) and (8.4) imply for the diagonal components p_{ii} that

$$p_{ii} = s_i + (1 - s_i)m_{ii}$$

that is, each probability on the main diagonal will be *increased*, each probability m_{ii} by a constant linear transformation $s_i + (1 - s_i)m_{ii}$.

Thus we see that the new model has characteristics that are desirable in view of the fact that the original model's most serious shortcoming concerned the main diagonal. In principle at least, the new model should be capable of overcoming this shortcoming, since by altering s_i one can alter the relative size of each component on the main diagonal.

However, the new model does not in fact remedy this limitation. After describing a procedure for estimating S and M from the data,

Blumen et al. proceed to compare various $P^{(t)}$'s with the actual observations. They report that, although $P^{(8)}$ fits the observations quite well, $P^{(t)}$ for t lower and higher than $t = 8$ does not. Specifically, $P^{(4)}$ underestimates the proportion of stayers, $P^{(11)}$ overestimates it. Thus the new model appears to have a built-in systematic error, just as did the original model. Both models suffer from systematic error with respect to the components on the main diagonal of matrix P.

The authors conclude that the reason why the new model still fails is the assumption that a stayer never changes his industry code group, and they develop a general model eliminating such an assumption. However, no attempt is made to test the new model against the data, and hence we cannot say whether their remedy will work. It is hoped that future research will resolve some of the problems which block the application of the model at this time, and that it will actually be tested against the data. In the concluding section of this chapter we shall consider some recent attempts in this direction.

8.2   MIGRATION

We shall now apply the theory of Markov chains to migration between different geographical areas. The application of the theory of Markov chains will be novel in that we shall consider not only probabilities but also frequencies. Following Rogers' (1965) work, we shall use transition matrices to predict the *number* of persons who will be in a given state at a given time.

A Model

Rogers considers a variety of problems of practical importance. For example, he presents a number of 7×7 transition matrices, the states of which are five regions in California (San Francisco-Oakland, San Jose, Sacramento, Los Angeles-Long Beach, and San Diego), the rest of California and the rest of the United States. Matrices are presented for different time periods, for different racial groups, and for different age groups. Comparison of these matrices suggests many interesting hypotheses about migration.

All of these matrices represent regular Markov chains and constitute a good first approximation to the study of migration. But quite often one is not interested in migration per se; one studies migration because one wishes to predict the population size in a given region. When this is the objective, then a model that takes into account only migration between regions is likely to be deficient, because it ignores two important processes that influence population size: the process of birth and death. In order to incorporate these two processes into the model, we turn to *absorbing* Markov chains.

The basic idea is quite simple: Since being dead satisfies both requirements of an absorbing state (once dead, always dead, and people die in all regions[4]) we simply add to the matrix one more state—"death." The transition matrix, for the simplest case of two regions, is as follows:

$$
\begin{array}{c}
\qquad\qquad\text{Region } A \quad \text{Region } B \quad \text{Death} \\
(8.5) \quad P = \begin{array}{c} \text{Region } A \\ \text{Region } B \\ \text{Death} \end{array}
\left[
\begin{array}{ccc}
p_{11} & p_{12} & p_{13} \\
p_{21} & p_{22} & p_{23} \\
0 & 0 & 1
\end{array}
\right]
\end{array}
$$

Using the convention described earlier, we can divide (8.5) into four submatrices as indicated by the dotted lines. Labeling the upper left submatrix Q,

$$
Q = \begin{bmatrix} p_{11} & p_{12} \\ p_{21} & p_{22} \end{bmatrix}
$$

We can now predict the *number* of persons living in region A or B at any time t if we know the number living in these regions at the time the process is assumed to begin, $t = 0$. It can be shown that if the number living in the two regions at time $t = 0$ is $w^{(0)} = [w_1^{(0)}, w_2^{(0)}]$, then we can compute the expected number $\bar{w}^{(t)}$ for any time $t = 1, 2, \ldots$ from

$$(8.6) \qquad\qquad \bar{w}^{(t)} = w^{(0)}Q^t$$

---

[4] Which corresponds to the requirement that there be at least one state which the process cannot leave, and that the process should be able to reach an absorbing state from every nonabsorbing state.

where Q is the submatrix in eq. 8.5.[5] It is not difficult to see that Q^t approaches zero as t approaches infinity. Hence we are in fact predicting that $\bar{w}^{(t)}$ approaches zero, too, i.e., that the population is dying out in both regions.

This indeed would be the case in real life if it were not for the process of birth, which must also be considered. Let us designate the number of babies born during period t in the two areas[6] by $x^{(t)} = [x_1^{(t)} x_2^{(t)}]$; then we take births into account by adding the birth vector $x^{(t)}$ to each population vector $\bar{w}^{(t)}$, thus obtaining a revised population vector, $\bar{w}^{(t)}$:

$$(8.7) \qquad\qquad w^{(t)} = \bar{w}^{(t)} + x^{(t)}$$

Let us inquire what consequences (8.7) has for the process. At time $t = 1$, eq. 8.6 implies

$$\bar{w}^{(1)} = w^{(0)}Q$$

Equation 8.7, however, allows us to write

$$w^{(1)} = \bar{w}^{(1)} + x^{(1)} = w^{(0)}Q + x^{(1)}$$

For $t = 2$ we obtain by (8.6)

$$\bar{w}^{(2)} = w^{(1)}Q = w^{(0)}Q^2 + x^{(1)}Q$$

From (8.7),

$$w^{(2)} = \bar{w}^{(2)} + x^{(2)} = w^{(0)}Q^2 + x^{(1)}Q + x^{(2)}$$

We conjecture (correctly) that

$$(8.8) \qquad w^{(t)} = w^{(0)}Q^t + x^{(1)}Q^{t-1} + x^{(2)}Q^{t-2} + \cdots + x^{(t)}$$

This is an unwieldy equation, but it can be used to compute $w^{(t)}$, and that is all we shall need.

[5] It is easy to show that a transition matrix can be used to compute either the proportion or the number of persons. According to the fundamental equation that holds for all Markov chains, $p^{(t+1)} = p^{(t)}P$. This equality is not altered if we multiply both sides by the same number N; hence we can write $Np^{(t+1)} = Np^{(t)}P$. Now let N be the total population in the United States, $p_k^{(t)}$ and $p_k^{(t+1)}$ the probability that an American is in state (area) k. Then $Np_k^{(t)}$ is the expected number of persons in state at time t, $Np_k^{(t+1)}$ the expected number in state k at time $t + 1$. If we designate these expected numbers as $w^{(t)} = Np^{(t)}$ and $w^{(t+1)} = Np^{(t+1)}$, then we can write $w^{(t+1)} = w^{(t)}P$, using P to predict directly the number of persons in each state $w^{(t+1)}$. This result holds when P is a transition matrix. Rogers (1965) shows that it holds also for transition submatrices Q.

[6] Our "time t" is always a discrete time interval, such as the period from 1935 to 1940.

Evaluation of the Model

Rogers chose to consider a simple problem—migration into and from California. Thus he was dealing with three states: two regions (California and the rest of the United States) and the state of death. Given the definitions of the three states and the availability of census statistics, estimation of the transition matrix posed no problem. Using the five-year periods 1935–1940, Rogers arrived at the following transition matrix:

$$1940$$

$$\text{Calif.} \quad \text{U.S.} \quad \text{Death}$$

$$(8.9) \qquad P = 1935 \quad \begin{matrix} \text{Calif.} \\ \text{U.S.} \\ \text{Death} \end{matrix} \begin{bmatrix} .9041 & .0331 & .0628 \\ .0068 & .9352 & .0580 \\ 0 & 0 & 1 \end{bmatrix}$$

The starting population vector $w^{(0)}$ for the year 1935 was

$$w^{(0)} = (6,175,000; 121,075,000)$$

The various birth vectors $x^{(t)}$ are given in Table 8.7. With this information, it is possible to apply eq. 8.8 to compute the predicted population vector $w^{(t)}$ for 1940, 1945, 1950, 1955, and 1960. Table 8.8 shows these computations.

Table 8.8 shows, among other things, the predicted and the actual populations for 1960. Note that the model underestimates both the California and the United States population: for California by about three and a half million, for the rest of the United States by almost one million. These discrepancies seem to be too large to

Table 8.7. Birth Vectors $x^{(t)}$

Period	Calif.	U.S.
1935–1939	$x^{(1)} = (464,000;$	$12,177,000)$
1940–1944	$x^{(2)} = (740,000;$	$14,293,000)$
1945–1949	$x^{(3)} = (1,128,000;$	$17,372,000)$
1950–1954	$x^{(4)} = (1,389,000;$	$19,410,000)$
1955–1959	$x^{(5)} = (1,705,000;$	$21,180,000)$

REPRINTED from Rogers (1965), by permission of the author.

Table 8.8.

	Calif.	U.S.	Calif.	U.S.		Calif.	U.S.

$$1935: (6{,}175{,}000\,;\,121{,}075{,}000) \begin{bmatrix} .9041 & .0331 \\ .0068 & .9352 \end{bmatrix} = \begin{array}{l} (6{,}406{,}000\,;\,113{,}434{,}000) \\ +(464{,}000\,;\;\;12{,}177{,}000) \\ \hline (6{,}870{,}000\,;\,125{,}611{,}000) \end{array}$$

$$1940: (6{,}870{,}000\,;\,125{,}611{,}000) \begin{bmatrix} .9041 & .0331 \\ .0068 & .9352 \end{bmatrix} = \begin{array}{l} (7{,}065{,}000\,;\,117{,}699{,}000) \\ +(740{,}000\,;\;\;14{,}293{,}000) \\ \hline (7{,}805{,}000\,;\,131{,}992{,}000) \end{array}$$

$$1945: (7{,}805{,}000\,;\,131{,}992{,}000) \begin{bmatrix} .9041 & .0331 \\ .0068 & .9352 \end{bmatrix} = \begin{array}{l} (7{,}954{,}000\,;\,123{,}697{,}000) \\ +(1{,}128{,}000\,;\;\;17{,}372{,}000) \\ \hline (9{,}082{,}000\,;\,141{,}069{,}000) \end{array}$$

$$1950: (9{,}082{,}000\,;\,141{,}069{,}000) \begin{bmatrix} .9041 & .0331 \\ .0068 & .9352 \end{bmatrix} = \begin{array}{l} (9{,}170{,}000\,;\,132{,}228{,}000) \\ +(1{,}389{,}000\,;\;\;19{,}410{,}000) \\ \hline (10{,}559{,}000\,;\,151{,}639{,}000) \end{array}$$

$$1955: (10{,}559{,}000\,;\,151{,}639{,}000) \begin{bmatrix} .9041 & .0331 \\ .0068 & .9352 \end{bmatrix} = \begin{array}{l} (10{,}578{,}000\,;\,142{,}162{,}000) \\ +(1{,}705{,}000\,;\;\;21{,}180{,}000) \\ \hline (12{,}283{,}000\,;\,163{,}342{,}000) \end{array}$$

Theoretical 1960 Population Distribution: (12,283,000; 163,342,000)
Actual 1960 Population Distribution: (15,717,000; 164,266,000)

REPRINTED from Rogers (1965), by permission of the author.

allow us to view our model as a realistic representation of the migration process. Why does the model fail?

It is clear that the size of population in any region is fully determined by three processes: birth, death, and migration. Thus the failure of the model must be attributable to the assumptions we made about these three processes. We see immediately that our assumptions about the birth process could not have been at fault, simply because we made no arbitrary assumptions, for we used the actual census data to determine $x^{(t)}$. Hence the fault must lie with either the death or the migration process.

There are two possible sources of error, an error due to incomplete definition of the states and an error due to the (false) assumption that the process is Markovian. The fact that our model may be deficient in the first respect is obvious. We should have considered as a state not only "the rest of the United States" but also "the rest of the world." In other words, our transition matrix should have been:

$$
\begin{array}{c}
 \quad\;\; \text{Calif.} \quad\;\; \text{U.S.} \quad\;\; \text{World} \quad\;\; \text{Death} \\
\begin{array}{c} \text{Calif.} \\ \text{U.S.} \\ \text{World} \\ \text{Death} \end{array}
\left[
\begin{array}{cccc}
p_{11} & p_{12} & p_{13} & p_{14} \\
p_{21} & p_{22} & p_{23} & p_{24} \\
p_{31} & p_{32} & p_{33} & p_{34} \\
0 & 0 & 0 & 1
\end{array}
\right]
\end{array}
$$

Had we considered such a process, we would have taken into account, for example, migration into the United States (from the rest of the world), this immigration being governed by the probability p_{31}. Since migration into the United States has been consistently much higher than migration out of the country, the omission of "world" as a state undoubtedly accounts for some of the underestimates.

The second potential fault is that the process may not be a Markov chain. It will be recalled that the defining characteristic of a Markov chain is that the probability matrix remains constant for all trials. Is this assumption justified? Rogers gives a matrix analogous to that of (8.9), except that it was estimated from the data of the 1955–1960 period:

$$
\begin{array}{c}
 1960 \\
 \text{Calif.} \quad\;\; \text{U.S.} \quad\;\; \text{Death} \\
\begin{array}{c} \text{Calif.} \\ \text{1955} \quad \text{U.S.} \\ \text{Death} \end{array}
\left[
\begin{array}{ccc}
.8902 & .0627 & .0471 \\
.0127 & .9385 & .0488 \\
0 & 0 & 1
\end{array}
\right]
\end{array}
$$

(8.10)

Since Rogers does not give the frequencies on which matrixes (8.9) and (8.10) were based, it is not possible to compute a statistic which would tell us exactly whether the two matrices are significantly different.[7] However, we know that a very large number of persons

[7] If we knew the frequencies N_{ij} that form the part of the estimate $p_{ij}(N_{ij}/N_i)$ we could use a statistic such as chi-square to determine whether the two matrices are significantly different.

was involved in computing the two matrices, and thus it is safe to conclude that the two matrices are indeed different.

Comparison of (8.9) and (8.10) suggests an additional reason why our model underestimates the population of 1960: The probability of dying is smaller for the 1955–1960 period than for the 1935–1940 period. As a result, the process overestimates the number of deaths at each period, this mistake being compounded as time goes on. Note also that the probabilities of migrating from and into California have both changed, have both about doubled. The probability of outmigration has increased from .0331 to .0627, the probability of inmigration from .0068 to .0127. If the population in the two regions, California and the rest of United States, were about the same, this change would not be noticeable. But since the population of California is much smaller than that of the rest of United States, this almost equal increase in transition probabilities means that the *number* of those migrating into California has increased much more than the number leaving California. Thus, use of the 1935–1940 matrix is bound to result in a larger underestimate of the population of California than of the population of the rest of the United States.

Our analysis thus suggests that in order to make the model of migration realistic, we should increase the number of states and abandon the Markovian assumption of constant p_{ij}. Provided that adequate data is available for the additional state ("the rest of the world") the first modification is relatively easy. The second modification, however, represents some difficulties, stemming from the fact that as soon as we abandon the simplicity of the finite Markov chains, a whole range of possibilities opens up. And it is not easy to determine which path should be followed. We shall consider briefly some of these alternatives.

8.3   TOWARDS A REALISTIC MODEL OF MOBILITY

There is little doubt that the models discussed in this chapter are not altogether satisfactory. Not only do they yield faulty predictions, but also many of the discrepancies between prediction and observation are systematic in nature. Undoubtedly the fit of some models could be further improved without any radical revisions. The model of migration, for example, might be considerably improved if one were to add the state "world" to the process. However, there is a general feeling among those working with the application of Markov chains to social mobility that the theory of *regular* Markov chains represent, at best, only the first approximation to realistic models of social mobility.

Coleman (1964) has applied the theory of regular Markov chains to a variety of subjects: consumers' "brand loyalty" (the tendency to purchase the same brand time after time), unemployment, and the changes in opinions of persons interviewed successively (panel analysis). And he reports the same result in all of these cases, that is, regular Markov chains models tend to underestimate the proportion of individuals remaining in a given state. Thus the failing of the occupational mobility model discussed in this chapter appears to be typical of that type of a model.

Accepting these results, Coleman turns his attention to possible remedies. And he recognizes several main types of revision that are possible, some- representing only slight modifications, others a rather radical departure from the theory of Markov chains. We shall consider briefly these alternatives, adding one which Coleman does not discuss.

Processes of Higher Order

Perhaps the least radical revision of the models discussed so far consists of increasing the time-dependency of the process. Essentially, this approach is based on the belief that the predictions fail to fit the data because a person's behavior at time $t + 1$ depends not only on his behavior at a time t (as assumed by the models discussed so far), but also on his behavior prior to that time. The remedy is to consider Markov chains of a higher order, that is, the chains with transition probabilities p_{ij} depending not only on what happened at time t but also on what happened at time $t - 1, t - 2, \ldots$.

Although higher-order chains are rather unwieldy, the basic idea is illustrated easily enough for a chain of second order. Let us use a simple example, one in which there is mobility between two occupations, A and B. One of the simplest models of mobility is given by a 2×2 matrix,

$$
\begin{array}{cc}
 & A \quad\; B \\
P = \begin{array}{c} A \\ B \end{array}\!\! & \left[\begin{array}{cc} p_{11} & p_{12} \\ p_{21} & p_{22} \end{array}\right]
\end{array}
$$

This model represents a Markov chain of the first order.

In order to formulate a model of the second order, we must redefine our states i and j. State i will refer to the two subsequent occupations, the one held at time $t - 1$ and the other at time t; state j will refer to the occupation held at time t and at time $t + 1$. Note that there is an overlap between the two states, for both include the occupation held at time t. The consequences of this fact are obvious when we write the resulting 4×4 transition matrix:

$$
\begin{array}{c}
\quad\quad AA \quad AB \quad BA \quad BB \\
P = \begin{array}{c} AA \\ AB \\ BA \\ BB \end{array}\!\! \left[\begin{array}{cccc} p_{11} & p_{12} & 0 & 0 \\ 0 & 0 & p_{23} & p_{24} \\ p_{31} & p_{32} & 0 & 0 \\ 0 & 0 & p_{43} & p_{44} \end{array}\right]
\end{array}
$$

Note that several of the probabilities are zero. The reason is precisely this overlap. For example, consider probability p_{13}, the probability that a person who had occupation A at time $t - 1$ and A *at time* t will have occupation B *at time* t and A at time $t + 1$. Clearly, if a person had occupation A at time t (as the row label states) he cannot have held occupation B at the same time (as the column label states). Hence $p_{13} = 0$. These considerations suggest that $p_{ij} = 0$ if the last letter of the label applying to the row i is different from the first letter of the label applying to the column j.

Kuehn (1958) applied this approach to brand loyalty of consumers purchasing orange juice and found that even a third-order chain did not remedy the tendency of the model to underestimate consumers' brand loyalty. Coleman, noting this empirical failure of the model, adds some conceptual criticisms as well. He argues that attempts to improve the model by increasing its order is "intellectually unrewarding for it makes no effort to develop a model of ... a memory trace and thus translate the individual's history into his present state. It is more like blind curve fitting, in which increase in pre-dictability of an extrapolation is sought through an increase in the number of points used.... Little is learned from such blind extrapolation...."[8]

The point Coleman is making seems to be based on two assumptions: first, that a good model should be capable not only of predicting but also of explaining; second, that the explanation should be theoretical in nature, that is, it should be in terms of some self-contained theory. In other words, Coleman seems to suggest that if a model has to be made more complex in order to fit the data, one should have good theoretical reasons for introducing certain complications. His objection against using higher-order processes is that no compelling theoretical argument can be made in favor of such a modification. The argument that the individual's behavior *may* depend on more remote past trials than the one immediately preceding is one of possibility, not likelihood, and hence is deemed insufficient.

Partitioning of the Population

Another possible approach is a fairly radical departure from the theory of the regular Markov chains. It attempts to remedy the systematic underestimates of the "stayers" by assuming that every member of the population is not necessarily governed by the same transition probabilities p_{ij}.

The basic version of this approach was discussed in connection with the stayer-mover model of occupational mobility. We noted that Blumen et al. (1955), the originators of that model, found it unsatis-factory and suggested a more general version to be investigated later. Their pioneering work has been continued by a group of theoreticians, most of whom are affiliated with Cornell University. For this reason, the model resulting from this particular approach is sometimes referred to as the *Cornell Mobility Model*.

As reported by McGinnis (1966), the Cornell model departs from the theory of regular Markov chains by assuming that the probability of a person's *remaining* in state i, p_{ii}, *increases* as duration of prior occupancy of that state increases. The reason for this assumption,

[8] Coleman (1964), p. 15.

notes the author, is not mathematical but sociological, since empirical evidence suggests that it is factually true.

We shall not give here a detailed description of the model. Suffice it to say that it is quite complex—so complex, in fact, that McGinnis has not been able to explore its implication by logical reasoning alone and had to resort to the "brute force" of computer simulation.

The chief result to date is the implication that under most circumstances, although by no means all, the population tends to turn into one of stayers. The longer the process continues (with the same population), the closer to 1 are the probabilities on the main diagonal of the transition matrix, p_{ii}.

Coleman discusses another way in which to build a model, using the assumption that different individuals have different transition probabilities. However, since this approach uses tools we have not discussed (differential and integral calculus, differential equations), we refer the interested reader to Coleman's book.

Response–Uncertainty Models

Another avenue is opened when one assumes that the reason why the regular Markov chains do not fit the data on social mobility is the existence of a gap between what is going on "inside" an individual and what he does overtly. Essentially, this approach assumes that two processes operate in each individual: a latent process which defines the probability that he is in a given state k at time t, $p_k^{(t)}$, and a process which links this unobservable state with an observable response.

Coleman develops this approach in some detail; however, since again he uses mathematical tools which are beyond the scope of this book, we shall not discuss it here. Instead, we shall represent some of his ideas through the methods we have developed by assuming that both processes are finite stochastic processes.

Let us start by considering a simple case, say, a migration that involves only two areas, A and B. Let us define a regular Markov chain over these two areas so that we obtain a transition matrix

$$P = \begin{array}{c} \bar{A} \\ \bar{B} \end{array} \begin{bmatrix} \overset{\bar{A}}{p_{11}} & \overset{\bar{B}}{p_{12}} \\ p_{21} & p_{22} \end{bmatrix} .$$

This matrix differs from the one discussed previously in connection with migration in that the two states of the process, $\bar{A}$ and $\bar{B}$, do not correspond to the physical presence of the individual in area A or B—they represent his being there "mentally." More specifically, we can interpret the statement "the process is in state $\bar{A}$" as meaning "the individual has decided to move into area A."

The response-uncertainty is now introduced because we must assume that it is by no means certain that the individual who decides to be in area j at time $t + 1$ will actually be there at that time. This is accomplished by defining the following matrix:

$$
\begin{array}{c}
t + 1 \\[4pt]
\begin{array}{cc} A & B \end{array} \\[2pt]
Q = t + 1 \quad \begin{array}{c} \bar{A} \\ \bar{B} \end{array} \left[\begin{array}{cc} q_{11} & q_{12} \\ q_{21} & q_{22} \end{array} \right]
\end{array}
$$

Note that this is not a Markov chain, since the column labels do not correspond to the labels of the rows: each probability q_{ij} refers to a transition from a "mental" state, $\bar{A}$ or $\bar{B}$, to a "physical" state, A or B. In other words, q_{ii} specifies the probabilities that the individual will actually do what he has decided to do, $q_{ij} \neq q_{ii}$ specifies the probabilities that he will not do it. Furthermore, matrix Q is intended to specify "instant" probabilities. Both the rows and the columns refer to time $t + 1$.[9]

In our simple illustration, matrix P is a regular Markov chain and hence we can calculate the probability that an individual will be in mental state k for any time t by using

$$
p^{(t)} = p^{(0)} P^t
$$

The application of matrix Q is such that when we know $p^{(t)}$, we can compute the probability that the individual will be in the (physical)

---

[9] Our response-uncertainty model is formally identical with the learning model described by Atkinson et al. (1965). In that model the subject can be in one of two mental states: He either knows the correct response or he does not (states analogous to our $\bar{A}$ and $\bar{B}$ of matrix P). It is further assumed that to each mental state corresponds a distinct probability of response. If the subject knows the correct response, he answers correctly with probability of one; if he does not know the correct answer, he answers correctly with probability g. It is perhaps clear that these response probabilities can be represented by a matrix which is a special case of our matrix Q.

area k at time t, $q_k^{(t)}$, by multiplying $p^{(t)}$ and Q:

$$q^{(t)} = p^{(t)}Q$$

Substituting, we obtain the new model:

(8.11) $$q^{(t)} = p^{(0)}P^tQ$$

Thus, if the starting vector $p^{(0)}$ and the two matrices P and Q are given, we can determine the probability that an individual will be in area k at time t.

Let us consider whether the model (8.11) can remedy the shortcomings of the regular Markov chain. To do this, let us assume that we know n_{ij}, the number of persons who were in area j at time $t + 1$ if, at time t, they were in state i. To avoid notational complexity, let us consider a specific example, letting

$$N = \begin{bmatrix} 700 & 300 \\ 200 & 800 \end{bmatrix}$$

The regular transition matrix estimated from this data (using "R" instead of "P" to avoid confusion) is

$$R = \begin{bmatrix} .70 & .30 \\ .20 & .80 \end{bmatrix}$$

Now our problem is to define P and Q for (8.11) so that P^tQ has higher probabilities along its main diagonal than does R^t. Can this be done?

Let us see what happens if we define Q as follows:

$$Q = \begin{bmatrix} .80 & .20 \\ .20 & .80 \end{bmatrix}$$

Equation 8.11 implies that our new model's *one-step* transition matrix is PQ and we write

$$PQ = \begin{bmatrix} .8p_{11} + .2p_{12} & .2p_{11} + .8p_{12} \\ .8p_{21} + .2p_{22} & .2p_{21} + .8p_{22} \end{bmatrix}$$

Since N represents one-step transitions, PQ may be estimated[10] from N and we write that

$$PQ = \begin{bmatrix} .70 & .30 \\ .10 & .80 \end{bmatrix}$$

As we discussed in Chapter 2, equality of two matrices with four components may be written as a system of four equations. However, it is sufficient to consider only two such equations:

$$.70 = .8p_{11} + .2p_{12} = .8p_{11} + .2(1 - p_{11}) = .6p_{11} + .2$$
$$.80 = .2p_{21} + .8p_{22} = .2(1 - p_{22}) + .8p_{22} = .6p_{22} + .2$$

Solving, we obtain

$$p_{11} = \frac{5}{6} = .8333\ldots$$

$$p_{22} = \frac{6}{6} = 1.00$$

and the matrix P governing the latent process is

$$P = \begin{bmatrix} .83 & .17 \\ 0 & 1 \end{bmatrix}$$

The last step is to determine whether the probabilities along the main diagonal after t steps will be larger for the revised model than for the original model. Consider the probabilities after two steps: The original model gives the transitional probabilities as

$$R^2 = \begin{bmatrix} .70 & .30 \\ .20 & .80 \end{bmatrix} \begin{bmatrix} .70 & .30 \\ .20 & .80 \end{bmatrix} = \begin{bmatrix} .55 & .45 \\ .30 & .70 \end{bmatrix}$$

while the modified model gives these transitional probabilities as

$$P^2Q = \begin{bmatrix} .83 & .17 \\ 0 & 1 \end{bmatrix} \begin{bmatrix} .83 & .17 \\ .0 & .1 \end{bmatrix} \begin{bmatrix} .80 & .20 \\ .20 & .80 \end{bmatrix} = \begin{bmatrix} .61 & .39 \\ .20 & .80 \end{bmatrix}$$

And we see that our modified model is indeed capable of remedying the deficiency of the regular Markov chain model. *The revised model*

[10] If we assume that at time $t = 0$ the person who is in state A (or B) is also in state $\bar{A}$ (or $\bar{B}$). In other words, we have to assume that the person who is, at time $t = 0$, in a given region physically is there "mentally" as well.

*is capable of predicting a higher proportion of stayers after two steps
than is predicted by a regular Markov chain.*

Note that we say that the revised model is "capable of predicting"
more stayers; we do not say that it actually does so. The point is
that the matrix Q was not estimated from the data; it was chosen
arbitrarily to make our point. Thus it remains to be shown that the
revised model predicts more stayers than does the original model
when Q is estimated from the data. Since the process of estimation
in this case is somewhat complex, we shall not discuss it here.

Absorbing Markov Chains

There is one more avenue which may yield a realistic model of
social mobility—that of viewing social mobility as an *absorbing*
Markov chains process. The model we have in mind is a synthesis
of the approaches developed by Cohen (1963) for social conflict
and the one used by Rogers (1965) for the study of migration.

Our point of departure is the observation that older men are more
likely to stay put, in occupation and social class as well as in places
of residence, than are young men. It would seem reasonable, therefore, that an occupation, region, or a social class should serve in
dual capacities, that is, as nonabsorbing state and as an absorbing
state. One could assume that when a young man or woman enters
the mobility process (usually by leaving his family), he enters it in
the nonabsorbing state; as he grows older, he becomes progressively
more likely to be "captured" by an occupation, class, or region
(defined as an absorbing state). To illustrate, consider a mobility
process with only two nonabsorbing states, A and B; one can
follow Cohen's lead and define a 4×4 absorbing Markov chain:

$$(8.12) \qquad P = \begin{array}{c} \\ \mathscr{A} \\ A \\ B \\ \mathscr{B} \end{array} \begin{array}{c} \mathscr{A} \quad\; A \quad\;\; B \quad\; \mathscr{B} \\ \left[\begin{array}{cccc} 1 & 0 & 0 & 0 \\ p_{21} & p_{22} & p_{23} & 0 \\ 0 & p_{32} & p_{33} & p_{34} \\ 0 & 0 & 0 & 1 \end{array} \right] \end{array}$$

where $\mathscr{A}$ and $\mathscr{B}$ are the two states viewed as being absorbing and A
and B as being nonabsorbing. For example, suppose that the two

states refer to occupations; then to say that "the individual is in state A" means that he has occupation A but has not yet decided to make it his life career; to say "the individual is in state $\mathscr{A}$" means that he not only has occupation A but has decided (irrevocably) to keep it.

The theory of absorbing Markov chains, as described in Chapter 7, is directly applicable. Above all, we can use (7.3) to define matrix Q specifying the transition probabilities from nonabsorbing to nonabsorbings states:

$$
\begin{array}{cc}
& A \quad\;\; B \\
Q = \begin{array}{c} A \\ B \end{array} & \left[\begin{array}{cc} p_{22} & p_{23} \\ p_{32} & p_{33} \end{array} \right]
\end{array}
$$

We now denote the number of individuals who are in the four states at an arbitrary time $t = 0$ as $w^{(0)}$; as noted in the discussion of Rogers' (1966) model of migration, the expected number of persons in the four states after t steps, $\bar{w}^{(t)}$ is

$$\bar{w}^{(t)} = \bar{w}^{(0)} Q^t$$

Since all q_{ij} in Q^t approach zero as n grows large, we know that our model predicts that all individuals ultimately become absorbed, that all mobility ultimately will cease. This is clearly an unrealistic result. Noting that our process is continuously "rejuvenated" by the young men and women who enter it for the first time, we follow Robers and define an *entry vector* $x^{(t)}$—analogous to his "birth vector"—to specify the number of men and women who enter the process for the first time at time t:

$$x^{(t)} = (0, x_2^{(t)}, x_3^{(t)}, 0)$$

Here we are assuming that all young persons enter the process undecided, still capable of mobility. We now use Rogers' result and state the number of persons who are still potentially mobile (still in one of the nonabsorbing states) after t steps:

(8.13) $w^{(t)} = w^{(0)} Q^t + x^{(1)} Q^{t-1} + x^{(2)} Q^{t-2} + \cdots + x^{(t)}$

It should be noted that each term of (8.13) represents the fate of a given *age cohort*. For example, $x^{(1)} Q^{t-1}$ represents the expected number of those who entered the process at time 1 and are still potentially mobile at time t, after $t - 1$ steps.

One more modification is needed to make the model realistic. As it is, the model predicts that everybody ultimately accumulates in one of the absorbing states $\mathscr{A}$ and $\mathscr{B}$. This is unrealistic, since as time goes by, older individuals either retire or die. Again we follow Rogers and add an *exit state E* (analogous to his "death" state) to the matrix 8.12:

$$
(8.14) \qquad P = \begin{array}{c} \\ \mathscr{A} \\ A \\ B \\ \mathscr{B} \\ E \end{array}
\begin{array}{c}
\begin{array}{ccccc} \mathscr{A} & A & B & \mathscr{B} & E \end{array} \\
\left[\begin{array}{ccccc}
p_{11} & 0 & 0 & 0 & p_{15} \\
p_{21} & p_{22} & p_{23} & 0 & p_{25} \\
0 & p_{32} & p_{33} & p_{34} & p_{35} \\
0 & 0 & 0 & p_{44} & p_{45} \\
0 & 0 & 0 & 0 & 1
\end{array}\right]
\end{array}
$$

Several comments are in order. First, note that E can be entered from any one of the states. This means that we are assuming that young men (who predominate in the nonabsorbing states A or B) can also leave the mobility process (through death), although probably with lesser frequency than do old men (who are mainly in $\mathscr{A}$ or $\mathscr{B}$). Second, note that, by adding E, we have changed $\mathscr{A}$ and $\mathscr{B}$ into nonabsorbing states since now it is possible to leave them. However, $\mathscr{A}$ and $\mathscr{B}$ are still different from A and B, for once $\mathscr{A}$ or $\mathscr{B}$ is entered, it is impossible to return to either A or B. To put it somewhat differently, it is possible to view $\mathscr{A}$ or $\mathscr{B}$ as each forming an *absorbing set* with state E. It is impossible to leave either one of these two absorbing sets, $\{\mathscr{A}, E\}$ or $\{\mathscr{B}, E\}$. As a result, matrix Q is still defined as above, and eq. 8.13 still determines the expected number of potentially mobile individuals.

To the best of our knowledge, the model (8.14) has not yet been applied to social mobility. It remains to be determined whether it can surmount the difficulties encountered when regular Markov chains are used. The appealing feature of (8.14) is that the theory of absorbing Markov chains can apply to it directly. Since the procedure described in the Appendix is directly applicable to (8.13), it should be relatively easy to estimate the transition probabilities of (8.14) as well. Hence the goodness of fit between this model and the mobility data should be easy to establish.

EXERCISES

1. Consider a country for which data is available for the social class status of fathers and their sons. Imagine that a cross-tabulation of this data is as follows:

Son's class

Upper   Lower

$$\text{Father's class} \quad \begin{matrix} \text{Upper} \\ \text{Lower} \end{matrix} \begin{bmatrix} 210 & 90 \\ 240 & 360 \end{bmatrix}$$

where n_{ij} is the number of sons in class j whose father belonged to class i. (a) Use the data to estimate a regular Markov chains matrix and call that matrix R. (b) What is the equilibrium vector r^* ($r^* = r^*R$)? (c) What is the meaning of r^*?

2. Now consider Blumen et al.'s "mover-stayer" model. Assuming that

$$S = \begin{bmatrix} .5 & 0 \\ 0 & .4 \end{bmatrix}$$

what is the "movers' matrix" M? [Hint: Assume that it holds for R of exercise 1 that $R = S + (I - S)M$.]

3. Compute the equilibrium distribution of movers, m^*. (Hint: Use the fact that $m^* = m^*M$.)

4. Using eq. 8.4 compute P^∞. (Hint: Since M is a probability matrix, $M^\infty = M^*$ where M^* is a matrix each row of which is m^*.) Is it possible to compute an equilibrium vector p^* for this stayer-mover model? (Ans.: No, because S of exercise 2 specifies that $s_{11} \neq s_{22}$). Compare your results with those of exercise 1.

5. Now consider Coleman's model as discussed in Chapter 8. Assume that a son of upper-class father is determined to remain upper-class, while many lower-class sons wish to move upwards. Let us assume that these considerations are given by

$$P = \begin{bmatrix} 1 & 0 \\ .4 & .6 \end{bmatrix}$$

What is matrix Q of eq. 8.11? (Hint: Assume that it holds for matrix R of exercise 1 that $R = PQ$). What is the meaning of matrix Q?

6. Given the results of exercise 5, what will be the ultimate distribution of sons in the two social classes? (Hint: Note that P of exercise 5 represents an absorbing process—all sons will ultimately want to belong to the upper class. Note that P need not always be absorbing.)

PART THREE

GAME–THEORETICAL MODELS

The theory of games, originally codified by von Neumann and Morgenstern (1947), represents an approach that is, in many respects, new to most behavioral scientists. Instead of attempting to describe how men actually behave or to predict how they will behave, the theory of games is used chiefly to determine how men should behave. Thus the behavioral scientist is provided with an approach permitting him to consider questions which he might otherwise dismiss as being outside the scope of scientific inquiry, for the study of how men should behave has been thought to involve value judgements, and hence to be unscientific.

Whether or not the game-theoretical approach can be reconciled with basic beliefs concerning the nature and function of science will be considered in Part IV. In this Part we shall attempt to acquaint the reader with the theory of games itself: with two-person zero-sum games (Chapter 9) and with two-person nonzero-sum games (Chapter 12). Contrary to the usual practice, however, we shall not discuss *n*-person games since the inclusion of that part of the theory would make our discussion too complicated and too lengthy without correspondingly increasing the reader's understanding. Those interested should consult Luce and Raiffa (1957) or any of several texts covering *n*-person games.

We shall emphasize the application of the theory of games to group behavior. Admittedly, since we limit ourselves to two-person games, we shall have to be satisfied with two-man groups or with groups that are divided into two camps. Even with this limitation, however, we shall discover many topics of interest to the social scientist. Chapter 11 discusses the application of the theory of zero sum games to warfare, the testing of the theory under experimental conditions, and even the general implications of the theory for the study of human interaction; Chapter 13 suggests that such presumably value-laden concepts as justice can be analyzed in a value-free fashion; Chapter 14 describes some additional experiments designed to confront the theory of games with empirical observations, and furthermore, it shows how the concepts of the theory can be helpful in clarifying some of the most puzzling dilemmas that often beset a man in his attempts to relate to his fellow men.

CHAPTER 9

Extreme Social Conflict:
The Problem

There are situations in which two persons or two groups find their most dominant interests diametrically opposed. Segregationists want the separation of the whites and the Negroes, Negroes want integration; labor wants wage increases and fringe benefits, management wishes to keep the cost down; in a war, each combatant wishes to destroy his opponent's means of continuing the war while keeping his own means intact; and so on.

It is true that in many such cases the two opponents have some interests in common. For example, both management and labor have an interest in keeping production going, since only then does management make a profit and labor earn wages. But it is also true that, as a conflict intensifies, the common interests tend to be more and more ignored and the differences tend to be emphasized. Whether or not this trend is desirable is a serious moral problem; we merely note that there are many situations in which the participants behave as if their interests were diametrically opposed, whether or not such conflict of interests does in fact exist. The study of behavior when the interests are diametrically opposed will be called the study of extreme social conflict.[1]

---

[1] There are social conflicts in which some payoffs are opposed, others are in harmony with each other. Such conflicts can be represented by nonzero sum games and will be discussed in Chapters 12 to 14.

One can learn how one should behave under conditions of extreme social conflict from, of all things, the study of parlor games such as poker. The reader may feel that to apply what one learns from studying trivial games to serious problems, such as a war, is absurd and dangerous. But this may be only because he does not fully appreciate the significance of games in a man's life. As we shall argue later (Chapter 11), it is possible to maintain that social interaction, the very foundation of societal life, is best understood when it is viewed as a game.

What is learned from the study of parlor games, and what this lesson means for economic behavior, was first stated in a comprehensive fashion by von Neumann and Morgenstern (1947). Their work has profound implications, however, not only for economics but also for all behavioral sciences. The reason for this is that the authors decided to apply the analysis of games to economic problems: The fact that they chose to study parlor games means that, if the importance of games for understanding social behavior is as profound as we believe it to be (see Chapter 11), their analysis is applicable to all social sciences. The fact that they chose to apply it to economic problems (and that one of the authors was an economist) meant that the apparatus of traditional economic theory was brought to bear upon the problem. And prominent in that apparatus is the tradition of analyzing economic behavior in terms of *how a rational man ought to behave*. Thus the social sciences are confronted with a theory that deals with a problem which is, or ought to be, the very center of their interest, but which deals with it in a manner that is foreign to their traditions, the traditions of a descriptive, empirical research.

We shall illustrate the manner in which a conflict is analyzed in the game-theoretical manner by discussing a semirealistic example of two officers playing a war game. We use this example to isolate the main tools of the game-theoretical approach and to show how these tools differ from those traditionally used by social scientists.

9.1 EXAMPLE OF A ZERO-SUM GAME

Suppose that two officers, Richard and Carl, are playing a simple war game in which Richard is in charge of the strategic air force of nation X, Carl in charge of the antiaircraft weapons of nation Y. Each player is given only two choices during a given "play of the game": Richard can decide only between sending his airplanes "flying high" and sending them "flying low"; Carl has only the choice between ordering "shoot" and ordering "do not shoot."

The Payoffs

The commanding officer who assigned the game wished to make it realistic in the sense of specifying the gains or losses each officer could expect to experience. In arriving at these gains and losses, he may or may not have used some statistics gathered from actual combat; in any case, he decided on the following "payoff matrices":

$$
\begin{array}{cc}
& \text{Shoot} \quad \text{Do not} \\
& \qquad\qquad \text{shoot} \\
& 1 \qquad\quad 2 \\
\begin{array}{c} \text{Fly high } 1 \\ \text{Fly low } 2 \end{array} &
\left[\begin{array}{cc} -1 & 4 \\ 2 & 0 \end{array} \right]
\end{array}
\qquad
\begin{array}{cc}
& \text{Shoot} \quad \text{Do not} \\
& \qquad\qquad \text{shoot} \\
& 1 \qquad\quad 2 \\
\begin{array}{c} \text{Fly high } 1 \\ \text{Fly low } 2 \end{array} &
\left[\begin{array}{cc} 1 & -4 \\ -2 & 0 \end{array} \right]
\end{array}
$$

Richard's   Carl's
payoff   payoff

Let us take a good look at the two payoff matrices. As the name "payoff" suggests, each component of the matrix represents a quantity of a commodity that is valuable to the player. In this particular example, since two officers are involved, one can think of the payoffs as points that enter into overall officers rating: The more points an officer makes in the game, the higher his rating. Thus, for example, if Richard chooses to send his planes "flying low" and Carl chooses to "shoot," then Richard receives 2 points (see the left matrix) and Carl receives -2 points (see the right matrix).

Notice that the two matrices are so selected that Richard's gains are always equal to Carl's losses, and vice versa. Carl's matrix has exactly the same components as Richard's, but their signs are opposite. As a result, were we to add the two matrices together, we would obtain a matrix with all zero components. This feature of the game is responsible for its name, the *zero-sum game*; since only two players are involved, it is known as a *two-person* zero-sum game.

This assignment of labels to our game is not merely a pointless exercise in classification, although it may seem so at this time. As we shall show in subsequent chapters, games that are not zero (or constant) sum, or that involve more than two persons, present some unique problems of their own. Let us add that now we can state more precisely what we mean by diametrically opposed interests. The interests of two individuals are *diametrically opposed* if they can be represented by payoffs that always add up to zero, that is, when one individual's gain is always the other person's loss.

The fact that our game is a zero-sum two-person game has one immediate consequence, which is that the game can be fully represented by a single matrix. If we accept the convention that the payoffs shown in the matrix are *those of the player who controls the rows*, we can represent the game by Richard's matrix ("Richard" for rows):

$$(9.1) \qquad V = \begin{bmatrix} -1 & 4 \\ 2 & 0 \end{bmatrix}$$

It follows from this convention and from the fact that the game is zero sum that the player who controls the columns ("Carl" for columns) will receive payoffs which are $-V$, i.e., the *negative* of the payoffs shown in eq. 9.1.

A Random Device

Let us return to the description of the game. After it has been explained to the two officers, each man goes into his room to ponder the game in complete privacy. Each man is given a *random device* which makes it possible for him to choose a particular strategy (in Carl's case, say, the strategy to "shoot") with any probability between 0 and 1. One such device, represented in Figure 9.1, consists of a disc divided into segments numbered from 0 to 9, with a free-turning pointer at the center. The device is used by spinning the pointer and noting the segment at which it comes to rest.

Use of the random device is not required, but should an officer decide to use it in arriving at his decision, he knows the procedure. To consider an arbitrary example, suppose that he decides to play strategy 1 with probability .71 (and hence play strategy 2 with probability $1.00 - .71 = .29$). He spins the pointer. If it comes to

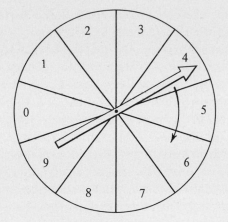

Figure 9.1. A random device.

rest in segment 0, 1, 2, 3, 4, 5, or 6, he plays his first strategy; if it
stops in segment 8 or 9, he plays strategy 2; if it rests in segment 7,
then he spins again. That this procedure assures that strategy 1
is played with a probability .71 can be seen as intuitively plausible
when it is realized that there are many more segments between .00
and .71 than between .71 and 1.00; hence the pointer has more
"chances" of stopping between .00 to .71 than between .71 and 1.00.

Whether an officer uses his random device or not, he writes his
decision (such as, for Carl, to "shoot") on a piece of paper. After
both men have made their decisions, the commanding officer collects
the two papers and announces the outcome of the game. For example,
if Richard chose to send his planes "flying high" and Carl chose
"do not shoot," these two decisions are announced and Richard
receives +4 points, Carl −4 points. And the game is over.

The Security-Level Principle

Let us now return to the room where Richard ponders the game,
and let us read his thoughts. If he is an intelligent man his reasoning
might go something like this:

"I have to choose between sending my planes flying high (strategy
1, first row) and flying them low (strategy 2, second row). I have no
way of predicting what Carl will do, *and so I might just as well assume
that he will always do the thing that is best for him (and, hence, worst*

for me): if I choose strategy 1, I may find that he has chosen his strategy 1, and I will receive -1 point; if I choose strategy 2, I may discover that he chose his strategy 2, which will result in a tie, and I will get 0 points. Is there anything I can do to improve my chances so that I can get more than the 0 points I might receive if I played strategy 2"?

Let us interrupt Richard's meditation for a moment and note that he jumps from the assumption that Carl's behavior is unpredictable to the conclusion that he might as well assume that Carl's choice will turn out to be Carl's best answer against his own, Richard's, choice. Notice that this conclusion is not based on any belief in Carl's clairvoyance (which would assume that Carl knows ahead of time what Richard will do), it is based merely on the fact that anything can happen, and therefore one might as well count on the worst thing happening. Does this conclusion follow from the premise? This is a crucial question, and one that is difficult to answer. But such is the reasoning implicit in the game-theoretical solution. The theory of games does assume[2] that a rational player will always consider the *security level* of any one of his strategies, the security level being defined as the lowest payoff he can receive if he uses a given strategy. Assuming that Richard accepts this principle, let us listen to some more of his reasoning.

"I know what my security level is when I use the first strategy (-1 point) and when I use the second strategy (0 points). But suppose I use this random device? Could I possibly increase my security level? Let me see ... If I do use this device, I actually extend the number of strategies available to me, from two to an infinite number. With the device I can decide to play strategy 1 with probability p_1 and strategy 2 with probability $1 - p_1$. Since p_1 can be any number between 0 and 1, an infinite number of distinct strategies is at my disposal—one for each p_1."

Graphic Representation of the Game

Richard stops for a moment to contemplate how the random device might be useful to him. After some thought he decides to

[2] More precisely, the solution to two-person zero-sum games is obtained by assuming that the players maximize their security level. Although other assumptions are possible, none of the other assumptions leads to as satisfactory a solution as the security level principle.

Figure 9.2

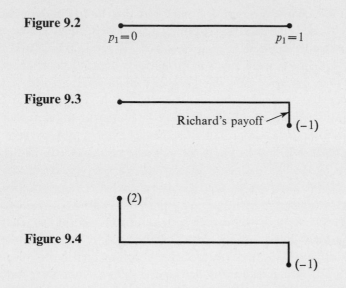

$p_1 = 0$ $p_1 = 1$

Figure 9.3

Richard's payoff → • (-1)

• (2)

Figure 9.4

• (-1)

record some of his thinking graphically, and he accepts the following conventions: He is going to draw a horizontal line segment to represent his strategies, as shown in Figure 9.2.

The point 0 represents strategy $p_1 = 0$, the decision to play his *first* strategy with probability $p_1 = 0$; point 1 represents strategy $p_1 = 1$ (when he plays his first strategy with probability $p_1 = 1$). Any point on the segment represents an arbitrary strategy p_1. The closer p_1 is to the right-hand end of the segment, the higher is p_1. And Richard continues to ponder the game.

"Now suppose that I decide to play my first strategy and Carl plays his first strategy; then I know that my payoff will be -1. I guess I can represent this payoff by a vertical line segment originating at the point 1 of the horizontal segment (1, because playing the first strategy means that $p_1 = 1$), as shown in Figure 9.3. If, on the other hand, I were to play my second strategy while Carl still played his first, I know I would receive 2 points." And, following the same reasoning as before, Richard adds a vertical segment originating at point 0 of the horizontal line, in Figure 9.4. "However, I don't want to limit myself to playing either 1 or 2, I want to consider what will happen if I play 1 with *any* probability p_1, always assuming that Carl continues to play his first strategy. Let's see what happens if I

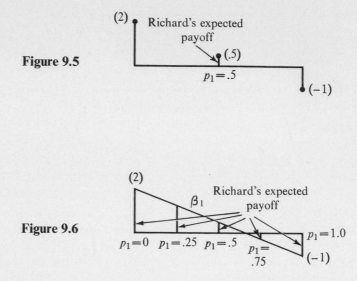

Figure 9.5

Figure 9.6

play $p_1 = .5$." Remembering a course in probability theory he took at one time, Richard proceeds, "In that case, my *expected payoff* would be $.5 \times -1 + .5 \times 2 = .5$." And he records the expected payoff, just as he recorded the previous payoff, by drawing a vertical segment from the midpoint (because $p_1 = .5$) of the horizontal segment, in Figure 9.5.

He now studies the pictures he has drawn and he is struck by the fact that the payoff he drew first (-1), the payoff he drew second $(+2)$, and the expected payoff $(.5)$ *all lie on a straight line.* And he jumps to the (correct) assumption that his expected payoff for any p_1, as long as Carl continues to play his first strategy, will be determined the straight line β_1 as shown in Figure 9.6.[3]

Inspection of the last graph suggests what he knows already, that if he could be certain that Carl would play his first strategy, his optimal choice would be $p_1 = 0$ (that is, playing his *second* strategy), since the line β_1 is further above the horizontal axis when $p_1 = 0$ than it is for any other value of p_1. But of course Richard cannot be certain that Carl will play his first strategy, so he proceeds to consider what will happen if Carl plays his second strategy. By following analogous reasoning, he obtains the graph shown in

[3] For a proof, see Luce and Raiffa (1958), pp. 395–99.

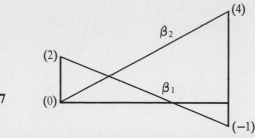

Figure 9.7

Figure 9.7. Now line β_2 determines Richard's expected payoff, if Carl uses his second strategy; the line β_1 determines Richard's expected payoff if Carl uses his first strategy.

But Richard still is not happy. He knows only too well that Carl may play neither his first strategy nor his second, but, being just as intelligent as Richard, he may end up playing any "mixture" of the two—that is, playing strategy 1 with probability q_1 (conversely playing strategy 2 with probability $q_2 = 1 - q_1$). How would this eventuality be represented graphically? We do not wish to expect too much from Richard, but perhaps he had a course in mathematics which helps him to reach the correct conclusion. His expected payoff for any strategy q_1 is determined by a straight line that goes through the intersection of β_1 and β_2, and intersects the left vertical boundary of the last graph *between* the points $+2$ and 0. In other words, his payoff is determined by a family of lines β_q that lie "between" the lines β_1 and β_2 (see Figure 9.8).[4]

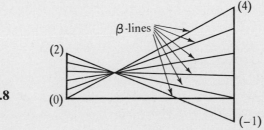

Figure 9.8

[4] *Ibid.*, for a proof.

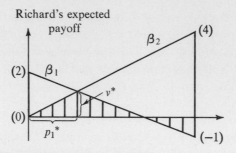

Figure 9.9. Richard's security levels.

The last graph represents the payoff to Richard that corresponds to any pair of strategies (the payoff is represented by a vertical line segment originating at the appropriate point p_1 of the horizontal segment and ending at the point where it intersects the appropriate line β).

Richard now remembers his earlier resolution to be concerned about his security level, that is, with the payoff he will receive if he plays strategy p_1 and Carl plays his best response to p_1. Accordingly he considers some arbitrary points p_1 along the horizontal line and draws the corresponding security levels as vertical segments, in Figure 9.9. Immediately his best strategy becomes clear: He should play strategy p_1^*, *because at point p_1^* his security level is highest.*

Computation of the Optimal Strategy

It remains for Richard to compute p_1^*. He could do so simply by dividing the distance between point 0 and p_1^* by the total distance between 0 and 1, but he prefers to do his computations algebraically. Observing that p_1^* lies directly below the intersection of lines β_1 and β_2, he knows that p_1^* is simply the horizontal coordinate of the point of intersection. Therefore, he proceeds in a standard fashion to find this coordinate.

First he writes the equation for line β_1. He notes that the two axes are his own strategy, p_1 (the horizontal axis), and the corresponding expected payoff to him, v (the vertical axis). He notes that β_1 is a straight line, and thus he knows that the equation for β_1 will have the form

(9.2) $v = Bp_1 + A$

where A and B are constants to be computed. On further inspection of the last graph he finds that when $p_1 = 0$ and when Carl plays $q_1 = 1$, his payoff will be $v = 2$ (the vertical distance between the left end of the horizontal line segment and line β_1). Substituting these values of p_1 and v into (9.2), he obtains the equation

$$2 = B(0) + A$$

which he simplifies to $A = 2$. Now he notes that when $p_1 = 1$ (and when Carl plays $q_1 = 1$), then $v = -1$. Using these values for v and p_1 and the fact that $A = 2$, he writes (9.2) as

$$-1 = B(1) + 2$$

and, solving, he finds that $B = -3$. Now he can write the equation for line β_1 by substituting the computed values of A and B:

(9.3) $\qquad v = -3p_1 + 2 \qquad$ (when Carl plays $q_1 = 1$)

In an analogous way, he proceeds to determine the equation for line β_2, and he finds that

(9.4) $\qquad v = 4p_1 \qquad$ (when Carl plays $q_1 = 0$)

It remains for him to determine the horizontal coordinate of the point of intersection between lines β_1 and β_2. The point of intersection, he observes, occurs at the point where the vertical distance between the horizontal axis p_1 and line β_1 *is the same* as the vertical distance between p_1 and line β_2. Since the vertical distance is, by definition, his expected payoff v, he concludes that, at the point of intersection, v of eq. 9.3 must be equal to v of eq. 9.4, and he writes

$$-3p_1{}^* + 2 = 4p_1{}^*$$

where $p_1{}^*$ is the horizontal coordinate of the point of intersection. Solving this equation he obtains $p^* = \frac{2}{7}$; since he knows that $p_1{}^* + p_2{}^* = 1$, he writes his final result:

$$p^* = (\tfrac{2}{7}, \tfrac{5}{7})$$

Playing the Optimal Strategy

Having identified his optimal strategy, $p^* = (\tfrac{2}{7}, \tfrac{5}{7})$, Richard proceeds to play it. He spins the pointer shown in Figure 9.1 and observes where it stops. If it stops in either segment 0 or segment 1, he plays his first strategy, fly high (since $\frac{2}{7} = .28\ldots$); if it stops in any segment between 3 and 9, he plays his second strategy, fly low; if it stops in segment 2, he spins the pointer again (to obtain the second digit of .28) and decides his strategy accordingly (for outcomes 0–7 he plays strategy 1, for 9 he plays strategy 2, for 8 he spins for a third time, and so on).

Actually, "playing" the strategy consists of writing on a piece of paper the number of the strategy Richard has chosen. Note that the commanding officer and Carl have no way of knowing that Richard went through all the labor of thinking, drawing graphs, and using a random device. The play of the game shows no trace of the effort that has gone into his choice of strategy. Worse yet, in any given play of the game, Richard may discover that all this effort has earned him a defeat, that he might have done better without using the random device at all. To be specific, the strategy $p^* = (\frac{2}{7}, \frac{5}{7})$ has a "tangible" meaning only as a general tendency which (as with any probability) is manifested as a certain "average" value over a very large number of plays of the game; in any *single* play of the game p^* does not guarantee anything. It is perfectly possible that p^* will lead Richard to play strategy 1 at the very time when Carl happens to play his first strategy, and that Richard thus will lose 1 point. Had he played his strategy 2, he would have been certain to receive no less than 0. It is thus of considerable interest to examine carefully the grounds on which one can recommend that Richard play p^* (see Section 10.2).

9.2   OPTIMAL STRATEGIES

It would be possible to determine the optimal strategy for Carl, the player who controls the columns, by following a procedure analogous to that applied to Richard. By drawing a graph in which Carl's expected payoffs are shown as a function of his strategy we could determine his security levels for each strategy; his optimal strategy would again be that with the highest security level. However, it is preferable at this point to switch to an algebraic mode of presentation and to discuss optimal strategies in general.

Expected Payoff

In arriving at Richard's optimal strategy p^* we used the concept of "expected payoff." Let us now define expected payoff algebraically. Consider a two-person zero-sum game in which each player has only two alternatives,

$$(9.5) \qquad V = \begin{bmatrix} v_{11} & v_{12} \\ v_{21} & v_{22} \end{bmatrix}$$

and let us assume that Richard (the player controlling the two rows) can play any strategy p, Carl (the player controlling the two columns) can play strategy q', where p and q' are probability vectors;

$$p = (p_1, p_2), \qquad q' = \begin{bmatrix} q_1 \\ q_2 \end{bmatrix}$$

As will become obvious presently, p is defined over the *rows* of the payoff matrix so that p_i refers to the probability that Richard will play row i. Similarly, q' is defined over the *columns* of V, and q_j refers to the probability that Carl will play column j.

Now remember the standard definition of expected value. If in an experiment the possible outcomes are numbers $a_1, a_2, \ldots, a_k$, occurring with probability $p_1, p_2, \ldots, p_k$, then the *expected value* is defined as

$$E = a_1 p_1 + a_2 p_2 + \cdots + a_k p_k$$

In our case, the "experiment" is a play of the game in which each player makes a choice; an outcome of that experiment is one of the cells of the payoff matrix V; the number associated with an outcome is the payoff within a given cell, v_{ij}. Hence, were we to associate a probability p_{ij} with each payoff v_{ij}, then the expected payoff v would be

$$v = p_{11} v_{11} + p_{12} v_{12} + p_{21} v_{21} + p_{22} v_{22}$$

Is it possible to define a probability distribution over the outcomes of the game so that probability p_{ij} is associated with the cell in the ith row and jth column of the payoff matrix? It certainly is. Whenever Richard plays p and Carl plays q, they are in fact associating the probability $p_{ij} = p_i q_j$ with each payoff v_{ij}.[5] In other words, when p and q' are played, we obtain the following probability distribution P defined over the four cells of matrix (9.5):

$$P = \begin{bmatrix} p_1 q_1 & p_1 q_2 \\ p_2 q_1 & p_2 q_2 \end{bmatrix}$$

(Matrix P is not a matrix of transition probabilities, since each row does not sum up to 1. Instead, all four products sum up to 1—$\Sigma\, p_i q_j = 1$.) Hence, when p and q are played, the expected payoff is

$$v = p_1 q_1 v_{11} + p_1 q_2 v_{12} + p_2 q_1 v_{21} + p_2 q_2 v_{22}$$

However, note that we can use matrix notation to obtain the same result, that

$$v = (p_1, p_2) \begin{bmatrix} v_{11} & v_{12} \\ v_{21} & v_{22} \end{bmatrix} \begin{bmatrix} q_1 \\ q_2 \end{bmatrix} = (p_1 v_{11} + p_2 v_{21}, p_1 v_{12} + p_2 v_{22}) \begin{bmatrix} q_1 \\ q_2 \end{bmatrix}$$

$$= p_1 q_1 v_{11} + p_2 q_1 v_{21} + p_1 q_2 v_{12} + p_2 q_2 v_{22}$$

In other words, we can write quite simply that Richard's expected payoff v will always be

$$(9.6) \qquad\qquad\qquad v = pVq'$$

Since Carl's payoff is always the negative of Richard's payoff, his expected payoff w will always be

$$(9.7) \qquad\qquad\qquad w = -pVq'$$

Optimal Strategies Defined

We now use our previous discussion to define the optimal strategies of a zero-sum game. We start by noting that it is possible to associate with each of Richard's strategies p the lowest expected payoff he can receive while playing it. As before, we shall term such

[5] Remember that Richard and Carl choose their strategies independently, and each chooses in ignorance of his opponent's choice. Consequently, if Richard chooses the first row with probability p_1 and Carl chooses the first column with probability q_1, then the probability that the first row *and* the first column will be chosen (i.e., that the upper-left cell of matrix V will be chosen) is $p_1 q_1$.

lowest payoff Richard's security level from strategy p and denote it by $\bar{v}$. Since, by playing p, Richard can secure for himself at least $\bar{v}$, we can write that

$$(9.8) \qquad \bar{v} \le pVq'$$

where pVq' is Richard's expected payoff when he plays p and Carl plays any strategy q'. If we denote the security level of Carl's strategy q' by $\bar{w}$, then it is obvious that

$$(9.9) \qquad \bar{w} \le -pVq'$$

since, as we noted in (9.7), $-pVq'$ is Carl's expected payoff if he plays q' and Richard plays p.

We now can define optimal strategies formally. Two strategies, p and q, are said to be *optimal strategies*, p^* and q^*, if the security level of p^*, $\bar{v}^*$, and the negative of the security level of q^*, $-\bar{w}^*$, are the same:

$$(9.10) \qquad \bar{v}^* = -\bar{w}^* = v^*$$

The expected payoff v^* for which (9.10) holds is called the *value of the game*.

Let us consider what this definition says. It states, first of all, that if Richard plays p^*, he can secure for himself at least v^*. Substituting v^* for $\bar{v}$ in (9.8), we write

$$(9.11) \qquad v^* \le p^*Vq'$$

Furthermore, it implies that if Carl plays q^*, he can secure for himself at least $-v^*$. Substituting $-v^*$ for $\bar{w}$ of (9.9), we write

$$-v^* \le -pVq'^*$$

The last inequality may be written as

$$(9.12) \qquad pVq'^* \le v^*$$

And, using (9.11) and (9.12), we can write that

$$(9.13) \qquad pVq'^* \le v^* \le p^*Vq'$$

i.e., that, if Carl plays his optimal strategy, he can keep Richard's expected payoff down to v^* *or less*; if Richard plays his optimal strategy, he can secure for himself v^* *or more*.

Solution of a Game

Several theorems are of importance to the theory of zero-sum two-person games. The first one asserts that when both players use their optimal strategies, p^* and q'^*, then Richard's expected payoff is the value of the game (and Carl's payoff is the negative of that value):

$$(9.14) \qquad\qquad p^*Vq'^* = v^*$$

The second theorem, known as the *Minimax Theorem*, asserts that every zero-sum two-person game has one and only one value of the game v^*, and at least one pair of optimal strategies p^* and q^*. The reader interested in the proof of these two theorems should consult a more advanced text on the Theory of Games, such as that by Luce and Raiffa (1958). We shall be interested here only in the significance of these two theorems.

The first important consequence is that it now makes sense to speak of a "solution" of zero-sum two-person games, since we know that each such game must have one v^* and at least one pair of p^* and q'^*. Thus we define a *solution* of a game as a set $(p^*, q'^*; v^*)$—that is, a set consisting of the value of the game and a pair of optimal strategies. Hence to "solve a game" means to find the value of the game and all pairs of optimal strategies.

The second consequence of the two theorems is that, although a game may have more than one pair of optimal strategies p^* and q'^*, any one pair will do for practical purposes: No matter which pair is used, the value of the game remains the same, v^*. Thus, if a game happens to have more than one pair p^* and q'^*, each player can use any random device to decide which one of his optimal strategies to play.

Finally, it should be noted that eq. 9.14 states that Richard's expected payoff will be reduced to v^* if both players use their optimal strategies. If Richard uses his optimal strategy while Carl does not, Richard's expected payoff is determined by (9.11) and it may be higher than v^*.

Computing a Solution

It is possible to define a standard procedure for solving zero-sum two-person games algebraically, without having to represent the game graphically. This procedure, however, deals with concepts which are of importance to the theory of games but which we have not dealt with systematically as yet: the concepts of "pure" and "mixed" strategy and the concept of a "saddle point." A *pure strategy* is a strategy that assigns the probability of 1 to one of the alternatives available to the player; a *mixed strategy* is any other than a pure strategy. For example, $p = (0, 1, 0, 0)$ is a pure strategy because it states that the second strategy is certain to be chosen; strategy

$$p = (\tfrac{1}{8}, 0, \tfrac{2}{8}, \tfrac{5}{8})$$

is a mixed strategy. It is perhaps clear that we have been considering so far only mixed strategies. A *saddle point* is the value of a game which has pure optimal strategies.

The recommended procedure for solving a zero-sum two-person game starts by determining whether the game has a saddle point. It is useful to enter to the right of the payoff matrix a column vector whose components are the smallest payoffs for each row (the *row minima*), and to enter below the matrix a row vector that contains the largest payoffs of each column (the *column maxima*). Let us illustrate by using a 3×3 matrix:

$$\text{Row Minima}$$

$$V = \begin{bmatrix} 0 & -8 & 6 \\ 2 & 7 & -1 \\ 3 & 9 & 4 \end{bmatrix} \qquad \begin{bmatrix} 0 \\ -1 \\ 3 \end{bmatrix}$$

$$\text{Column Maxima } (3 \quad 9 \quad 6)$$

We now inspect the row minima and the column maxima, searching for a saddle point, that is, for an outcome the payoff of which is both a row minimum and a column maximum. And we see that $v_{31} = 3$ is both the smallest payoff of the row in which it appears (third row) and the largest payoff of the column in which it appears (first column). Thus the above game has a saddle point; the value of the game is the value of the saddle point $v^* = 3$; and the pure strategies, the intersection of which forms the saddle point, are the optimal strategies $p^* = (0, 0, 1)$ and $q'^* = (1, 0, 0)$.

It should be clear why the saddle point identifies the solution of the game. Since the payoff associated with the saddle point is, by definition, the smallest payoff in the chosen row (third row in the above game), Richard, by playing the chosen row, is certain to receive at least that payoff; since the payoff associated with the saddle point is, by definition, the largest payoff in the chosen column (first column in our example), Carl, by playing the chosen column, is certain to keep Richard from getting more than that payoff (and hence is keeping his own payoffs no lower than the negative of that payoff). Thus the two strategies associated with the saddle point maximize both players' security levels, and hence constitute the game-theoretical solution.

If a game has a saddle point, the above procedure is sufficient to arrive at the solution. If, however, this procedure fails to yield a solution, any 2×2 game can be solved as follows: Designating the payoffs by

(9.15) $$V = \begin{bmatrix} a & b \\ c & d \end{bmatrix}$$

the solution is given by

$$p^* = \left(\frac{d - c}{a + d - b - c}, \frac{a - b}{a + d - b - c} \right)$$

(9.16) $$q^* = \left(\frac{d - b}{a + d - b - c}, \frac{a - c}{a + d - b - c} \right)$$

$$v^* = \frac{ad - bc}{a + d - b - c}$$

Let us apply this procedure to the game of eq. 9.1:

Row Minima

$$V = \begin{bmatrix} -1 & 4 \\ 2 & 0 \end{bmatrix} \qquad \begin{bmatrix} -1 \\ 0 \end{bmatrix}$$

Column Maxima (2   4)

We see that this game does not have a saddle point since the components of the row minima vector are all different from the components of the column maxima vector. Using (9.15), we identify $a = -1, b = 4, c = 2, d = 0$. Using (9.16), we write the solution,

$$p^* = \left(\frac{0 - 2}{-7}, \frac{-1 - 4}{-7}\right) = \left(\frac{2}{7}, \frac{5}{7}\right)$$

$$q^* = \left(\frac{0 - 4}{-7}, \frac{-1 - 2}{-7}\right) = \left(\frac{4}{7}, \frac{3}{7}\right)$$

$$v^* = \frac{0 - 8}{-7} = \frac{8}{7}$$

And we conclude that by playing his optimal strategy p^*, Richard can secure for himself at least the expected payoff of $\frac{8}{7}$; by playing his optimal strategy q'^*, Carl can secure for himself an expected payoff of at least $-\frac{8}{7}$; if both play their optimal strategies, the expected payoff is $\frac{8}{7}$ for Richard, $-\frac{8}{7}$ for Carl.

To solve games larger than 2×2 is more difficult. Any $2 \times n$ or $m \times 2$ game can be solved by using the graphical methods outlined in this chapter. For a general $m \times n$ zero-sum two-person game the computations become involved, and several alternative procedures are available. One of the easiest procedures is the so-called simplex method, well explained, for example, by Kemeny et al. (1962).

EXERCISES

1. Which one(s) of the following games has (have) a solution in pure strategies?

$$A = \begin{bmatrix} 7 & -3 & 4 \\ 2 & 9 & -7 \end{bmatrix} \qquad B = \begin{bmatrix} -3 & 1 & 4 \\ -4 & 7 & -1 \end{bmatrix} \qquad C = \begin{bmatrix} 8 & 3 \\ 0 & 2 \\ 4 & 2 \end{bmatrix}$$

What are the pure optimal strategies?

2. Using the results of exercise 1 (for the games with pure strategies), show that if one player employs his optimal strategy he is certain to receive at

least v^*, but may receive more. Under what circumstances will he receive more than v^*?

3. Represent game A of exercise 1 graphically from the row player's point of view. What is the relationship between the column player's first and third strategies? Represent v^* and p_i^* graphically.

4. Find algebraically p^*, q^*, and v^* for game A of exercise 1. (*Hint:* the column player's first strategy may be discarded.)

5. Using a random device and the results of exercise 4, simulate 20 consecutive plays of game A when p^* and q^* are played. In other words, using p^* and q^* and a random device, determine a sequence of 20 pairs of choices, such as:

Play Number	R's Choice	C's Choice
1	2	1
2	1	1
.	.	.
.	.	.
.	.	.
20	2	2

For each play, determine R's payoff. What is the mean payoff to R for the 20 plays? How does it compare with v^*?

6. Keep R's choices as you simulated them in exercise 5, but change C's choices so that he always plays the second column. What is R's mean payoff now? Is it larger than it was in exercise 5? Would you expect it to be larger? If your expectation was not met, why not?

CHAPTER 10

The Game–Theoretical Approach

The theory of zero-sum two-person games has become the basis for the entire theory of games. Many of the assumptions and principles used when solving these games are also used, with some modifications, to solve both the n-person and the nonzero-sum games. We now turn to these assumptions and principles. To some extent, we shall be going over the same material we covered in Chapter 9. However, our emphasis will be different, for we shall be concerned primarily with the mathematical significance of the serious problems and solutions that are considered by the theory of games.

10.1   DECISION–MAKING

It is instructive to consider the theory of games as a special version of a problem which is of considerable interest to both the layman and the social scientist, the problem of decision-making. The game-theoretical approach is unique in that it is concerned with determining the decisions that *should* be made under certain circumstances rather than with predicting what decisions *will* be made. The difference in objective presupposes a difference in conceptualization; and we shall attempt to characterize the formulation typical of the game-theoretical approach.

Decision–Making under Certainty

Perhaps the simplest illustration of the characteristics of the game-theoretical approach is the so-called decision-making under certainty. Imagine a man who has to choose between several alternatives—say, between working and going to a movie. If he prefers going to the movie, can we not say that he should go?

The problem and the suggested solution are deceptively simple. For example, one may object that men would like to do many things which in fact they never do. Who does not prefer playing to working, and yet how many of us actually have quit working? It might seem that this objection immediately disposes of our suggested solution, but this is not necessarily so. We can save it by altering the nature of the problem. Instead of asking whether a man prefers to go to a movie or to work, we will ask whether he prefers the *consequences* of having chosen to go to a movie to those of having chosen to work. Thus we separate the act of deciding from the consequences of that decision.

Let us consider exactly how we have altered the problem. First, we have eliminated ambiguities and at the same time we have arrived at a conceptual scheme basic to the entire theory of games. We have moved in the direction of distinguishing between alternatives for a choice and outcomes of a choice. As we shall see in the next section, a choice may have more than one outcome; but decision-making under certainty is, by definition, a problem in which each alternative has associated with it only one outcome, this outcome being the set of all the consequences associated with the choice of the given alternative. Now we can represent our example in a standard fashion:

$$\begin{array}{cc} \text{Alternatives} & \text{Outcomes} \\ \text{Going to movies } 1 & \begin{bmatrix} O_1 \\ O_2 \end{bmatrix} \\ \text{Working} \quad\quad 2 & \end{array}$$

where O_i is the outcome of having chosen alternative i (1 or 2)—or, simply, the outcome of alternative i. The above representation is complete if we specify the preferences over the outcomes. In our example, we shall assume that the decision-maker prefers the outcome of having chosen to go to the movies to the outcome of having chosen to work.

And we come to the second modification of the original problem. We are now considering all of the consequences of a choice, while before we seemed to be considering only some of the consequences. Specifically, in the original problem we asked whether our man preferred going to a movie to working; now we are asking whether he prefers going to the movie and prefers also all additional consequences of this decision (such as the consequence of not completing his work) to working and all the consequences that stem from the decision to work (such as, possibly, becoming tired and tense from lack of relaxation).

We now can see how we have disposed of the objection that, although we would usually rather play, yet most of us work. This objection implicitly separates the pleasure derived from playing from its other consequences—something that should not be done. We now use a conceptual scheme in which such separation is not permissible. This being the case, the objection is really directed not against our conclusion that our man should go to the movies (if he prefers O_1 to O_2), but rather against the problem itself. The objection has a semblance of plausibility because we know it to be a fact that most men do not prefer all the consequences of playing to all the consequences of working—most of us are too poor to be able not to work. But, once it is realized that we are taking exception to the problem rather than to its solution, the objection becomes groundless as long as we do not assert that we are dealing with a typical problem. As long as we view our problem as no more than a mental exercise, a toy that may, but need not, have practical relevance, there is precious little one can criticize. The problems begin, as we shall see in subsequent chapters, when our mathematical toy is applied to real life. Then, and only then, it becomes of critical importance to determine whether the preferences are in fact what we assume them to be.

It might seem that, having defined outcomes so that all possible consequences of an act are included, we have left our problem utterly uninteresting. Naturally, one might say, if you stack the cards like this, if you define preferences over all possible outcomes, what else can the man do but choose the alternative with the most preferred outcome? This is so obvious that it is hardly worth mentioning.

But, again, we shall counter this objection. We shall assume that there is a gap between preferences and action: To say that a certain outcome is most preferred is not the same as to say that it has to be chosen. Since this assumption more than any other separates the theory of games from much of empirical social science theory, we shall discuss it at some length.

To start with, this assumption is related to the all-important distinction between "rational" and "nonrational" behavior. In order to avoid the triviality that would result if it were assumed that all men by necessity choose the alternative with the most preferred outcome, the theory of games makes no such assumption whatsoever. For reasons that are more obvious when games of strategy are considered, the game-theoretical approach assumes that a man is completely free to decide which alternative to choose. This fundamental assumption means that *it is absolutely impossible to state, in an a priori fashion,*[1] *how likely a given decision-maker is to choose a given alternative.* In other words, it is basic to the game-theoretical approach that the decision-maker be viewed as a free agent, as a man whose decision is absolutely unpredictable.

If it were assumed that a man always chooses the alternative with the most preferred outcome, then, once his preferences are given, his behavior would follow automatically. And then what purpose would there be in developing a theory of decision-making in the first place? If all men always chose what is best for them, what else could the theory find except that this is so? If, however, the assumption of free choice is extended to include even the freedom from being ruled by one's own preferences, then there is a very good reason for pursuing the analysis further. If one assumes that men do not always do what is "best for them," then it makes sense to attempt to find out what the best choice is—then one can hope to improve a man's decision-making.

---

[1] The expression "a priori" describes something that has been defined before the problem is submitted for consideration. Hence an a priori probability is given; it cannot be considered a variable of the problem.

At the same time, however, the theory of games is interested in those who do choose the alternative with the most preferred outcome. The solution of this problem is simplicity itself. The choice of the most preferred outcome, is labeled "rational," the remaining choices "nonrational." And we arrive at the concept of rationality that is common to all of the branches of the theory of games we shall discuss: A man is said to be *rational* if he chooses the alternative having the outcome he most prefers.

Let us return to our man who must choose between going to a movie and working. The game-theoretical approach consists of the following main steps:

1. We assume that the man, when making his choice, is taking into account all the consequences of his decision. These consequences are called the outcomes of the decision problem.
2. We assume that the man can rank the outcomes in order of his preference.
3. He may, but he need not, choose the alternative with the outcome he prefers most (in our example, going to the movies); if he does, he is said to have made a rational choice.

Decision–Making under Uncertainty

The example of decision-making under certainty, simple as it was, allowed us to display some of the most fundamental features of the game-theoretical approach. From here on, the road leading into the proper domain of the theory, the games of strategy, is already charted. We shall merely add assumptions as needed to deal with each specific problem as it is considered.

The problem which forms a logical bridge between games of strategy and those of decision-making under certainty is decision-making under *un*certainty. One can think of the progress from decisions under certainty to those under uncertainty as a progress in the direction of realism. Uncertainty seems to be a far more prevalent condition than certainty for most of us. Stated most simply, we propose to modify the problem considered in the previous section so that:

1. Each alternative has more than one outcome associated with it (the number of outcomes being the same, n, for each alternative).

2. There is an event s_j that determines which one of the n outcomes associated with an alternative will occur.

Let us illustrate. Consider again a man who has to decide whether to go to a movie or to work. But this time, he is a student who has been warned that he may have an examination on the very next day. He also knows that if he does not work, he will fail. His decision problem may be represented as follows:

Event

	Examination takes place	Examination does not take place
Going to a movie	O_{11}	O_{12}
Working	O_{21}	O_{22}

Notice that there are now four outcomes, and that the student does not know which of the two events will occur—whether the examination will or will not take place. As before, we assume that the decision-maker can rank the outcomes with respect to his preference. Suppose that he prefers most going to the movie should there be no examination (that is, that his first preference is outcome O_{12}) that his second choice is the consequence of having worked when the examination does take place (e.g., passing, or O_{21}); and that he likes least of all the consequence of having studied in the event the examination does not take place (e.g., failing the examination, O_{22}). In other words, let us assume that $O_{12} > O_{21} > O_{11} > O_{22}$ where $O' > O''$ means O' is preferred to O''. What shall he do?

There is no agreement in the literature on this point. The reader interested in decision-making under uncertainty per se should consult the various texts on the subject.[2] We shall consider a special version of the problem, one on which there is general agreement and one which will also serve as a stepping stone for the discussion of games of strategy. We shall now assume that:

3. The decision-maker knows the a priori probability q_j that event s_j will occur.

[2] Chapter 13 of Luce and Raiffa (1958) contains a good introductory discussion.

In other words, we shall assume that there exists, at the time of the decision, a probability vector the components of which are the unchangeable (a priori) probabilities that a given event will occur. In our example, we assume the existence of a probability vector $q = (q_1, q_2)$, where q_1 is the probability that the examination will take place and q_2 the probability that it will not take place.

This assumption helps, but it is insufficient to solve the problem. The next ingredient we need is the assumption that the decision-maker knows not only that he prefers outcome O' to outcome O'' but also *how much more* he prefers it. It is customary to express this new assumption by saying that:

4. Each outcome O_{ij} has associated with it one and only one payoff v_{ij} such that when O' is preferred to O'', then v' is larger than v''; moreover, the payoffs form an *interval scale*.[3]

Now, perhaps, the reader sees something familiar about our problem—it is beginning to look more and more like a game which can be represented by a payoff matrix V. Using arbitrary numbers for the sake of illustration (numbers which nevertheless preserve the preference ranking we postulated earlier), we represent the problem as

$$V = \begin{array}{c} \\ 1 \\ 2 \end{array} \begin{array}{cc} s_1 & s_2 \\ \begin{bmatrix} 3 & 9 \\ 7 & 1 \end{bmatrix} \end{array}$$

The differences between this matrix and the payoff matrices considered in Chapter 9 should be noted, too. *The columns of the above matrix are not controlled by an opponent*, they are events which occur with a known probability. Decision-problems of this kind are sometimes called "games against Nature"—"Nature" being different from an opponent in that it does not possess the freedom of choice all decision-makers are assumed to possess. Its "decisions" are stochastically determined, the probabilities of Nature's "choices" being given by vector q. The events s_j are sometimes referred to as the "states of Nature."

[3] A "scale" is an instrument that permits us to assign numbers according to certain rules. If the rules specify that the assigned numbers can be used to determine by how many units the measured object (in our case, the preference) is larger than another object, then the scale is said to be an interval scale.

Our final assumption is already familiar to the reader from Chapter 9. We shall assume that:

5. A rational player prefers an outcome with a high expected payoff to an outcome with a low expected payoff.

Thus it is possible to define an expected payoff vector v' which assigns one and only one expected payoff to each alternative i. This is accomplished by multiplying the payoff matrix V by a column vector q' the components of which are the a priori probabilities q_j:

$$v' = Vq'$$

In our example, we can write that

$$v' = \begin{bmatrix} 3 & 9 \\ 7 & 1 \end{bmatrix} \begin{bmatrix} q_1 \\ q_2 \end{bmatrix} = \begin{bmatrix} 3q_1 & +9q_2 \\ 7q_1 & +q_2 \end{bmatrix}$$

Notice that the last assumption reduces our problem to a problem reminiscent of decision-making under certainty. It is now possible to say which set of outcomes the decision-maker prefers more, the outcomes in the first row of the outcome matrix or those in the second row. He prefers going to the movies to working if $v_1' > v_2'$, that is, if

$$3q_1 + 9q_2 > 7q_1 + q_2$$

We note that this inequality holds for any vector q such that $q_1 < \frac{2}{3}$,[4] and conclude that, given the payoff matrix V, the student should go to the movies only if the probability that the examination will be given is less than $\frac{2}{3}$.

Thus we see that decision-making under uncertainty can be transformed into a version of decision-making under certainty if the a priori probabilities q are given: (a) Using $v' = Vq'$, we associate a single expected payoff with each alternative, and (b) we call "rational" the decision-maker who chooses the alternative with the highest expected payoff.[5]

[4] Since $q_2 = 1 - q_1$, we can write this inequality as

$$3q_1 + 9(1 - q_1) > 7q_1 + (1 - q_1)$$

Simplifying, we write $8 > 12q_1$, and we obtain that $q_1 < \frac{2}{3}$.

[5] Luce and Raiffa (1958) discuss some of the experiments conducted to test whether men actually act so as to maximize their expected payoff (pp. 34–38).

Games of Strategy

It is perhaps obvious by now how a decision problem under uncertainty may be transformed into a game of strategy. We replace "Nature," which controls the columns of the payoff matrix, by an intelligent opponent, a person who (1) has a payoff function defined over the very same outcomes as the man who controls the rows, and who (2) is just as free to choose any one of the columns he controls as the row player is with respect to the rows.

This replacement of Nature by an intelligent opponent has several consequences. First of all, the fact that the opponent has freedom of choice means, by definition, that it is no longer possible to define the a priori probabilities over the columns of the payoff matrix. Consequently, it is no longer possible to reduce the matrix V into a payoff vector $v' = Vq'$ and thereby determine which alternative is more preferred. We have to search for a different approach to solve the present problem.

The second consequence concerns terminology. Our procedure, the one outlined in Chapter 9, requires some additional distinctions. Remember that we have termed rational the man who chooses the alternative which maximizes his expected payoff, and that this concept of rationality was sufficient to identify the solution for all decision problems under certainty and for some decision problems under uncertainty. However, this concept is not sufficient when our decision-maker faces an intelligent opponent. As we stated in Chapter 9, a solution is arrived at only through the concept of optimal strategies—a concept that presupposes not only that the decision-maker is rational but also that he abides by the *security-level principle*, choosing the alternative which maximizes his security level.

For historical reasons, decision problems involving an intelligent opponent are called "games." It is through the study of parlor games such as chess and poker that much of the theory of games began. To distinguish these problems from problems in which the decision-maker "plays" against Nature (games of chance), it is customary to speak of games involving intelligent opponents as of *games of strategy*. Clearly, this means that the concept of optimal strategies has to be invoked in addition to the concept of rationality if these games are to be solved.

The reasoning behind the concept of optimal strategies and the computational procedures for determining optimal strategies can be found in Chapter 9, and need not be repeated here. However, we do want to list all the assumptions which must be made if the solutions discussed in Chapter 9 are to be mathematically impeccable.

In order to solve zero-sum two-person games one has to assume that:

1. Two players are playing a game which can be represented by a single payoff matrix with n rows and m columns, as discussed in Chapter 9.
2. Each player knows the entire payoff matrix.
3. Each player's subjective preferences for the outcomes of the game are completely characterized by a *utility function* that is linear with the (expected) payoff function of the game.
4. Each player is free to make his choice; that is, it is impossible to define a priori probabilities of his choice.
5. Each player makes his choice without knowing his opponent's choice.

Of these assumptions, the third deserves some attention since it introduces an all-important game-theoretical concept of a utility function.

Utility Function

It should be noted that we are using the terms "expected payoffs" and "utility function" somewhat differently than is customary. While the usual practice is to use the two terms more or less interchangeably, we draw definite distinctions. We start from the observation that a given game is usually defined by a matrix whose components are *specific numbers*. Since this is customary, and since these specific numbers are often given objective meaning (they often represent a valuable commodity such as money), we call them the payoffs v_{ij}.

However, it is customary for a game-theoretician to assume that a player's subjective preferences are not defined in such a unique way. The reason for this is mainly historical. Experience has convinced many economists that it is not reasonable to assume that a man's subjective preferences are so specific. Particularly, it seemed unreasonable to assume that everybody's preference for money is the same, that a millionaire derives the same amount of "satisfaction" (utility) from a dollar as does a beggar. On the other hand, it did seem reasonable to assume that both a millionaire and a beggar prefer more money to less money. The solution that some economists accept, one which has been incorporated into the theory of games, is that a man's subjective utility of money is not a unique number but a whole set of numbers. Specifically, the game-theoretical approach assumes that, if the payoff matrix for a given matrix is V, then the subjective preferences of the player are given by a set of utility matrices U such that

$$U = aV + B$$

where a is a positive number, B is a matrix of the same size as V, whose components are all the same number b (positive, negative, or zero). As a result, the subjective preference for outcome O_{ij} is given by a *non-unique* utility index u_{ij}:

$$u_{ij} = av_{ij} + b$$

The utility index u_{ij} is clearly non-unique (is not a specific number but rather a whole set of numbers) because a and b can be any numbers (a any positive number). To illustrate, consider again the game of (9.1):

$$V = \begin{bmatrix} -1 & 4 \\ 2 & 0 \end{bmatrix}$$

When we say that the player's utilities are linear with his payoffs we mean that, for example, Richard's utility matrix could be

$$U = \begin{bmatrix} -2 & 8 \\ 4 & 0 \end{bmatrix}$$

(note that we multiply each payoff by 2) or it could be

$$U = \begin{bmatrix} 3 & 13 \\ 9 & 5 \end{bmatrix}$$

(note that we added 5 to each payoff). In general, his utility matrix is

$$U = \begin{bmatrix} -1a + b & 4a + b \\ 2a + b & b \end{bmatrix}$$

The very same reasoning that applies to Richard applies to Carl as well. His utility function U' could also be given by any one of the possible linear transformations $U' = -(a'V + B')$. It should be noted that the subjective utilities of the two players are diametrically opposed if and only if it is possible to choose a, a', B, and B' so that the resulting payoff matrix is zero-sum. In other words, the utility functions U and U' are diametrically opposed if and only if it holds that

$$U = aV + B$$
$$U' = a'V' + B'$$
$$V = -V'$$

where V is a matrix describing Richard's payoffs and V' a matrix describing Carl's payoffs.

One consequence of the linearity assumption will be important in later chapters. It follows from this assumption that we cannot say that one player prefers an outcome more than another player does, even if the payoff from that outcome to the first player is larger than the payoff (from that outcome) to the other player. To be sure, we can say that a given player (subjectively) prefers outcome O' to O'' if his payoff from O' is larger than his payoff from O''. But in this case we are comparing two outcomes for the given player; what cannot be done is to compare a given outcome for two players. Why cannot such "interpersonal comparisons of utility" be made? Precisely because the payoff function does not determine utility function uniquely. Even if player 1's payoff v_{ij} from a given outcome is higher than player 2's payoff v'_{ij} from that outcome, it does not follow that player 1's utility index u_{ij} is higher than player 2's utility index u'_{ij}. In other words, if $v_{ij} > v'_{ij}$, then it is not necessarily true that $u_{ij} > u'_{ij}$.

For the theory of zero-sum two-person games this impossibility to compare subjective preferences of different players presents no problem. However, we shall see in Chapter 13 that it does become a problem when the so-called nonzero-sum games are considered. It then becomes imperative to find some way to circumvent this limitation imposed upon the utility functions.

It will be recalled that it is customary to assume not only that the utility function is linear with the payoff function, but also that it describes a player's preferences *completely*. This is again an important assumption, for it means that all of a player's motivations are described by his utility function. This assumption will quite often mean that the players are not motivated by extraneous considerations such as the excitement inherent in taking a chance or feelings of friendship or compassion for the opponent. To make this point perfectly clear: We are not saying that a player cannot be motivated by considerations such as feelings of compassion for the opponent; we are merely saying that, if he is motivated by such feelings, then this motivation has to be incorporated in the utility function (and therefore also in the payoff function) of the game. Consequently, it is assumed that the utility function describes the preferences that result from all the various motivations a player can have.

Classification of Games

Today the theory of games is an impressive edifice, comprising a large number of topics, many of which are not true games of strategy. We shall mention here only a few of the important problems considered to be in the mainstream of the development of the theory.

The most obvious extension of the zero-sum two-person games is to zero-sum n-person games. Is it possible to solve games of strategy when the number of players is increased beyond two? Some such games can be solved, but the theory of n-person games is generally considered to be less satisfactory than the two-person theory. The main difficulty stems from the fact that, as soon as more than two players participate, a totally new phenomenon emerges—the possibility of *coalitions*. And no altogether satisfactory method has been found for taking into account the strategic significance of coalitions. ·

Somewhat unexpectedly, the problems encountered when the number of players is allowed to increase are similar to those encountered when the zero-sum assumption is relaxed and the nonzero-sum games are considered.[6] However, the way in which the problem manifests itself is different. When the payoffs do not sum to zero, the

---

[6] The reason for this similarity is that an n-person nonzero-sum game can be always treated as an $n + 1$-person *zero*-sum game by adding a "dummy" player.

whole security-level principle collapses—it is no longer sufficient to obtain a solution. We shall discuss this problem in Chapter 12.

It has been found that one of the most important classificatory dimensions for nonzero-sum games is the amount of communication permitted. When communication is allowed, and when the participants are permitted to commit themselves with respect to the choices they will make, then solutions which seem reasonable are quite different from those obtained when no communication is allowed. This, too, will be considered later, in Chapters 12 and 13.

Finally, a considerable amount of work has been done in the area of *continuous* games—games in which each player has an infinite number of choices available to him, and payoffs are a fairly simple function of this "choice variable." This area has been quite rewarding, both because it is possible to apply some fairly powerful mathematical methods (such as differential equations) and because its practical applications are many (primarily to warfare). The interested reader may wish to consult any one of a number of standard texts in this area.[7]

10.2   MEANING OF OPTIMALITY

A mathematician is usually satisfied with proving that a problem he has set up to consider has a solution; if he can show also that this solution is unique, his accomplishment is even greater. For this reason, the Minimax Theorem, discussed in Chapter 9, is an accomplishment which has received considerable attention in the literature. The social scientist, however, finds himself in a somewhat different position. He may appreciate the elegance of the mathematical solution, but he is interested also in its "practical" significance. Above all, he will wonder about the precise meaning of the word of "optimality": exactly why should a player choose the optimal strategy?

Since we are now concerned more with the application of the theory of games than with its mathematical structure, it will be convenient to base our discussion on a specific example. We shall consider again the example used in Chapter 9, the war game in

[7] Luce and Raiffa (1958) discuss such games in their Appendix 7.

which two officers, Richard and Carl, were pitted against each other. The game is defined as follows:

$$
\begin{array}{c}
\text{Carl's strategies} \\
\text{Shoot} \quad \text{Do not shoot}
\end{array}
$$

(10.1)   Richard's strategies

$$
\begin{array}{c}
\text{Fly high} \\
\text{Fly low}
\end{array}
\begin{bmatrix}
-1 & 4 \\
2 & 0
\end{bmatrix}
$$

It will be recalled that the solution of this game consisted of Richard's optimal strategy $p^* = (\frac{2}{7}, \frac{5}{7})$, Carl's optimal strategy $q'^* = (\frac{4}{7}, \frac{3}{7})$, and the value of the game $v^* = \frac{8}{7}$. We now turn to the reasons why p^* and q'^* should be chosen, starting with a review of some of their purely mathematical properties: their stability, equivalence, and interchangeability.

Some Mathematical Properties

The strongest argument recommending the optimal strategies p^* and q'^* may be the fact that the solution $(p^*, q'^*; v^*)$ is *stable*, or, as it is often phrased, that p^* and q'^* are in equilibrium, for when one of the players uses his optimal strategy, then his opponent cannot possibly gain (and may actually lose) by not playing his optimal strategy. In other words, there is a certain compulsion for a rational player to use p^* whether he wants to or not. This compulsion is generated precisely by the rational considerations that we identified as the spirit of the game-theoretical approach. If Richard is a fully rational being who not only wishes to maximize his own utility, but can also put himself into his opponent's shoes, then he will be drawn the conclusions that his opponent (1) may be a rational being, (2) may identify his optimal strategy q'^*, (3) may play q'^*.

Now if the opponent indeed plays q'^*, then, by virtue of the above-stated stability of $(p^*, q'^*; v^*)$, Richard would be foolish not to play his optimal strategy p^*. But, let us admit, there is a very real temptation not to play p^*, and this temptation has its roots in the fact that if the opponent does not play q'^*, then p^* may not be the best strategy to play. The reader should note well the fact that the property of stability does not guarantee that p^* is Richard's best answer against *any* q', it merely guarantees that if Richard sticks to p^*, he will receive at least v^* no matter what his opponent does. For example, in the game (10.1), if Carl were to play his strategy $q_1 = 0$ rather than his optimal strategy $q_1^* = \frac{4}{7}$, then Richard's best answer would be to play $p_1 = 1$, thus securing for himself a payoff of $+4$ rather than the expected payoff $v = \frac{8}{7}$ which he would have if he played his optimal strategy $p^* = \frac{2}{7}$. Thus the compulsion to play p^* is limited to instances in which opponent plays his optimal strategy.

But can Richard ever expect Carl not to play q'^*? Not if the assumptions of the Theory of Games are met and if Carl is a free agent. If Carl is completely free so that no a priori reasoning can reveal what Carl is "bound" to do, then there is not even the slightest reason for expecting Carl not to play q'^*. Furthermore, if for any reason Carl does in fact fail to play q'^*, there is absolutely no way for Richard to find out which strategy q' Carl did play, and hence he cannot possibly play his best answer to Carl's q'. After considering these arguments, a rational player is compelled to fall back upon p^* as the safest strategy under the circumstances.

Note that the Minimax Theorem does not guarantee that every zero-sum two-person game will have only one optimal strategy for each player; a player may in fact have at his disposal more than one optimal strategy. But the Theorem does guarantee that, in case there are two or more equilibrium pairs (i.e., two or more "associated" optimal strategies), $(p^*, q^*), (p^{**}, q^{**}), \ldots$, then the expected payoff from (p^*, q^*) is the same as that from (p^{**}, q^{**}). We say that all equilibrium pairs are *equivalent*.

An even more important property of the solution is its *interchangeability*. Each optimal strategy yields value v^* not only against the "associated" counter-strategy (p^* against q'^*, p^{**} against q'^{**}), but also against any one of the counter-strategies. So, for example, when Richard uses p^* he is certain to receive v^* no matter which one of his optimal strategies (if there are several) Carl uses.

The practical consequences of these two properties is that, even if there are several alternative optimal ways by which the game can be played, the player need not worry which one of these optimal strategies to follow. He can choose any one of them; his payoff will always be the same.

Should Expected Payoff Be Maximized?

So far we have discussed the mathematical properties of optimal strategies and we have found them to be quite compelling. However, these properties rest on a foundation which in itself may be rather shaky. Is it really reasonable to assume that men should act in such a way as to maximize their *expected* payoff? Consider again the game (10.1);

$$V = \begin{bmatrix} -1 & 4 \\ 2 & 0 \end{bmatrix}$$

We know that the optimal strategy for Richard is $p^* = (\frac{2}{7}, \frac{5}{7})$. But is this strategy really a good one from a common sense point of view? Note that by playing p^* Richard may receive as little as -1 point (if the less likely, but still possible, result of spinning the random device is the decision to play his first strategy, and if Carl decided to play his first strategy also); but if Richard plays his pure strategy $p = (0, 1)$, then he is certain to receive no less than 0 points. Which is better—the certainty of having at least 0 points, or the mathematical expectation of having at least $v^* = \frac{8}{7}$, an expectation that nevertheless permits the payoff of -1 to occur on any one play of the game?

The answer to this question depends on how one views the play of a game. If one wishes to consider one play in isolation, then to play it safe by using the best *pure* strategy might be the sensible thing to do, even though one could object to such a strategy on logical grounds.[8] But if one is willing to admit that the very same game may be played again, then it might be more sensible to take a long-range view. Instead of worrying about any single play of the game, one would begin to think of the total or the average payoff over a number of plays of the game. And once the player becomes concerned about the average payoff, then the expected payoff acquires crucial importance. It can be shown that the larger the number of plays of the game, the closer will be the actual mean payoff to the expected value of the game, v^*, provided that both players play their optimal strategies. If Richard alone plays his

---

[8] When the optimal strategy is in fact a mixed strategy, then the best pure strategy is not stable; that is, the opponent can improve his payoff by playing a strategy other than his best pure strategy.

optimal strategy p^*, then his actual mean payoff will be, with increasing probability as the number of plays increases, v^* or more.[9]

Optimality in Repeated Plays

Although the concept of a solution presupposes a single play of a game, we have just seen that it helps us to accept game-theoretical solutions as reasonable if we consider repeated plays. We shall now outline an argument that to some readers may seem more relevant than anything we had to say so far in support of the concept of optimality. We shall show that if, in repeated plays of a game, each player interprets his opponent's past choices in a certain way, the players will inevitably end up playing their optimal strategies.

We suggest the following: Let us assume for a moment that each player views a zero-sum two-person game not as a game of strategy, but as a "game" against Nature—that is, as a decision problem under uncertainty. This means that, before he plays the game at time t, he uses his opponent's previous choices to define the a priori probabilities of opponent's choice at time t. For example, Richard assumes that Carl will choose his alternative j with probability $\bar{q}_j = N_j/N$, where N_j is the number of times Carl chose j up to time t and N is the total number of plays of the game up to time t. In other words, Richard assumes that the opponent's probability of choosing j "now" is the same as the proportion of plays on which he chose j in the past.

To illustrate, let us again consider game (10.1),

$$V = \begin{bmatrix} -1 & 4 \\ 2 & 0 \end{bmatrix}$$

[9] The law of large numbers states that, if a given outcome O_{ij} occurs repeatedly with the same probability p_{ij}, then the proportion of times O_{ij} has occurred approaches p_{ij} as the number of trials grows large (see, for example, Mosteller et al., 1961, p. 292). This means that, after N plays of the game in which the same strategies p and q are used (so that O_{ij} occurs always with the probability p_iq_j), outcome O_{ij} occurs in about N_{ij} trials where $N_{ij}/N \approx p_iq_j$. Multiplying both sides by v_{ij} we obtain

$$\frac{N_{ij}}{N} v_{ij} \approx p_iq_jv_{ij}$$

when N is large. Since the left side of the near equality represents the average payoff for all trials on which outcome O_{ij} has occurred, the average payoff for all trials must be close to $p_1q_1v_{11} + p_1q_2v_{12} + \cdots + p_iq_jv_{ij} + \cdots$. That is, it must be close to the expected payoff.

On the very first play of the game there are no "previous" choices, and hence it is impossible for Richard to estimate Carl's probability vector $\bar{q}$, and for Carl to estimate Richard's probability vector $\bar{p}$. For our argument, however, it makes no difference which alternatives the two players choose on their very first play, so let us assume that Richard chooses his second strategy, Carl his first:

$$p^{(1)} = (0, 1), \qquad q^{(1)} = (1, 0)$$

After these results are announced, both players prepare themselves for the second play. Richard now has some basis for estimating Carl's choice at time $t = 2$ for since Carl chose alternative $j = 1$ once "in the past" and $j = 2$ not at all, it follows that $N_1 = 1$, $N_2 = 0$, and $N = 1$. And he defines the following a priori probabilities for Carl:

$$q = \left(\frac{N_1}{N}, \frac{N_2}{N}\right) = (1, 0)$$

Given these probabilities, he can now treat the game as a decision problem under uncertainty. He determines his expected payoff from each alternative

$$v' = V\bar{q}' = \begin{bmatrix} -1 & 4 \\ 2 & 0 \end{bmatrix}\begin{bmatrix} 1 \\ 0 \end{bmatrix} = \begin{bmatrix} -1 \\ 2 \end{bmatrix}$$

and chooses (if he is rational) his second alternative since his expected payoff from that alternative, 2, is higher than that from his first alternative, -1:

$$p^{(2)} = (0, 1)$$

Carl proceeds in similar fashion. Using Richard's first choice, he notes that Richard has chosen "in the past" his first alternative zero times, $M_1 = 0$, and his second alternative once, $M_2 = 1$. He defines a priori probabilities for Richard,

$$\bar{p} = \left(\frac{M_1}{M}, \frac{M_2}{M}\right) = (0, 1)$$

and computes his own expected payoffs

$$w = -v = \bar{p}(-V) = (0, 1)\begin{bmatrix} 1 & -4 \\ -2 & 0 \end{bmatrix} = (-2, 0)$$

Since his second alternative has a higher expected payoff than the first, he chooses the second alternative:

$$q^{(2)} = (0, 1)$$

The subsequent plays of the game proceed in the same fashion. The quantities relevant for the third play of the game are

$$N_1 = 1, \qquad N_2 = 1, \qquad N = 2; \qquad \bar{q} = (\tfrac{1}{2}, \tfrac{1}{2})$$
$$M_1 = 0, \qquad M_2 = 2, \qquad M = 2, \qquad \bar{p} = (0, 1)$$

Using these a priori probabilities $\bar{q}$ and $\bar{p}$, we could compute expected payoff for each player and his rational choice for time $t = 3$. And so on.

Brown (1951) has shown that as time t grows large, the a priori probabilities $\bar{q}$ and $\bar{p}$ (estimated by each player on the basis of opponent's past choices) approach the optimal strategies q^* and p^*. In other words, each player becomes more and more convinced that his opponent is playing a strategy which is (in fact) optimal. To see the reason why this will happen, consider at what point Richard (who in our example has been playing his second alternative repeatedly) will switch to his first alternative. We know that this will happen (if he is rational) as soon as the expected payoff from his first strategy is larger than that from his second strategy, that is, when $v_1 > v_2$. Since his expected payoffs if Carl's a priori probabilities are $\bar{q}'$ is

$$v = \begin{bmatrix} -1 & 4 \\ 2 & 0 \end{bmatrix} \begin{bmatrix} \bar{q}_1 \\ \bar{q}_2 \end{bmatrix} = \begin{bmatrix} -\bar{q}_1 + 4\bar{q}_2 \\ 2\bar{q}_1 \end{bmatrix}$$

the condition $v_1 > v_2$ may be written as

$$-\bar{q}_1 + 4\bar{q}_2 > 2\bar{q}_1$$

Recalling that $\bar{q}_2 = 1 - \bar{q}_1$, we write the above inequality as

$$\tfrac{4}{7} > \bar{q}_1$$

But what is $\bar{q}_1 = \tfrac{4}{7}$? As we showed in Chapter 9, $(\tfrac{4}{7}, \tfrac{3}{7})$ is Carl's optimal strategy! Thus we see that Richard's "switching point" is determined by Carl's optimal strategies. And we could show that Carl's "switching point" is determined by Richard's optimal strategy. Thus we have the following situation: If the inequality relationship between $\bar{p}_1$ and $p_1{}^*$ (or $\bar{q}$ and $q_1{}^*$) is reversed between time $t-1$ and time t, then Richard (or Carl) has to play a different alternative at time t than he did at time $t-1$. But if the opponent has played a different strategy at time t than at time $t-1$, then the stage is set for another switch of alternative now, and the inequality between $\bar{p}_1$ and $p_1{}^*$ (or $\bar{q}_1$ and $q_1{}^*$) is again in danger of being reversed. Thus, intuitively, we feel that the strategies of the two players will oscillate around p^* and q^*. The result of such oscillation will be that each strategy is played in the "recommended" proportions of trials, p^* and q^*.

Concepts Related to Optimality

By now the reader should understand the concept of optimality well enough to realize the following:

1. Optimality is related to the security-level principle. The optimal strategy is that which maximizes the player's security level.
2. The assertion that a player should maximize his security level is plausible in zero-sum two-person games, but it need not be plausible in other games.
3. The security-level principle was used to define optimal strategies not only because this principle is plausible in zero-sum games, but also because it helps to define a solution with highly desirable mathematical properties.

It follows that in games in which it is not plausible to assert that the player should maximize his level of security, or in which such an assumption is of no help in defining a solution, a different principle has to be invoked.

We shall see (in Chapters 12 and 13) that the security-level principle is neither plausible nor helpful in nonzero-sum games. Since the payoffs of the players are not diametrically opposed in such games, it does not make much sense to assume that the opponent will choose that alternative which gives the player the worst possible payoff. Such an assumption would mean (when the payoffs are not diametrically opposed) that the opponent is interested more in punishing the player than in maximizing his own payoffs. Furthermore, this assumption is no longer helpful since to assume that each player maximizes his security level leads to a solution which (when the game is nonzero-sum) has none of the properties described earlier, for the resulting strategies are neither stable nor equivalent nor interchangeable.

For this reason, solutions for nonzero-sum games are based on some new principles. We shall see that the strategies that are a part of the solution of a nonzero-sum game are usually labeled "fair" rather than "optimal." Thus the concept of optimality is, by and large, reserved for the recommended strategies in zero-sum games.

EXERCISES

1. The City of New York has been experiencing race riots for several days and the Mayor has to decide whether or not to ask for the National Guard to be called in. He knows that the riots are likely to continue if the hot weather continues, and he knows that calling the National Guard uselessly is politically dangerous. He arrives at the following evaluation of the situation:

Hot weather

Continues   Ends

$$\begin{array}{l} \text{Call National Guard} \\ \text{Do not call National Guard} \end{array} \begin{bmatrix} -2 & -3 \\ -10 & 8 \end{bmatrix}$$

(a) Suppose that the Weather Bureau tells him that the probability that the hot weather will stop is $q_2 = .5$; should he ask for the National Guard? (b) What weather prediction will make him indifferent between calling and not calling the National Guard? (*Hint:* he will be indifferent if his expected payoff for the first row is the same as for the second.)

2. Find the optimal strategies and the value for the following zero-sum game:

$$V = \begin{bmatrix} 3 & 1 \\ 7 & 10 \end{bmatrix}$$

3. Subtract 1 from each of the four payoffs of the game of exercise 2, and compute p^*, q^*, and v^* for this new game. Are the strategies for the new game the same as for the original game? Is the value v^* the same?

4. Multiply matrix V of exercise 2 by 2 (i.e., multiply each v_{ij} by 2) and compute p^*, q^*, and v^* for the new game. Are the optimal strategies the same as in the original game? Is the value the same?

5. Consider the example discussed in Chapter 10. Game V is played repeatedly and each player is acting as if he was confronted with decision-making under uncertainty. He always assumes that his opponent will make his choice with probabilities $q_1 = N_1/N$, $q_2 = N_2/N$ (where N_i is the number of times the opponent has chosen alternative i in the past). Suppose that the game is

$$V = \begin{bmatrix} -1 & 4 \\ 2 & 0 \end{bmatrix}$$

and that the early choices have been as follows:

Play	Richard's Choice	Carl's Choice
1	2nd row	1st column
2	2nd row	2nd column

Determine Richard's and Carl's choices for plays 3 to 10.

6. Using the results of exercise 5, compute $\bar{p}_1 = N_1/N$ and $\bar{q}_1 = M_1/M$ for plays 3 to 10. Is $\bar{p}_1$ approaching $p_1{}^*$ and $\bar{q}_1$ approaching $q_1{}^*$?

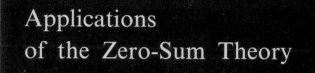

CHAPTER 11

Applications
of the Zero-Sum Theory

As was stated in Chapter 10, the theory of zero-sum two-person games can be applied fully only to conflicts in which five main assumptions are met:

1. Two players are playing a game which can be represented by a single payoff matrix with n rows and m columns.
2. Each player knows the entire matrix.
3. Each player's subjective preferences for the outcomes of the game are completely characterized by a utility function that satisfies certain specific requirements[1] and is linear with the payoff function of the game.
4. Each player is free to make his choice; that is, it is impossible to define a priori probabilities of his choice.
5. Each player makes his choice without knowing his opponent's choice.

Only when these assumptions are met can the optimal strategies be identified. It is possible, however, to apply the theory with some profit even when these conditions are not satisfied or when it is uncertain whether they are satisfied.

[1] Since the utility function is assumed to be linear with the payoff function, it has to meet the same requirements as the payoff function. It has to describe preferences completely and it has to form an interval scale.

We shall discuss three such applications. The first one is in some respects the most modest and in others the most ambitious. It is modest because it does not attempt to determine the solution to any particular game—it merely attempts to view social interaction as a game; it is ambitious because it maintains that the game-theoretical approach may be the best approach for the study of human interaction.

The second example involves application of the zero-sum theory on its own terms. Payoffs are defined, optimal strategies are identified and executed. It is no accident that our example will deal with military conflict, since the assumptions of the zero-sum theory (in particular, the assumption that the interests are diametrically opposed) are most nearly met in warfare.

The third example involves "testing" the theory of zero-sum two-person games by investigating whether men in fact play such games as the theory recommends. Such applications are relatively abundant, even though this approach actually violates the spirit of the theory of games. The theory never claims that men actually behave in accordance with its prescriptions; it merely states that they should.

Just for the record, it should be noted that the first example does not deal with the application of theory of zero-sum two-person games alone but rather with the application of the game-theoretical point of view as a whole. Thus, strictly speaking, it does not belong in this chapter. However, given the importance of the views expressed in this example and their general applicability, we could think of no better place for it than here.

11.1 SOCIAL INTERACTION AND THE THEORY OF GAMES

The theory of games has already exercised considerable influence upon the thinking and the interests of many behavioral scientists. But few authors have been influenced more profoundly and have drawn more basic conclusions from the theory than have Anderson and Moore (1960, 1962). They suggest that the study of man and his society might be more profitable if it were based on the game-theoretical approach than if it were continued along the lines presently employed.

To a large extent, to study society "scientifically" means today to study it in ways that have proven successful in the physical sciences. The scientist defines his problem, assumes that the conditions defining his problem are constant, and proceeds to find a solution. Anderson and Moore feel that to assume that the conditions *are* stable and that they will not change as a result of the investigation is highly questionable when man and his society are studied. Man is such an adaptable creature that almost nothing about him can be taken for granted. When we least expect it, he can change his behavior so profoundly as to change the very conditions we have assumed to be stable, thus making the solution inapplicable.

It seems to us that Anderson and Moore are arguing that the game-theoretical assumption that man is free to make choices is correct more often than has been commonly assumed. It will be recalled that the assumption of free choice means that it is impossible to define a priori probabilities which apply to the alternatives from which the decision-maker has to choose. It is the a priori status of such probabilities that the authors question. They suggest that in many cases it is impossible to define such probabilities, or, alternately, that if one does assume the existence of such a priori alternatives, one often finds that the resulting solution fails to correspond to the actual decision. Since the freedom of choice is one of the cornerstones of the theory of games, the game-theoretical approach should be employed to the study of society.

Anderson and Moore offer more than a simple opinion, however; they make several observations about society to support their view. The most fundamental of these is their observation that all known societies have so-called autotellic folk models and that these models are designed to train the members of the society to cope with some basic human problems.

Before we deal with the significance of this observation, let us explain that the authors feel that problem solving is one of the most basic of human activities. Some of the problems facing man involve his natural environment, others involve his fellow men, still others the affective life, his own as well as that of others. These problems are difficult in the sense that their solution is by no means obvious to those without experience. Consequently, all societies are confronted with the task of teaching their children how to solve these difficult problems.

But how should one teach children to solve problems? On-the-job training is often impractical if for no other reason than that mistakes are likely to be costly. One cannot allow an inexperienced man to design houses, for they may collapse. Nor can one allow inexperienced warriors to do battle, for they will be defeated. Similarly, an inexperienced priest might inspire confusion rather than a feeling of devotion and solidarity among his fellow men. Clearly then, training activities have to be separated from real-life problem solving.

But once training activities are separated from real life, what is going to motivate the trainees to learn? In real life the solution of a problem usually leads to a reward: The family can find shelter in a house, the victors can enrich themselves in the conquered territory, the priest helps to maintain order and a sense of fellowship. In the training period there can be no such real-life rewards and therefore substitute rewards have to be found. One of the most universal, and usually the least expensive, of these substitutes is fun, having a good time. It is thus not surprising that the serious business of training is very often transacted through the misleadingly whimsical and trivial vehicle of games. Children learn how to solve serious adult problems by playing games that are fun.

Let us pause now to consider the consequences of this argument. In the first place, we have come to a point where we can understand what Anderson and Moore mean by "autotelic folk models." An *autotelic* activity is one which is self-rewarding, which needs no additional reward beyond the pleasure derived from the very performance of the activity. Solving a puzzle or building a house of wooden blocks is enjoyable in itself, just as much as is playing poker or listening to music. And a folk model is a part of the "prescientific culture" of a society; it is that segment of the culture which formalizes certain autotelic activities. In short, autotelic folk models are the various games which form a part of the culture and which play a dual role: entertaining the children while preparing them for solving some serious problems of adult life.

In the second place one ought to note certain formal similarities between autotelic folk models and the game-theoretical approach. Recall that the game-theoretical approach assumes that each game is self-contained in the sense that the utility function completely describes the preferences of a player. It may be difficult to satisfy this assumption in real life, but when it comes to autotelic folk models the assumption is amply met. "Having fun" does have the properties of a simple utility function as assumed by the Theory of Games, since having fun is autotelic. It is intrinsic to the playing of the game itself.

The similarity, however, does not stop there. Problem solving under certainty and under uncertainty, the two basic versions of the game-theoretical approach, are appropriate for training men to cope with their natural environment precisely because the "opponent" in these games is "Nature," the a priori probabilities of which are assumed to be known. Games of strategy are appropriate for the second category of human problems, those involving interaction among men. The last category of human problems, those dealing with affective aspects of our lives, has no satisfactory analog in the theory of games at the present time. To be sure, autotelic folk models do exist. Music, poetry, and drama all may be viewed as culturally formalized devices enriching man's emotional life and, perhaps, enlarging his repertoire of emotional responses. Anderson and Moore venture a guess that some of these aesthetic activities may find analogs in games of strategy or games of chance. For example, a murder mystery is not altogether dissimilar to a puzzle since both seem to require putting together various pieces in order to obtain a solution. Much pleasure is derived in both instances from the neat fitting into place of the various parts.

Now for the third, and perhaps crucial, consequence of the Anderson-Moore argument. If it is true that autotelic folk models have been used from time immemorial to train children in the serious business of problem solving, and if this has been done successfully, should we not continue this practice? Note that if these attempts were successful in the past, if playing the various games did in fact prepare children for adult life, then it must have been because these games are a close enough representation of man's society. And since the game-theoretical approach historically stems from and is conceptually similar to the autotelic folk models, does it not follow that the game-theoretical approach is appropriate to the study of man's society? And therefore that we should continue training children and young adults within the game-theoretical framework?

If we answer these questions in the affirmative, as Anderson and Moore do, then we ought to develop new ways of studying man's behavior. Sociological and psychological experimentation should be seen in a new light, the participants being not "subjects" whose behavior one wishes to predict, but rather "colleagues" from whom one is learning. Instead of exposing the participants in an experiment to a simple set of stimuli, we ought to surround them with a rich and challenging environment. We should study not how men *react* to a set of stimuli but rather how they *master* a rich and unstable environment. In short, the scientist should do what "societies" have done in the past, creating games that resemble some aspects of societal life, and noting the participants' solutions to these games.

Moore's own experiments with "dynamic autotelic responsive environment" are an example of such an approach. For example, by constructing a responsive electronically controlled environment, Moore (1963) succeeded in teaching some preschool children to read and to type on an electric typewriter, all in a matter of weeks. On the purely theoretical side, the approach advocated by the authors is exemplified by attempts to establish the so-called deontic logic, the logic of norms. That one should be interested in studying social norms is hardly surprising when one realizes that the game-theoretical approach is normative. Its objective is to determine how men should behave, not how they do in fact behave. Although the present state of deontic logic is not considered to be completely satisfactory, a number of logicians have been working in this area. Perhaps the most basic work of this kind is a paper by von Wright (1951).

Finally, the game-theoretical approach may prove to be rewarding to social scientists interested in the study of cultures. If it is true that autotelic folk models are devices for training children in solving important problems, then the prevalence of games of certain types might provide an important insight into the culture. For example, one could hypothesize that games of the zero-sum variety would be much more prevalent in a highly competitive society than in one which emphasizes cooperation. One could even pursue the intriguing notion that cultural norms themselves may be viewed as game-theoretical solutions. For example, could those aspects of social organization which vary considerably from culture to culture be conceptualized as games that allow for a variety of solutions, while on the other hand certain nearly universal norms, such as the incest taboo, occur under circumstances that can be represented by games with a single set of optimal strategies? The assumption underlying such a query is that societies ultimately prescribe and sanction as their norms those forms of behavior which have been found, over the centuries, to be the most rewarding.

11.2   MILITARY STRATEGIES

Considerable controversy has arisen concerning the usefulness of the zero-sum theory to actual life. Most of the criticism centers around the contention that the assumptions upon which the theory is built are so restrictive that they are satisfied only very rarely by social conflicts of any significance. Perhaps the best reply to this criticism is to cite examples in which the theory can be applied to important problems. While serving as a colonel in the U. S. Air Force and as a student at the Air War College, Haywood (1954) analyzed two World War II battles, attempting to show that the game-theoretical approach was applicable to them and that the strategy prescribed by the theory agrees with the military-decision doctrine currently approved by the Joint Chiefs of Staff.

The Battle of the Bismarck Sea: A Case of Pure Strategies

In February, 1943, the struggle for New Guinea reached a critical point, the Allies controlling the southern part of New Guinea, the Japanese the northern part. At this time, intelligence reports indicated that the Japanese were assembling a troop and supply convoy at Rabaul, located at the eastern tip of the nearby island of New Britain, with the intention of reinforcing their position in New Guinea. The destination of the convoy was to be Lae in New Guinea.

General Kenney, the commander of the Allied Air Forces in the South Pacific area, was ordered by General MacArthur to inflict maximum destruction on the convoy.

Kenney and his staff analyzed the situation. It was perfectly obvious that the Japanese commander had two choices for routing his convoy; he could sail either north of New Britain, or south. Either route required about three days. Since the detection of a convoy from the air is most likely when the planes are concentrated along its route, Kenney, also, had two choices for deployment of his reconnaissance aircraft. He could deploy them predominantly either along the northern route or along the southern route.

At this point a critical factor was pointed out by Kenney's staff: rain and poor visibility were predicted for the area north of New Britain, while visibility south of the island was expected to be good. This meant that it would take Kenney's planes longer to locate the convoy if it followed the northern route, and as a result, Kenney's bombing force (which was to strike as soon as the convoy was located) would have only a short time to inflict damage. The problem was further complicated by the fact that if Kenney happened to deploy most of his reconnaissance planes along one route while the Japanese chose the other, the detection of the convoy would also be delayed considerably.

Figure 11.1 shows the four outcomes that were possible in view of the two strategies available to each commander. Note that the point at which the convoy was likely to be sighted is indicated on each of the four maps. Since the point of sighting determines the length of time the convoy could be bombed and since the damage inflicted upon the convoy may be assumed to be proportional to the length of bombing, it is plausible to consider the length of bombing as Kenney's payoff in this situation. Given the estimated length of bombing shown in Figure 11.1, the military conflict of the Bismarck Sea can be represented by the following matrix:

Japanese strategies

Sail north   Sail south

		Sail north	Sail south
Kenney	Search north	2 days	2 days
strategies	Search south	1 day	3 days

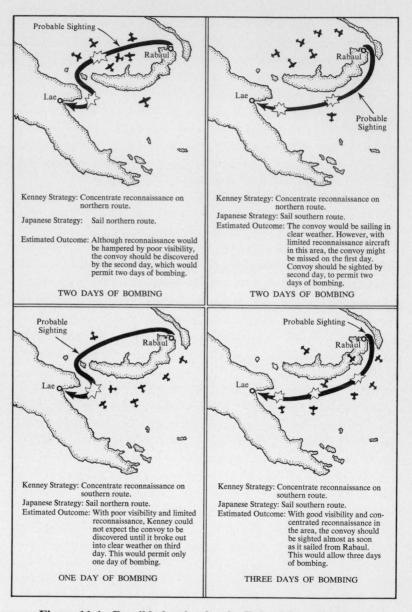

Figure 11.1. Possible battles for the Rabaul-Lae situation.

REDRAWN from Haywood (1954), by permission of the Operations Research Society of America.

Given the representation of the conflict by the above matrix, what strategy should Kenney have chosen? The zero-sum game theory clearly prescribes that he should choose his first strategy, to deploy his reconnaissance craft along the northern route. The reader can verify this conclusion by noting that the upper-left cell of the matrix is the "saddle point" of the game (see Chapter 10). The minimum of the first row (2 days) is the same as the maximum of the first column (2 days). Recall that whenever this is the case (whenever payoff in the ith row and jth column, v_{ij}, is both the minimum of the ith row and the maximum of the jth row), then the game has a solution in pure strategies, the row i and column j being the optimal strategies.

We can verify that the first row (search along the northern route) and the first column (sail along the northern route) are optimal strategies, since this combination of strategies is stable in the sense described before. Unilateral deviation from the optimal strategy is not profitable and may even be damaging. For example, if the Japanese commander chose his optimal strategy and sent the convoy going north, but at the same time Kenney chose the non-optimal strategy of searching south, then he would have only one day of bombing instead of the two he could have had from his optimal strategy.

The actual decisions made by the two commanders were those prescribed by the zero-sum theory, both commanders choosing the northern route. As expected, the convoy was sighted about one day after it sailed, allowing about two days for bombing. The battle was a disastrous defeat for the Japanese, with very high losses to the convoy. This fact may lead the reader to wonder whether the decision of the Japanese commander was indeed optimal. How can a decision that ends in a disastrous defeat be called a good decision?

Two points can be made in reply. First of all, the choices available to the commander were only to sail south or to sail north; the alternative choice, not sailing at all, was not his to make at that point, since this decision had already been made. Now perhaps the decision to sail at all was wrong, and there are some indications that this may have been so. The Japanese did not know that Kenney had modified a number of his aircraft for low-level bombing and had perfected a deadly technique. As a result, the expectations of the

Japanese concerning the probable losses to their convoy were too optimistic. To put it somewhat differently, the decision to sail or not to sail may be conceptualized as a part of a different game, the payoffs of which were not only the losses to the convoy but also the deterioration of the Japanese situation in New Guinea (if no reinforcements arrived). Where the Japanese may have failed was in assigning wrong payoffs to this larger game, expecting a greater part of the convoy to come through than actually did.

In the second place, the correctness of a decision cannot be judged in terms of the value of the actual outcome. Not all games are fair, and this one in the Bismarck Sea was very unfair to the Japanese. No matter what alternative they chose, their convoy would suffer losses. To eliminate such losses completely was not in the Japanese commander's power; the best he could do was minimize them. Hence it would be completely mistaken to assume that the application of the zero-sum game to military conflicts is a guarantee of victory. Quite often victory is not in the cards at all, and one can only make the best of a bad situation. Or—and this is apparently overlooked by some critics of the application of the zero-sum theory to international affairs—if the game-theoretical analysis of a military conflict reveals that the game which represents it is unfair to us (i.e., that we can expect a defeat even if we do our best), then the rational conclusion may be not to play the game at all, to avoid that conflict altogether.

The Battle of Avranches: A Case of Mixed Strategies

In August, 1944, shortly after the Allies invaded Normandy from Great Britain, their forces broke out of their beachhead near Avranches, forming a narrow gap in German fortifications at that point. The U. S. First Army and the British Army, penetrating northeast of Avranches, were threatening the western flank of the German Ninth Army; the U. S. Third Army was located south of Avranches and was beginning its sweep west, south, and east.

The U. S. forces in this area were commanded by General Omar Bradley, the German forces by General von Kluge. It was at this point that both commanders had to make some rather crucial decisions. Von Kluge had to decide whether to attack to the west in order to secure his west flank and cut off U. S. forces south of the gap, or to withdraw to the east to take up a more defensive position near the Seine River. Bradley's problem was what to do with his reserve of four divisions just south of the gap at Avranches. According to his own account, Bradley considered three alternatives:

1. To order his reserve back to defend the gap.
2. To send the reserve eastward to harass or possibly cut off withdrawal of the German Ninth Army.
3. To leave it where it was and uncommitted for one day, prepared to go eastward or westward, as necessary. (Bradley believed that if the gap was attacked it would hold without reinforcement for one day and later reinforcement would not be necessary.)[2]

The six possible outcomes, resulting from the application of the available strategies, are shown in Figure 11.2. These outcomes were predicted by Bradley on the strength of his long military experience; we merely display them in Figure 11.2. It goes without saying, perhaps, that had these predictions been wrong, any decision based on them might have been wrong also; but the judgment of a seasoned officer on the likely outcome for each contingency may be the best that can be made in actual battle.

Bradley's next step was to evaluate the six possible outcomes in terms of their impact upon Allied overall objectives. He did not undertake to assign precise payoffs to each outcome, but he could rank them in the order of his preference. Thus, using Bradley's ranking, we can represent the situation at Avranches with a matrix the components of which are numbers from 1 to 6, where 6 designates the most favorable outcome for the Allies, and 1, their least favorable outcome:

$$
\begin{array}{cc}
 & \text{von Kluge strategies} \\
 & \begin{array}{cc} \text{Attack} & \text{Withdraw} \end{array} \\
\begin{array}{l}
\text{Reinforce gap} \\
\text{Bradley strategies} \quad \text{Move eastward} \\
\text{Do not move}
\end{array}
&
\begin{bmatrix}
2 & 3 \\
1 & 5 \\
6 & 4
\end{bmatrix}
\end{array}
$$

[2] See Haywood (1954).

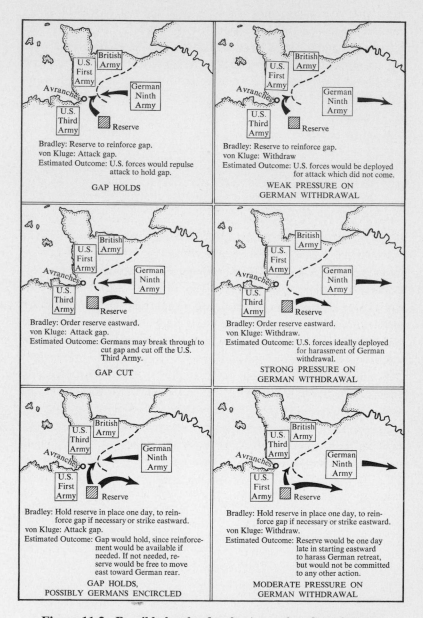

Figure 11.2. Possible battles for the Avranches Gap situation.

REDRAWN from Haywood (1954), by permission of the Operations Research Society of America.

Note that the components of this matrix have the properties of a ranking (we used "6" to designate the most favorable outcome, although usually "1" is so used, for the reason that, according to the game-theoretical convention, high numbers indicate desirable outcomes). For example, the "distance" between 5 and 6 cannot be assumed to be the same as the distance between 1 and 2. But let us proceed as if these numbers were true payoffs, not merely ranks, and worry about this difference later.

As our first step, we note that it would be totally irrational for Bradley even to consider his first strategy, that of reinforcing the gap. His third strategy is thoroughly superior to the first, since by using it he always receives a higher payoff than if he used his first strategy. If von Kluge were to "attack," Bradley's third strategy yields 6 points while the first yields only 2; if von Kluge were to "withdraw," then Bradley's third strategy yields 4 points while his first yields only 3. We say that the third strategy "strongly dominates" the first, which we omit from further consideration without changing the strategic properties of the game in any way (i.e., the solution of the game remains the same even if all strongly dominated strategies are removed). And we proceed to represent the game graphically as described before (see Chapter 9), using only the second and third of Bradley's strategies, as shown in Figure 11.3. Thus we see that if the payoffs are as given above, the best strategy for Bradley would be to use a probability mixture assigning a high probability to keeping the reserve uncommitted for one day (strategy 3) and a low probability to moving the reserves eastward (strategy 2). We could compute the strategy p^* exactly (using eq. 9.16), but we shall not

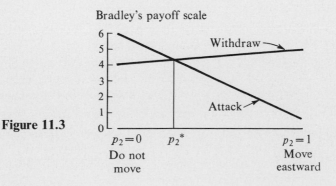

Figure 11.3

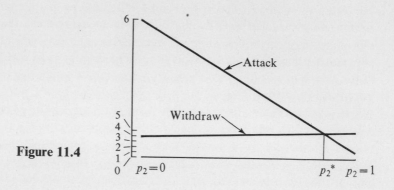

Figure 11.4

do so, precisely because the numbers in the above matrix are not "true" payoffs, but merely ranks.

When we say that the "payoffs" in the above graph are merely ranks, we mean that the numbers 1 through 6 indicate that Bradley preferred certain outcomes over others, but not how much he preferred them. Thus it is possible, for example, that he was almost indifferent between the outcomes ranked 1–5, but that he much preferred the outcome ranked 6 (his "best" outcome) to the one ranked 5. To represent this situation graphically, we contract the intervals 1–5 on the ranking scale so that they become very small, and expand the interval 5–6 so that it becomes large, as shown in Figure 11.4. Notice that the order of preference for the outcome has not changed in any way, so that this graph represents the very same game as did the preceding one. And yet the mixed strategy p^* has changed considerably. Now the best strategy for Bradley is to assign a high probability to moving eastward, whereas before the high probability was to be assigned to staying put.

The lesson to be learned from this example is that the solution in mixed strategies cannot be located if the payoffs are not defined as assumed by the theory of games, that is, as constituting an *interval* scale. If the payoffs are given as mere ranking of preferences (as a mere "ordinal scale"), the theory is applicable only if a solution in pure strategies exists; if no such solution exists, then it becomes more difficult to find the best approach. One could urge the commander to attempt to go beyond a mere ranking and to assign specific payoffs to each outcome, but it is doubtful whether this procedure should really be recommended. If it amounts to assigning specific numbers just for the sake of having such numbers, then one is engaging in an elaborate self-deception which may be very dangerous, precisely because it is elaborate. One may be dead wrong in the choice of strategy, but wrong with a precision which may be impressive to the uninitiated.

The other alternative is to forego altogether the search for mixed strategies, but to retain the principle of maximum security level as utilized by the theory of games. Such a strategy is to choose the pure strategy with maximum security level. For Bradley it is the strategy "do not move" (because the minimum of the third row, 4 points, is higher than the minimum of any other row), for von Kluge it is the strategy "withdraw" (because the maximum of the second column, 5 points, is lower than the maximum of the first column). But, it should be emphasized, these two strategies are not optimal in the sense described earlier—they are not stable. For example, it would be to Bradley's advantage to "move eastward" when von Kluge "withdraws," since by so doing he can raise his payoff from 4 points (accruing to him when he chooses "do not move") to 5 points.

As a matter of historical fact, Bradley did choose his third strategy (to keep his reserves uncommitted) and von Kluge did choose to withdraw. And history provides an ironical twist at this point. After von Kluge made his prudent decision to withdraw, Hitler overruled him and ordered him to attack, thus in effect handing to Bradley on a silver plate his very best outcome. The gap held for one day, and Bradley used his four divisions to encircle the Germans. After a battle that was disastrous for the Germans, von Kluge committed suicide.

11.3 EXPERIMENTS WITH ZERO-SUM GAMES

Although the theory of games never claims to be capable of predicting how men will behave (it claims merely to prescribe how they should behave) it is of considerable interest to investigate whether men behave in fact as the theory states they should. Such an investigation is simple enough. One needs merely to let subjects play a game and then observe whether they play their alternatives in proportions corresponding to their optimal strategies. We shall review here such experiments as conducted by Lieberman (1960, 1965).

Pure Optimal Strategies

In one set of experiments, Lieberman (1960) gave his subjects a game which has a solution in pure strategies:

$$V = \begin{bmatrix} 15 & 0 & -2 \\ 0 & -15 & -1 \\ 1 & 2 & 0 \end{bmatrix}$$

Note that this game has a saddle point, that the payoff of 0 in the third row and third column is both the minimum in the third row and the maximum in the third column. Thus the solution of this game is

$$v^* = 0, \qquad p^* = (0, 0, 1), \qquad q^* = (0, 0, 1)$$

That is, both players should always choose their third alternative. Will they in fact make this choice?

Lieberman asked 30 subjects, all undergraduate men at Harvard College, to play this game. Having formed 15 pairs, he let each pair play the game 200 times. The assumptions of the two-person zero-sum games were satisfied in that each player knew the entire payoff matrix, and the payoffs had objective value for him. Each point in the payoff matrix was worth one cent to him. Specifically, each player started the game with $2.50 to his credit; depending on the outcome of each play of the game, he either gave to his opponent (when he lost) or received from him (when he won) the amount associated with the outcome.[3] Each subject made his choice in ignorance of the choice his opponent was about to make.

It will be recalled that the game-theoretical solutions are independent of the opponent's behavior: the solution is arrived at from the assumption that it is impossible to specify a priori probabilities

[3] In actual practice, the subjects did not use real money while playing the game—they used poker chips. However, these chips were exchangeable for money at the end of the experiment.

defined over his alternatives. Since the optimal strategies p^* and q^* thus remain the same no matter what the opponent does, a rational player, after having analyzed the game, should be able (and willing) to commit himself to a "grand strategy" of playing his optimal strategy every time. The subjects were given an opportunity to do so. Each was given a blank card on which he could write, if he wished, how he planned to play the remaining turns of the game. Once this card was given to the experimenter, the player could not change his mind—from that point he had to follow the grand strategy he had chosen. The nature of his grand strategy was of course kept secret from the opponent.

The most fundamental finding emerging from the experiments is that the subjects chose the optimal strategies much more often towards the end of their 200 plays than in the early plays. Figure 11.5 shows that the proportion of players who chose the third alternative increased steadily from about 0.70 to about 0.93. Thus it would seem that *experience with the game taught the subjects to use their optimal strategies.*

This main observation, however, describes only the most general trend of the experiments. There were additional tendencies underlying, and at times contradicting, this general trend. First of all, the

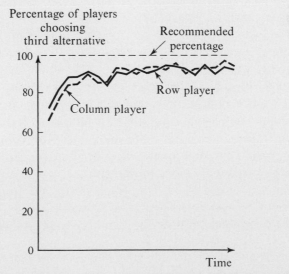

Figure 11.5. Choices of the optimal strategy (third alternative).

subjects differed with respect to how quickly they came to adopt the optimal solution. Twelve of the 30 subjects submitted grand strategy cards by the fifty-fifth trial, all committing themselves to play the optimal strategy p^* or q^*. Three subjects seemed to have adopted the optimal strategy in fact, even though they did not commit themselves to a grand strategy. All 3 played the recommended strategy consistently over the last 75 plays of the game. The remaining 15 subjects continued playing a wrong (the first or the second) choice occasionally even during the final 75 plays of the game. However, even these subjects continued to learn, playing the correct (third) choice more and more frequently.

Furthermore, the previous choices of the opponent did make a difference. If the opponent played repeatedly his optimal (third) strategy, the player tended to adopt his optimal (third) strategy also; if, however, the opponent played repeatedly a non-optimal strategy, the player tended to choose a strategy to exploit his opponent's weakness. For example, if the row player kept choosing the second row, the column player would often switch to choosing the second column, thus securing for himself the payoff of 15 cents.

Finally, an interesting finding stems from the interviews held at the close of each experiment. According to the author, *virtually all subjects gained an understanding of the game-theoretical solution after a few plays of the game*, realizing quickly that the third choice was the safe and conservative way of playing the game. Many even went so far as to state that the second alternative was to be avoided completely and that the first alternative was quite risky. Why then did a full one-half of them play non-optimal choices? Two of the most frequent reasons were that to continue playing the optimal strategy was *boring* and, on occasion, *unfair*. Many subjects deviated from what they knew was the safe course just to break the monotony of the experiment; others deviated in order to give their opponents a chance to win after a long losing streak.

Mixed Optimal Strategies

The second set of experiments of interest to us was performed by Lieberman (1965) with a game whose optimal strategies are mixed.

The payoffs of this game were

$$V = \begin{bmatrix} 3 & -1 \\ -9 & 3 \end{bmatrix}$$

Using eq. 9.16 to solve this game, we find that

$$v^* = 0, \qquad p^* = (\tfrac{3}{4}, \tfrac{1}{4}), \qquad q^* = (\tfrac{1}{4}, \tfrac{3}{4})$$

In other words, the game is fair (since the expected payoff to both players is 0) and the recommended strategy is for the player controlling the rows to play his first alternative on three-fourths of the trials, for the player controlling the columns to play his first alternative on one-fourth of the trials.

The general setting for these experiments was as before. The subjects were 18 men, all undergraduates at the State University of New York at Stony Brook; they were divided into 9 teams, and each team played the game 200 times. Each player received a credit of $2.50, and he gained or lost in accordance with the outcome of each play, each payoff point being worth one cent. One major difference from the previous design was that the subjects were not given an opportunity to commit themselves to a grand strategy.

As before, we start by asking whether the subjects played their alternatives in the recommended proportions and, if they did not, whether some learning nevertheless took place. The answer to the first question is negative. Although the subjects should have played their "better" alternative (first row for the row player, the second column for the column player) on 75% of the trials, the row players chose the first row on only 69% of the plays, the column players chose the second column on only 57% of the trials. As Figure 11.6 shows, however, there was a general tendency for the actual proportions to come closer to the recommended ones, even though the tendency is less pronounced than in Figure 11.5.

As before, the subjects differed with respect to how close they came to following their optimal strategies. According to Lieberman, analysis of the data shows that 10 of the 18 players (7 row players and 3 column players) played their last 75 trials in proportions sufficiently close to the recommended proportions to warrant the conclusion that they were in fact playing their optimal strategies.

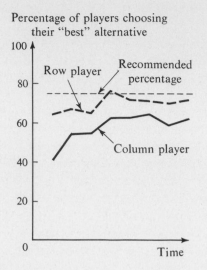

Figure 11.6. Choices of the "best" alternative (first row for the row player, second column for the column player).

Analysis of the post-session questionnaires indicated, however, that none of the subjects was playing his strategies with any fixed probabilities in mind. As before, each subject was playing against his opponent's past record, trying to use it to predict his next move and choosing his best alternative against the opponent's anticipated choice.

Interpretation of the Findings

What do these experiments show about the applicability of the theory of games? Do men in fact behave as the theory recommends? Before attempting to answer this question, let us summarize the most salient findings:

1. The subjects discovered the pure optimal strategies quite early, but they failed to arrive independently at the idea of a mixed strategy.
2. Even though the subjects recognized the optimal pure strategy, many deviated from it.

3. The subjects who did not commit themselves to a grand strategy
   (when they had an opportunity to do so) based their choices on
   an analysis of past choices by the opponent rather than on analysis
   of the payoff matrix alone.

The first finding raises an interesting problem. Is it necessary to
assume that the theory of games is applicable only if the subjects
discover independently the notion of "mixed strategy"? Lieberman
believes this to be so, but we are not so certain. Would it not be
better to supply the subjects with a random device like the one
described in Figure 9.1 and explain to them how to use it? This
could be done without mentioning expected payoff and the reasoning
that accompanies it. Or, at the very least, could one not give the
subjects an opportunity to decide on a grand strategy, noting that
the assignment of probabilities over the two alternatives is sufficient?
Surely it is not our intent that the subjects should discover the rules
of the game, since these are always given. And the fact that a grand
strategy can be decided upon or that a random device is permissible
is, in our opinion, one of these rules. If it were shown that, given
these opportunities, the subjects preferred not to use them, that
could be a definite strike against the applicability of the theory.
But to show merely that the subjects do not happen to think of an
innovation is, in our opinion, a much less convincing argument.

We thus come to the second finding. Even though the subjects
in the first set of experiments knew that their third choice was the
most secure choice of all, many continued to choose a different
alternative. Why? Two main reasons can be given: First, as the last
finding suggests, *some subjects played the game as if it were a decision
problem under uncertainty rather than a game of strategy.* They
continually tried to assign a priori probabilities to their opponent's
alternatives, they tried to guess what the opponent would do. Second,
as the post-session interviews indicated, *the payoffs did not characterize the subjects' motivation completely.* They were interested not
only in making as much money as possible, but also in avoiding
boredom and being fair to their opponents.

Let us consider these two reasons in some detail. It is perhaps
clear that the subjects were able to predict their opponents' choices
only because the game was played repeatedly. But the game-
theoretical analysis of a game of strategy is based on the assumption

that the game is played *only once*.[4] Hence the subjects were able to predict opponents' choices only because one of the rules has been violated. It is possible, of course, to study whether subjects learn to use optimal strategies without violating this rule by using a "round robin" design: After each play of the game, the players change partners and thus they are, at the same time, learning the game and playing with a player whose past record is unknown to them.

However, even when subjects are playing repeatedly against the same partners, and even if they act as if they were making decisions under uncertainty rather than playing a game of strategy, even then the theory of two-person zero-sum games is not necessarily contradicted. As was mentioned in Chapter 10, Brown (1951) shows that if a game is played repeatedly, and if each player, at time t, assigns to his opponent a priori probabilities which reflect the frequencies with which the opponent played a particular alternative, and if he chooses the (possibly mixed) strategy that is best against such a priori probabilities, then both players ultimately end up playing their optimal strategies. It is this fact that helps us understand why, in both sets of experiments, the subjects did in fact come progressively closer to playing their optimal strategies, even though they did not "use their head"—they did not analyze the game as a game of strategy.

Now consider the second explanation, that the subjects were motivated by considerations other than the payoff. Again we see that the basic assumption of the theory is violated in the experiments. Where, then, does the fault lie that the subjects did not behave more often in the recommended fashion? Does it lie in the theory or in the experiments which violated the assumptions?

Perhaps surprisingly, we maintain that both the theory and the experiments are at fault. Let us reiterate that, in principle, the theory of games cannot be tested empirically because it does not assert that anything will happen, but merely that certain behavior

[4] It is customary to distinguish between games in the "extensive" and the "normal" form: a game in the extensive form distinguishes between different moves (a game is viewed as a *time*-sequence of moves), while a game in the normal form "suppresses" time by substituting the concept of a "strategy" for a possible sequence of moves. Thus, even if the actual game involves a number of subsequent moves (e.g., chess), a player chooses a strategy only *once*. (See, for example, Luce and Raiffa, 1958, Chapter 3.)

should occur. To this extent anyone who tests the theory is at fault; he is not doing the theory justice. But let's look at it from a different point of view. A theory, whether descriptive or prescriptive, is just about useless if its assumptions are so esoteric that they are never met in real life. Of what use is it to know how one should behave under circumstances which never occur?

Thus we feel that it is legitimate to investigate whether men behave as the theory says they should, provided that all possible care is taken to make sure that the assumptions of the theory are met. What is ultimately decisive is not whether men in fact behave according to the theory but rather whether one can find or create real-life situations which satisfy the assumptions of the theory. And one of the shortcomings of the theory may be that the assumptions concerning the utility function are seldom satisfied in real life. In experimental or parlor games the players will often be motivated by considerations other than the payoffs given to them; in situations that are not clearly games, motivation may be so complex as to make it virtually impossible to assign each "player" a unique utility function.

11.4   DISCUSSION

These three examples of the application of the zero-sum theory suggest both the virtues and the deficiencies of such attempts. Perhaps the greatest virtue of the theory, as far as the social sciences are concerned, is that it provides for a rigorous *conceptualization* of problems which interest social scientists. This conceptualization in itself often leads to valuable results.

Consider, for example, the work of Anderson and Moore. The very fact that they think of social interaction as if it were a game means that their whole approach to the study of human behavior changes. The subjects in their experiments are no longer "subjects" in the true sense of the word; they become experimenters' partners, learned from rather than merely tested; the objective is no longer to predict human behavior but rather to invent new solutions to problems both new and old; the underlying view of man is no longer that of a particle driven by irresistible forces but rather of a person who is free to make decisions.

Or consider military conflicts. A systematic application of the game-theoretical approach forces the commanding officer to take into account many alternative courses of action rather than to rely on a standard response to a standard situation. It forces him to evaluate the many alternatives open to his opponent, thus minimizing the possibility of a surprise. All this is bound to increase the quality of his strategic decisions.

The theory of games has provided considerable inspiration to experimentalists. The simplicity of representing a game by a matrix, the variability of the payoffs within the matrix, and the fact that many games do not possess solutions are all features of the theory which have proven irresistible. As Lieberman's (1960) work illustrates, the experimenter may simply wish to determine whether men behave as the theory says they should. Or he may wish to supply empirical solutions to games that do not possess a game-theoretical solution. In either case human behavior is studied in novel ways, thus increasing our understanding of man.

On the more negative side, the theory of games appears to possess some serious weaknesses in its application to social conflicts. Three problems seem to be of paramount importance: the problems of using mixed strategies, of knowing the outcomes of the game, and of knowing the payoffs.

To some extent, these problems are related. Recall that in the Battle of Avranches General Bradley was unwilling or unable to estimate his own payoffs "exactly," that he estimated merely the ranking of these payoffs. Had this game had a saddle point, such estimates would have been sufficient to identify a solution in pure strategies. As it turned out, the game did not have a saddle point, and hence no game-theoretical solution was available.

To a considerable extent, however, each of these three weaknesses is a problem in its own right. Lieberman's (1965) experiments suggest that men hesitate to use mixed strategies. The reason may be, as in these experiments, that for most men, the concept of a mixed strategy is too sophisticated to be arrived at independently. But, on the other hand, there may be plausible arguments for refusing to use mixed strategies even when one knows what they are and how to play them. For example, Haywood (1954) argues that makers of routine strategic decisions, those that are repeated over and over again, should use mixed strategies whenever necessary, because the average outcome over a large number of simpler battles is important. However, when a major strategic decision is being made, one that is unique and may affect the entire war (and hence will not be repeated), then the gamble implicit in using a mixed strategy may be too great.

The next problem, that of knowing the outcomes of the game, arises because in real life the connection between strategy and outcome is not arbitrary and is often subject to empirical laws, the nature of which is not known to us. For example, prior to World War II much of United States military thinking was dominated by the "Douhet doctrine," a doctrine that maintained that the nation that controls the air ultimately wins the war. This doctrine was predicated upon certain assumptions later proven to be wrong. Bombing failed to inflict decisive damage upon German industry and it failed also to damage German morale seriously. As a result, the strategic decision to allocate top priorities to the production of airplanes may have been wrong to some extent. Let us add, however, that the development of nuclear bombs has made the Douhet doctrine much more realistic now than it was during World War II when only conventional bombs were available. But the problem is clear. When military decisions have to be made involving new and untested weapons, it is easy to miscalculate the effectiveness of these weapons, and hence the true outcomes may prove to be quite different from those expected.

This problem is further complicated by the fact that the opponent may have weapons about which we do not know, and which will curtail the effectiveness of our new weapons. An anti-missile may intercept our missiles, a bulletproof vest may stop our bullets, and so on. As we shall show later (see Chapter 15), the theory of negotiation may be seriously hampered by the fact that an opponent's behavior may be unpredictable. Under some conditions concessions generate concessions; under other conditions concessions are interpreted as a sign of weakness and thus serve to inhibit the opponent's concession making. In other words, the problem may be not only that we do not know the laws that govern the relationship between strategies and outcomes, but also that in some cases knowing such laws is almost impossible.

The third problem concerns knowing the payoffs. Even when one knows the outcomes associated with the possible strategies, the payoffs are not always certain. This problem arises even in the seemingly clear-cut case of a military conflict. It would seem that the outcome involving the largest enemy losses and the smallest losses to oneself is the outcome to be desired, but a moment's thought reveals that this is not always so. For example, occupation of a strategic hill may be a desirable outcome even if it results in heavy casualties to our side, because possession of that hill makes future casualties light. Or consider the famous Truman-MacArthur feud. In insisting on bombing the Chinese mainland, MacArthur was right in the sense that such bombing would indeed curtail American losses. Truman, however, had to consider other "payoffs" than simple military casualties; he was dealing with a different "game" and hence reached a different decision.

Not only is it often difficult to know one's own payoffs, it may often be difficult to know the opponent's payoffs. It seems to us that the assumption of complete knowledge seriously hampers experimental work using payoff matrices. As we shall discuss later (see Section 14.2), presenting the subjects with a payoff matrix which displays the opponent's payoffs may in many cases violate the assumption that subjective utility must be linear with (but not necessarily identical with) the payoffs.

But let us look again at the brighter side. It seems to us that these problems may be solvable for at least some important types of social conflict. In any case, these problems are often not unique to the theory of games; they are bound to beset any decision-maker. The theory of games actually helps a decision maker by showing in sharp relief what work needs to be done.

Thus, for example, the problem of not knowing the outcomes may be handled by changing the nature of the game somewhat. Given a limited knowledge about the outcomes, is it possible to identify a strategy that is optimal under these conditions?[5] The problem of not knowing the payoffs that are associated with the outcomes may also be treatable. For example, the problem of deciding whether the capture of a strategic hill is worth the casualties may be handled

[5] For some recent accomplishments in this area see, for example, Isaacs (1965), Chapter 12, or Wold (1964), Chapter 7.

by viewing the game in which occupying the hill is an outcome as being a part of a larger game, one that involves a sequence of related games.[6] The reader interested in the theory of games should keep abreast of current developments, many of which deal with these difficulties.[7]

[6] See, for example, Luce and Raiffa's (1958) discussion of the sequentially compounded games (Appendix 8).

[7] The reader should consult the various journals dealing with the game-theoretical approach. *The Journal of Conflict Resolution, Econometrica,* and *Behavioral Science* being among the most prominent such publications.

CHAPTER 12

Antagonistic Cooperation:
Some Nonzero–Sum Games

Sociologist Sumner (1907) popularized the concept of "antagonistic cooperation." According to Sumner, "antagonistic cooperation is the most productive form of combination in high civilization. It is a high action of the reason to overlook lesser antagonisms in order to work together for great interests."[1]

Most sociologists would probably agree that the study of antagonistic cooperation is of particular interest to the social sciences. Extreme conflicts, discussed in Chapters 9–11, are found relatively rarely in real life, precisely because the parties in conflict often do have some interests in common. And pure cooperation is not very intriguing from the theoretical point of view. When the interests of the two parties coincide perfectly, they will do what is in their mutual interest, and that's that. On the other hand, situations in which the interests are partly opposed, partly in harmony, are commonly found in human affairs and are theoretically challenging because the process of antagonistic cooperation is anything but obvious.

The matrix notation used to describe extreme conflicts can be used also to describe antagonistic cooperation. However, since the interests are no longer diametrically opposed, a single matrix with

[1] Sumner (1907), pp. 17–18.

single components is no longer sufficient. One of the accepted means of presenting antagonistic cooperation is through a single matrix containing double components such as shown in eq. 12.1 below.[2] Since at least some of these pairs of payoffs sum up to a nonzero number, these games are known as nonzero-sum games.

12.1   NONZERO–SUM GAMES

The games considered in Chapters 9–11 were zero-sum games, that is, games in which one player's gain always equals the opponent's loss and vice versa. This feature permitted a simple representation of the game (through a single matrix), allowed for a plausible definition of rationality, and led to a solution with some highly desirable properties.

Given the success of the game-theoretical approach to the zero-sum two-person games, it is natural to extend the approach to nonzero-sum games. This extension, however, leads to considerable difficulty, so much that there is no integrated theory of nonzero-sum games available at this time, and perhaps there never will be. The best one can do is to isolate certain types of games and to find a solution for them. As a result, the theory of nonzero-sum games abounds with such nicknames as "Battle of the Sexes," or "Prisoner's Dilemma," each name designating a certain type of game.

It turns out that what the players are allowed to do before the game is actually played has considerable bearing upon the analysis of nonzero-sum games. If the players are allowed to have "pre-play communication" so that they can make *binding commitments*[3] about the way the game is to be played, and are permitted to use *joint strategies*,[4] then the strategic aspects of the game are quite different from those when no such pre-play communication is permitted.

---

[2] It is also possible to represent antagonistic cooperation by two matrices, each with single entries.

[3] The question of when a commitment is binding is not easily answered in real life. In the theory of games, however, a binding commitment is defined without a difficulty. Here, a commitment is binding when the rules of the game specify that a player who agrees to play a particular strategy must in fact play it.

[4] The definition of a joint strategy is given below under the heading "Joint Strategies."

Since it is not our purpose to give an exhaustive coverage of the theory of games, but rather to single out a few of the most promising of its applications, we shall merely illustrate briefly some of the more important differences which pre-play communication make for the analysis of the nonzero-sum games. The two main differences are:

1. If the players are allowed to make binding commitments, the game may turn into a "battle of wills."
2. If the players are allowed to use joint strategies, then a whole set of new outcomes is added to the game.

Battle of Wills

To illustrate the first point, consider the game known as the Battle of the Sexes. This game is represented by the following matrix:

$$(12.1) \quad \text{Man} \quad \begin{array}{c} \\ \text{Prize fight} \\ \text{Ballet} \end{array} \begin{array}{cc} \text{Woman} & \\ \text{Prize fight} & \text{Ballet} \\ \begin{bmatrix} (2, 1) & (-1, -1) \\ (-1, -1) & (1, 2) \end{bmatrix} \end{array}$$

The reader should note that in this game, as in all nonzero-sum games, each outcome has associated with it a pair of payoffs (u, v), the first member of the pair, u, always designating the payoff to the player who controls the rows. So, for example, the payoffs $(2, 1)$ in the upper left cell mean that if the man and woman both go (together) to the prize fight, the man will receive 2 payoff points, the woman only 1. Note that in this game, as in many nonzero-sum games, both cooperation and conflict are possible. The man and woman can go together to the prize fight or together to the ballet (cooperation), or each can go alone to a different affair (conflict). When the two cooperate, both gain; when they engage in a conflict, both lose. What makes the game interesting is that to cooperate is not easy, because the man prefers the prize fight, the woman prefers the ballet.

From a formal point of view, the interesting fact here is that there are *two* pairs of strategies in equilibrium:

$$\text{1st pair:} \quad p^* = (1, 0) \quad\quad q^* = (1, 0)$$
$$\text{2d pair:} \quad p^{**} = (0, 1) \quad\quad q^{**} = (0, 1)$$

The first pair is in equilibrium because it does not pay for the opponent to use strategy other than $q*$ when the player uses $p*$ and vice versa; similarly, the second pair is in equilibrium because it does not pay to use strategy other than $q**$ when the player uses $p**$ and vice versa. Notice, however, that the two pairs are not *equivalent* since the first pair yields payoff (2, 1), and the second yields a different payoff, (1, 2). Nor are the two pairs interchangeable: strategy $p*$ is not in equilibrium with strategy $q**$, nor is $p**$ in equilibrium with strategy $q*$.[5]

It is precisely the lack of equivalence and interchangeability of the two pairs of equilibrium strategies that allows for a battle of wills when pre-play communication is permitted. Suppose that the man announces that he is going to the prize fight and that nothing will change his mind. Then the rational choice for the woman is to go along to the prize fight, since to go to the ballet alone brings her less satisfaction (-1 point) than going to the prize fight with her date ($+1$ point). But, if perchance the woman made her commitment first, then the rational decision for the man is to sit through the ballet, for the same reason. Thus, if the two players are allowed to discuss the game before they make their decision, it is in the interest of each player to be the first to make an ironclad commitment. And a battle of wills ensues, each person trying to be the first to make a commitment, each trying to shake the determination of the other.

Joint Strategies

The second effect of pre-play communication is that, customarily, it allows for the use of joint strategies. The use of joint strategies is important largely because it allows the players to secure outcomes they could never get by using their individual strategies p and q'. To understand this, and to see what we mean by a "joint strategy," consider again the Battle of the Sexes game as given in (12.1).

For simplicity's sake, let us start by representing that game as

$$(12.2) \qquad V = \begin{bmatrix} a & b \\ c & d \end{bmatrix}$$

[5] For the game-theoretical concept of an equilibrium see Sec. 10.2.

where $a = (2, 1)$, $b = (-1, -1)$, $c = (-1, -1)$, and $d = (1, 2)$. Now suppose that the man plays strategy $p = (p_1, p_2)$, and the woman plays $q = (q_1, q_2)$. Then, by definition, the expected payoff $E(v)$ is

$$E(v) = pVq' = p_1q_1a + p_2q_1c + p_1q_2b + p_2q_2d$$
$$= aP_a + bP_b + cP_c + dP_d$$

where P_a is the probability of payoff a occurring, P_b the probability of payoff b occurring, and so on, i.e., where

$$P_a = p_1q_1, \qquad P_b = p_1q_2, \qquad P_c = p_2q_1, \qquad P_d = p_2q_2$$

Now it is not difficult to see that, as long as P_a, P_b, P_c, and P_d are defined as above, it is impossible to have either

(i) $\qquad\qquad P_a > 0, \qquad P_b = 0, \qquad P_c = 0, \qquad P_d > 0$

or

(ii) $\qquad\qquad P_a = 0, \qquad P_b > 0, \qquad P_c > 0, \qquad P_d = 0$

To see that (i) cannot hold, consider that if $P_a = p_1q_1 > 0$, then both p_1 and q_1 must be larger than 0, i.e., $p_1 > 0$ and $q_1 > 0$. Furthermore, if $P_d = p_2q_2 > 0$, then $p_2 > 0$ and $q_2 > 0$. But, if both p_1 and q_2 are positive, then it is impossible that $P_b = p_2q_2 = 0$; similarly, if both p_2 and q_1 are positive, then it is impossible that $P_c = p_2q_1 = 0$. Thus we have shown that condition (i) cannot prevail. Similarly, we could show that (ii) cannot hold either.

To clarify what has just been demonstrated, let us represent P_a, P_b, P_c, and P_d in a matrix form that parallels eq. 12.2:

(12.3) $$P = \begin{bmatrix} P_a & P_b \\ P_c & P_d \end{bmatrix}$$

The reader should note well that the above matrix is *not* a matrix of transition probabilities, that each row of P does not sum to 1. Instead, all components of P sum to 1; that is,

$$P_a + P_b + P_c + P_d = 1 \qquad P_a, P_b, P_c, P_d \geq 0$$

We have shown above that, if the two players use their *individual* strategies, p and q', they can never play P in such a way that

(iii) $$P = \begin{bmatrix} P_a & 0 \\ 0 & P_d \end{bmatrix} \qquad P_a, P_d > 0$$

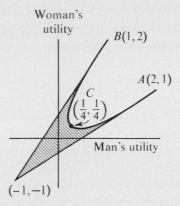

Figure 12.1. Battle of the Sexes without joint strategies.

or that

(iv) $$P = \begin{bmatrix} 0 & P_b \\ P_c & 0 \end{bmatrix} \qquad P_b, P_c > 0$$

Now we can define a *joint strategy* as a strategy that allows the players to assign *any* P_a through P_d (that sum up to 1) to P—which means a strategy that permits (iii) and (iv) to be played.

A graphic representation of the game shows that permitting (iii) alters the game materially since it adds many new outcomes to the game. Let us use a system of coordinates such that the horizontal axis represents the man's utilities, the vertical axis the woman's utilities. It can be shown that when only individual strategies p and q' are allowed all possible outcomes lie in the shaded set of

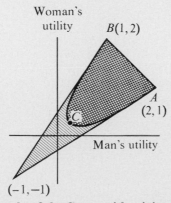

Figure 12.2. Battle of the Sexes with a joint strategy.

Figure 12.1. If, however, the players are allowed to agree on a joint strategy P as defined above, then the game is represented by Figure 12.2. Note that the entire crosshatched area BCA has been added to the game.

One meaning of the term joint strategy should perhaps be made clear. By being able to consider situation (iii) above, the players can agree to limit their choices to the cooperative outcomes alone. Graphically, this amounts to limiting their consideration to the points that lie along the straight line AB, the so-called negotiation set of the game.[6] For the mathematically inclined, let it be added that by permitting joint strategies, one makes certain that the game can always be represented by a "convex polygon,"[7] that is, that the set representing the game will never have a "gaping hole" such as BCA of Figure 12.1. This fact simplifies mathematical analysis considerably,[8] and is one of the reasons why games with pre-play communication have received a good deal of attention in the literature.

Classification of Nonzero–Sum Games

Depending on whether or not pre-play communication (with the possibility of binding commitments and joint strategies) is allowed, the nonzero-sum games are classified into two main categories, the *noncooperative games* (pre-play communication not allowed) and the *cooperative games* (pre-play communication allowed). We shall consider in some detail one example for each type, the so-called Prisoner's Dilemma to represent the noncooperative game, and Bargaining Games to represent the cooperative type.

12.2   PRISONER'S DILEMMA

The noncooperative games come in great variety, depending largely on the type of solution available. Some games have a number of

---

[6] A *negotiation set* consists of outcomes that are (1) Pareto optimal and (2) individually acceptable. A *Pareto optimal* outcome is one such that no other outcome has higher payoff for both players; an *individually acceptable* outcome is one that has, for a given player, at least as high a payoff as the one he would receive from his optimal individual (maximin) strategy. See also Luce and Raiffa (1958), p. 118.

[7] A *convex polygon* is defined as "the intersection of closed half planes" [Kemeny et al., (1957), p. 251].

[8] For example, one of the theorems states that a linear function that is defined over a convex polygon takes on its maximum (and minimum) value at a corner point of the convex polygon (*ibid.*, p. 256).

equilibrium strategies that are neither interchangeable nor equivalent (such as the Battle of the Sexes); in others the equilibrium strategies are interchangeable and equivalent.[9] It is clear perhaps that a game which has interchangeable and equivalent equilibrium strategies has a solution that is most satisfactory from the mathematical as well as from the practical point of view. In such games the equilibrium strategy comes close to being the same as an optimal strategy of a zero-sum game, since the player can secure for himself certain payoff v if he keeps using one of his equilibrium strategies.

Note that we say only that such strategies come "close" to being the optimal strategies of a zero-sum game. This is because even in games with equilibrium strategies there remain many unresolved problems. Briefly stated, the main problem is this: There are some noncooperative games in which to behave nonrationally is more profitable than to behave rationally. The outstanding example of such a game is the Prisoner's Dilemma.

An Example

The Prisoner's Dilemma is illustrated by the following matrix:

$$
\begin{array}{cc}
& \begin{matrix} \text{Not to} & \\ \text{confess} & \text{To confess} \end{matrix} \\
\begin{matrix} \text{Not to confess} \\ \text{To confess} \end{matrix} &
\begin{bmatrix} (1, 1) & (-2, 2) \\ (2, -2) & (-1, -1) \end{bmatrix}
\end{array}
$$

The story that goes with the game and accounts for its name is this: Two prisoners are held in separate cells, both charged with the same crime. They can be convicted only if at least one of them confesses. In order to extract a conviction, the prosecutor has promised that the man who confesses (while the other refuses to confess) will be set free and will be given a reward. This story is roughly reflected in the payoffs of the above matrix. If both prisoners remain silent, they both go free [the payoff $(1, 1)$]; if one prisoner talks while the other remains silent, he goes free and receives the

---

[9] For a definition of "interchangeability" and "equivalence" see Sec. 10.2.

reward (+2 points) while the "double-crossed" prisoner has the book thrown at him (−2 points); if both confess, both get mild sentences [the payoff (−1, −1)].

This game is called a dilemma not only because of its "to confess or not to confess" phrasing, but also because of the temptations implicit in it. Let us say, first of all, that to confess is a rational strategy for both prisoners, not because to confess is the "right" thing to do, but because these two strategies are the only two strategies that are in equilibrium. This becomes clear when one observes that if either one of the prisoners confesses, his accomplice is better off also confessing (−1 point) than not confessing (−2 points).

But the temptation is introduced precisely because the game is not zero-sum. If the two prisoners can trust each other (remember, they are not allowed to communicate!) then they both could profit by not confessing, both raising their payoffs from −1 to +1. But can they trust each other? The game is so designed that each prisoner is tempted to double-cross his colleague, the payoff for a double cross being even higher (+2 points) than the payoff for cooperating against the authorities (+1 point).

Let us recapitulate. We have here a situation in which being rational (in the sense of playing it safe i.e., playing the equilibrium strategy "to confess"[10]) leads to a low payoff, and in which ignoring safety and trusting the other player (i.e., by playing "not to confess") could increase one's own payoff. But to trust is difficult because there is a premium on violating the partner's trust. Does this situation have a familiar ring? It should, since political affairs are often subject to similar conditions. For example, is it not true that both the Soviet Union and the United States could benefit by reducing their expenditures for armaments (cooperation), but that each party could benefit even more by only pretending to disarm while the opponent did in fact disarm (double-cross), and that, as a result, both sides continue to spend vast sums on arms (playing it safe)?

---

[10] This strategy is safe because it guarantees the user at least −1 point (with the possibility of +2 points if the opponent does not play it safe).

Definition

Given the above interpretations of the payoffs in a Prisoner's Dilemma, we can represent the game as

(12.4)
$$
\begin{array}{cc}
 & \begin{array}{cc} C_2 & D_2 \end{array} \\
\begin{array}{c} C_1 \\ D_1 \end{array} & \begin{bmatrix} (R, R) & (S, T) \\ (T, S) & (P, P) \end{bmatrix}
\end{array}
$$

where R is "reward," T is the "temptation" (to double-cross), S is "sucker's payoff" (the payoff to the player who is double-crossed), P is "punishment" (for playing it safe).[11] Note the labeling of the two strategies: C stands for the cooperative strategy, D for the strategy of "defection." Clearly, the labels do not adequately define a Prisoner's Dilemma game. The game in (12.4) is a Prisoner's Dilemma if

(12.5)
$$S < P < R < T$$

The inequalities of (12.5) are nothing more than a definition of a Prisoner's Dilemma game. However, by contemplating this definition for a moment, we can understand the unique features of this game. First of all, let us rewrite (12.4) so that it represents only the row player's payoffs:

(12.6)
$$V = \begin{bmatrix} R & S \\ T & P \end{bmatrix}$$

Now note that (12.5) specifies that $T > R$ and that $P > S$—that the payoff in the second row is always higher than the (corresponding) payoff in the first row! Hence, if the row player is rational in the sense of preferring high payoff to low payoff, he will always choose the second row. Similar analysis shows that the column player who wishes to maximize his payoff will always choose the second column. Hence $D_1 D_2$ is the "recommended" outcome and the payoff to the two players is (P, P). However, note that eq. 12.5 states that $R > P$; as a result the outcome $C_1 C_2$, although not the recommended (rational) outcome, has a higher payoff for each player, (R, R), than does the recommended outcome $D_1 D_2$. It is this discrepancy between being rational (in the sense of choosing an alternative that is certain to have a higher payoff than any other

[11] This representation is from Rapoport (1965).

alternative) and receiving a high payoff that gives the Prisoner's Dilemma its special flavor.

12.3   BARGAINING GAMES

While the Prisoner's Dilemma is among the most interesting of the noncooperative games, *bargaining* games are, in our opinion, of equal importance among the cooperative games, for the same reason that the Prisoner's Dilemma has value. Bargaining games are simple enough that a game-theoretical solution of practical interest is available for them, and, furthermore, they resemble situations that occur often in real life, the situations of bargaining and negotiation.

There is one difference worth noting, however. The chief problem with the Prisoner's Dilemma is that the game-theoretical solution does not seem plausible, that it is not sensible to call "rational" the behavior that yields a lower payoff than does "nonrational" behavior. The main problem with the bargaining games, on the other hand, is that the traditional tools of the game-theoretical approach are not sufficient to identify the solution and that there is a disagreement regarding what additional assumptions should be made in arriving at a solution. These differences will be clarified in Chapter 14 when experimental evidence is cited. The chief motive for the experiments using the Prisoner's Dilemma design is to observe how men behave under the conditions of the dilemma; the experiments using the bargaining games design are motivated by the desire to test the different solutions which have been suggested in the literature.

An Example

Consider the heads of state of West Germany and Great Britain meeting at a summit conference to discuss two outstanding issues which plague their relations—German reunification and Great Britain's entry into the Common Market. Their agreed-upon agenda incorporates these two issues as two specific proposals: (1) that Great Britain actively support German reunification, and (2) that Germany actively support Britain's entry into the Common Market. As is well known, Great Britain does not like the idea of German reunification (while Germany is all for it), and at the same time Germany is only mildly interested in having Great Britain enter into the Common Market (Great Britain being highly interested in this possibility). Thus it might not be completely unrealistic to represent the summit meeting as a nonzero-sum game with the following payoffs:

(12.7)

	German reunification	Britain's entry into Common Market
Germany — German reunification	$(3.75, -1.70)$	$(0, 0)$
Germany — Britain's entry into Common Market	$(0, 0)$	$(0.25, 2.50)$

The purpose of the summit meeting is to agree on a strategy. Restated in game-theoretical terms, the purpose is to arrive at a strategy through pre-play communication, not through the actual play of the game. The players are allowed to agree on a joint strategy, and their agreements, although made privately and in secret, are assumed to be binding.[12]

Note that the payoffs in (12.7) which are not on the major diagonal are zero. This is because the outcomes that do not lie on the major diagonal correspond to disagreement, with one player insisting on one proposal, the other player on a different proposal. It is typical of what we shall call *bargaining games* that the payoff for disagreement is always zero, and therefore that *the payoffs not on the major diagonal are always zero.*

This being the case, one can always represent a bargaining game in a compact form by indicating the possible outcomes as the rows of a payoff matrix, the players as the columns. For example, the game (12.7) can be represented as

(12.8)

	Germany	Great Britain
No agreement	0.00	0.00
German reunification	3.75	-1.70
Britain's entry into Common Market	0.25	2.50

---

[12] When we say that the players agreed on a joint strategy, we are ipso facto saying that they will actually play that strategy when the time comes to play. In our example, the assumption is that the participants at the summit not only reach an agreement, but also put it into effect.

The advantage of the compact representation is its greater simplicity (only one payoff per cell), its smaller size [a game with n proposals can be represented by an $(n + 1) \times 2$ matrix instead of by an $n \times n$ matrix], and its ability to represent games with more than two players in a single matrix. Therefore, from now on we shall use only the compact representation, always remembering that there is a standard representation corresponding to it.

The players are allowed to use joint strategies. We define the "compact version" of the joint strategy (as opposed to the "standard version" of eq. 12.3) as

(12.9) $P = (P_0, P_1, P_2)$

the three components of P being defined over the *rows* of (12.8).

The problem facing the two heads of state in our example is to negotiate an agreement acceptable to both nations, but formally it is merely a special case of the general problem of finding the best joint strategy P^*. Formally, the joint strategy P is a probability vector that assigns a certain probability to each of the rows of (12.8), but there is no harm done if the reader thinks of P as representing the amount of diplomatic effort which each nation will exercise along the indicated lines. For example, one can interpret the joint strategy

$$P = (0, \tfrac{1}{4}, \tfrac{3}{4})$$

as an agreement that Germany's support of Britain's entry into the Common Market be three times as strong as Britain's support for German reunification. This interpretation can be justified if the payoff associated with this diplomatic activity is the same as the expected payoff from P, that is, if it is equal to

$$E(v) = PV = (0, \tfrac{1}{4}, \tfrac{3}{4}) \begin{bmatrix} 0.00 & 0.00 \\ 3.75 & -1.70 \\ 0.25 & 2.50 \end{bmatrix} = (1.125, 1.40)$$

Definition

Adhering to the spirit of this discussion, we define a *bargaining game* as a game that (1) can be represented by an $m \times n$ matrix, the m rows representing the possible outcomes, the n columns the players, (2) has zero payoffs in all components of the first row (the "no agreement" outcome), and (3) allows for the use of joint strategies $P = (P_0, P_1, \ldots, P_m)$. To this definition should be added the usual assumption that the players know the entire matrix; the customary assumption that the subjective utility is *linear* with payoff becomes the stronger assumption that (4) the subjective utilities of the players are *proportional* to their payoffs.

In order to understand the reasons for (4), a few words should be added about the history of these games. Our definition, and the discussion in Chapter 13, is based on the work of Nash (1950) with cooperative games. In his original article Nash described an elegant solution to cooperative games, providing that several assumptions are made in addition to those customarily made in the theory of games. One of the properties needed for the solution was that the utility functions of the players be defined not merely as an interval scale but more strongly as a ratio scale, that is, that the origin of the utility scale be given unambiguously.

Nash formulated his "bargaining problem" as follows: Two individuals are willing to trade, but since they have no money they can only barter goods. Each possible trade has a definite utility for both of them, the utility functions being defined over the possible trades (and over the probability mixtures of possible trades) and having the usual properties of an interval scale. However, the status quo "trade" (i.e., no trade at all) is distinguished among the possible trades in the sense that the utility of 0 can be assigned to it for both players.

In order to facilitate our discussion, we have changed Nash's formulation in several ways. First of all, we substituted the term "proposals" for Nash's "trades," thus making the terminology more general. Once this modification was made, it seemed reasonable to change the term "status quo" to "no agreement."

The second modification has to do with our assuming that utilities are *proportional* with payoff rather than, as Nash assumed, that they are linear with it. This change, however, is more apparent than real. Nash starts by assuming that

$$u_j = av_j + b$$

where v_j is player j's payoff function, u_j his utility function and a and b are arbitrary constants (a being positive). He then assumes that there exists an outcome which has both zero payoff and zero utility for *both* players (the status quo outcome)—in other words, he assumes that it is possible to add to every payoff of player j a constant b' that transforms the original payoff function v into a new payoff function v' such that

(i) $$v_{jR} = u_{jR} = 0$$

where R is the status quo outcome and

(ii) $$u_j = a'v_j$$

where a' is the new constant of proportionality. Our presentation omits the first step of Nash's formulation, the linearity assumption, and uses (i) and (ii) as the starting point of our formulation.

EXERCISES

1. Consider the game "Battle of the Sexes":

$$V = \begin{bmatrix} (2,1) & (-1,-1) \\ (-1,-1) & (1,2) \end{bmatrix}$$

Compute the expected payoff to the two players, (v_1, v_2) for the following pairs of individual strategies: (a) $p = (\frac{3}{4}, \frac{1}{4})$, $q = (\frac{3}{4}, \frac{1}{4})$; (b) $p = (\frac{1}{2}, \frac{1}{2})$, $q = (\frac{1}{2}, \frac{1}{2})$; (c) $p = (\frac{1}{4}, \frac{3}{4})$, $q = (\frac{1}{4}, \frac{3}{4})$. Plot the expected payoff graphically for these three pairs of strategies.

2. Suppose that the row player and the column player in exercise 1 play symmetrical strategy such that $p_1 = q_1 = a$ and $p_2 = q_2 = b$. What is the expected payoff for the two players? (*Ans.*: $2a^2 - 2ab + b^2$ for the row player, $a^2 - 2ab + 2b^2$ for the column player.) Show that the locus of such expected payoffs is the curve ACB of Figure 12.1.

3. Identify the Prisoner's Dilemma among the following three games:

$$A = \begin{bmatrix} (4,4) & (-5,6) \\ (6,-5) & (-3,-3) \end{bmatrix} \quad B = \begin{bmatrix} (8,4) & (-10,6) \\ (12,-5) & (-6,-3) \end{bmatrix}$$

$$C = \begin{bmatrix} (2,2) & (-3,3) \\ (3,-3) & (-4,-4) \end{bmatrix}$$

(*Ans.*: Games A and B). Use eq. 12.5 to explain your identifications.

4. Consider the three games of exercise 3. What is the row player's best strategy for each game if he knows that (a) his opponent will play the first column? (b) his opponent will play the second column? Is game C different from games A and B in this respect? Why?

5. Consider a general bargaining game V:

$$V = \begin{bmatrix} (a, b) & (0, 0) \\ (0, 0) & (c, d) \end{bmatrix}$$

Rewrite this game in the compact form such as given in (12.8).

6. Rewrite the following bargaining game

$$V = \begin{bmatrix} 0 & 0 \\ 5 & 1 \\ 3 & 2 \\ 1 & 7 \end{bmatrix}$$

in the standard form (matrix the components of which are pairs of payoffs).

CHAPTER 13

Principles of Justice: The Nash Solution

Noncooperative games, such as the Prisoner's Dilemma, have inspired a considerable amount of empirical research, but there is no prominent theoretical treatment which goes beyond the solutions based on equilibrium strategies. Cooperative games, on the other hand, have received much attention in the literature and several authors have proposed solutions for them.[1] It is true that different authors have arrived at different solutions and that, therefore, the theory of two-person cooperative games does not achieve the simplicity of the zero-sum two-person games. But the lack of agreement is less distressing than may appear at first. Although the difference in solutions stems from the fact that cooperative games allow for a variety of assumptions about what is "rational," upon closer examination it turns out that different assumptions actually reflect different types of social behavior. We shall discuss Nash's assumptions because, in our opinion, these assumptions may well specify the conditions under which social justice can prevail, and the treatment of social justice is an important topic which has been largely neglected by behavioral scientists.

---

[1] For a discussion of these solutions see, for example, Luce and Raiffa (1958), pp. 124–54.

13.1   NASH'S THEORY

When discussing the Prisoner's Dilemma, we mentioned that it is possible to have solutions based on presumably rational behavior which give the players a lower payoff than would presumably nonrational behavior. This fact has led some theoreticians to the conclusion that the definition of rationality which suffices for the zero-sum games does not suffice for the nonzero-sum games, that there is a need for rationality which transcends the "selfish" interests of individuals. The willingness to accept this point of view was strengthened particularly by the fact that "selfish" rationality is usually not sufficient to identify a unique solution for cooperative games.

At this point something of a schism occurs in the theory of games. The founding fathers of the theory, von Neumann and Morgenstern, have been unwilling to alter in any way their definition of rationality. They argued, quite plausibly, that the lack of unique solutions must be accepted as an inherent limitation of the theory, that actual agreement will always be determined by nonrational factors such as the norms of the society or psychological idiosyncrasies of the players. But others, including Nash, have ventured beyond the confines of the traditional theory in order to obtain a unique solution for cooperative games. We shall consider Nash's approach in some detail. To illustrate our discussion we shall consider the game described in Chapter 12:

$$
(13.1) \quad
\begin{array}{lc}
 & \begin{array}{cc} & \text{Great} \\ \text{Germany} & \text{Britain} \end{array} \\
\begin{array}{l} \text{No agreement} \\ \text{German reunification} \\ \text{British entry into} \\ \text{Common Market} \end{array}
\begin{array}{c} 0 \\ 1 \\ \\ 2 \end{array}
\left[\begin{array}{cc} 0.00 & 0.00 \\ 3.75 & -1.70 \\ \\ 0.25 & 2.50 \end{array}\right]
\end{array}
$$

Main Argument

Imagine that representatives of Germany and Great Britain meet to negotiate and that their objective is as indicated by (13.1). They have to agree on how much "weight" (how large a probability) to assign to each of the three alternatives before them. Recall also that both parties know the entire payoff matrix. Since the payoffs are assumed to characterize completely the motivation of the two parties, we can "translate" whatever transpires between them into the language of payoffs. No matter what noble ideas may be exchanged, it all boils down to the simple question of how large a payoff each party should receive.

Once the problem is phrased in this way, the solution appears quite simple: Why not agree on a joint strategy which gives the players equal payoff? Not only is such a solution patently fair, but also it is difficult to make objections to it. After all, how can either party justify receiving better terms than his opponent?

This reasoning is basically sound; equality is indeed often viewed as synonymous with fairness, and one should be concerned with the possible objections. However, it is not quite correct to state that neither participant can object to the equal-payoff solution. The very fact that the utility indices are assumed to be proportional to the payoffs (see Section 12.3) means that either party can object quite strenuously to the equal-payoff solution. Equal *payoff* does not necessarily give each party equal subjective *utility*. For example, it is perfectly consistent with the assumption of proportionality for Germany to argue that its utility function u_1 is obtained from its payoff function v_1 by multiplying v_1 by $\frac{1}{2}$, $u_1 = \frac{1}{2}v_1$. Consequently, the equal-payoff solution gives Germany only half the "satisfaction" it gives to Britain, and hence is *not* fair. To which Britain may respond that she obtains even less satisfaction from her payoffs than does Germany, that her utility function u_2 is given by, say, $u_2 = \frac{1}{4}v_2$. Therefore, the fair solution is the one which gives her twice as large a payoff (since $\frac{1}{4}$ is only one-half of $\frac{1}{2}$) as it gives to Germany. And the negotiation terns into a heated argument about the coefficient a_j in the equation

(13.2) $$u_j = a_j v_j$$

This equation determines the degree of "satisfaction" (the utility index) each player receives from the equal-payoff solution.

The basic problem, of course, is that subjective utilities for different players are assumed to be "interpersonally incomparable": presumably it does not make sense to say, "This solution has a lower utility for me than it does for you." As we have stated earlier, the lack of interpersonal comparability is inherent in the game-theoretical definition of utility.

Different authors have suggested various ways by which this lack of interpersonal comparability can be surmounted. Generally speaking, they all sought a standard situation which would allow them to assert that the utilities (in that particular standard situation) *are* interpersonally comparable. Some authors, for example Raiffa (1953) and Braithwaite (1955), feel that such a standard situation arises when each player considers his "best" and his "worst" payoff. Although the definition of "best" and "worst" may differ, the general idea is that each player should agree that his best payoff has for him a utility of 1, the worst payoff a utility of 0. Once both players are committed to this *unique* utility function, it is possible to find a solution giving each player equal utility.

These ideas could be applied to bargaining games, but there is a difficulty. If the players know that this procedure was to be used to compare their utilities, each would try to influence the agenda of the conference. (It can be shown, for example, that a player will benefit if he succeeds in having placed on the agenda only proposals having high payoff for him.) To use a term which will be explained shortly, we may say that the resulting solution is not "independent from irrelevant alternatives": Adding or omitting proposals in the agenda alters the nature of the solution.

The procedure suggested by Nash (1950) does not suffer from this weakness and is based on reasoning which, in our opinion, is highly plausible. In essence, his idea is that the players should agree on transformation coefficients a_j of (13.2) which give the players *completely symmetrical utility functions* (we shall define symmetry later in this chapter); the solution of the game is that outcome which gives both players equal utility (in this symmetrical transformation).

Such is the crux of Nash's approach. To explain it fully, we shall make several points: (1) We shall show that, when certain assumptions are made, every bargaining game can be made symmetrical. (2) We shall outline a simple procedure by which a Nash solution can be computed for a group with any number of participants. (3) We shall discuss the reasons why Nash's solution may be viewed as fair.

Simplification of the Game

Our objective is to show that any two-person game, the game of (13.1) in particular, can be made symmetrical in the sense that for every proposal with payoffs (a, b) there exists another proposal whose payoffs are (b, a).[2] This is a highly technical definition of symmetry, but we shall soon see that it has graphical meaning which is quite easy to understand.

The task of transforming (13.1) into a symmetrical game is not as simple as it may seem. Remember that our objective in making the game completely symmetrical is to arrive at standardized utility functions. In other words, we can consider only transformations consistent with the assumption that utilities are proportional with payoffs. We are limited to choosing positive numbers a_1 and a_2 and substituting them in eq. 13.2. The reader may wish to try to find a pair (a_1, a_2) which, when applied to (13.2), yields a symmetrical pair of utility functions. To do this, multiply the first column of (13.1) by a_1 and the second column by a_2, i.e.,

$$U = \begin{bmatrix} 0.00 & 0.00 \\ 3.75a_1 & -1.70a_2 \\ 0.25a_1 & 2.50a_2 \end{bmatrix}$$

We now have all the utility functions which are consistent with the assumption that utility is proportional to payoff. Now try to define a_1 and a_2 so that $3.75a_1 = 2.50a_2$ and $0.25a_1 = -1.70a_2$. If this can be done, we have found a pair $(a_1{}^*, a_2{}^*)$ which yields symmetrical utility functions. However, such a pair does not exist, if for no other reason than that a_1 and a_2 must both be positive.

To surmount this difficulty we shall make an assumption which will allow us to alter the agenda by adding or deleting proposals almost at will. We shall assume that we can add or discard any outcome as long as it is not the solution of the game. Such outcomes will be termed "irrelevant," and we shall refer to the assumption stating that they can be added or omitted at will as the *assumption of independence from irrelevant outcomes*.

In making this assumption we may appear to be putting the cart

[2] Although we shall deal only with two-person bargaining games, the same arguments can be applied to bargaining games with any number of participants.

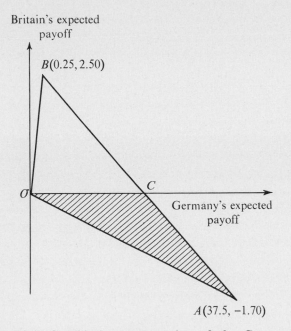

Figure 13.1. Graphical representation of the Germany–Great Britain bargaining game.

before the horse. How can adding or omitting irrelevant outcomes help us to find the solution if "irrelevance" is defined in terms of that solution, if an outcome is irrelevant only if it is not the solution? The answer is that while we may not know which outcome could be a solution, we can readily agree which ones cannot be one. Let us illustrate by considering the game of (13.1). To make our illustration even more vivid, let us represent the game graphically. Representing Germany's payoffs along the horizontal axis and Britain's payoffs along the vertical axis, we obtain the graph of Figure 13.1.

Let us now consider all the outcomes which lie in the shaded area *ACO*. Can we not discard all of them? We certainly can, since they are the outcomes having negative expected payoff for Britain, and Britain can always secure for herself at least zero payoff by refusing to come to an agreement [by choosing the first row of (13.1)]. If Britain is rational in the sense of preferring an alternative with a high expected payoff to an alternative with a low expected payoff, she will never agree to any one of the outcomes in the shaded area; thus none of them can ever become the solution. Consequently, we can limit ourselves to a game represented in Figure 13.1 through *OCB*.

Consider now whether there are any other outcomes which can be safely discarded. Take, for example, point *X* in Figure 13.2. Why should the two players ever agree on outcome *X* when it is obvious any one of the outcomes in the shaded area would be preferred by *both* players? Specifically, Germany prefers any outcome in the shaded area because her resulting payoff would be higher than that from *X*—it would have to be higher, since the outcomes in the shaded area lie to the right of *X*. Similarly, any outcome in the shaded area would have a higher expected payoff for Britain than would *X* because all outcomes in the shaded area lie higher than *X*. Thus, if both players are rational, they will never agree on *X*. But note that identical reasoning applies to any point *X* lying to the left and below the line $\overline{BC}$, and therefore, if the two players are rational, all those outcomes may be discarded as irrelevant. Thus we have reduced the game to the line $\overline{BC}$.

Notice that, in eliminating outcomes, we had no need to introduce new assumptions about the players; we merely pursued the customary game-theoretical definition of rationality. Our procedure so

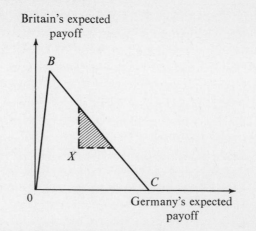

Figure 13.2. **Dominated outcomes *X*.**

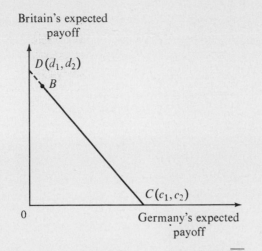

Figure 13.3. The extended Pareto optimal set $\overline{CD}$.

far has been identical with that which led to the definition of optimality in two-person zero-sum games. We have isolated a certain behavior (the one which maximizes expected payoff), termed it "rational," and investigated some consequences of so-defined rational behavior. And we have found that rationality implies that the game may be reduced to the outcomes along the line $\overline{BC}$.

Although we have made no new assumptions and supplied no new definitions, it is customary to use different terms than we have here. The set of outcomes along the line $\overline{BC}$ is known as the *Pareto optimal* (or "jointly optimal") set; pursuing the game-theoretical concept of rationality as we have done is often said to involve the *assumption of Pareto optimality*. Note that a Pareto optimal set contains outcomes which cannot be "jointly improved": If we choose an arbitrary point *on* the line $\overline{BC}$, then any outcome other than the chosen one will "hurt" one of the players. Points closer to B "hurt" Germany (since they lie to the left of the chosen point); points closer to C hurt Britain (since they lie below the chosen point).

We now make a last modification of the game before we transform it into a symmetrical game. As shown in Figure 13.3, we shall use the assumption of independence from irrelevant outcomes and add all the outcomes which constitute the extension $\overline{BD}$ of line $\overline{BC}$. We cannot be certain whether any one of the added outcomes will become a solution. Hence, to satisfy the assumption of independence from irrelevant alternatives (which states that we can add only outcomes that will *not* become solutions) we add the segment $\overline{BD}$ only conditionally. If the solution should turn out to be one of the points on $\overline{BD}$, we shall not accept it.

Our game is now represented by the line $\overline{CD}$. Since this is a straight line, we know that this game can be represented fully as one with *two* alternatives, C and D (see Chapter 9):

$$V' = \begin{array}{c} \text{Proposal } C \\ \text{Proposal } D \end{array} \overset{\text{Germany} \quad \text{Britain}}{\begin{bmatrix} c_1 & c_2 \\ d_1 & d_2 \end{bmatrix}}$$

If we can determine the above payoff matrix V', then any point lying on the line $\overline{CD}$ has the expected payoff coordinates (v_1, v_2)

$$(13.3) \qquad (v_1, v_2) = (P_C, P_D) \begin{bmatrix} c_1 & c_2 \\ d_1 & d_2 \end{bmatrix} = \begin{bmatrix} P_C c_1 + P_D d_1 \\ P_C c_2 + P_D d_2 \end{bmatrix}$$

where $P = (P_C, P_D)$ is the joint strategy of the two players which assigns probability P_C to proposal C and probability P_D to proposal D.

We shall now identify proposals C and D. This identification will not be in terms of "content." We shall not attempt to specify whether C and D are "new" proposals or merely some modification of the "German reunification" or "Britain's entry" proposals; we shall be satisfied with determining the payoffs which have to be associated with these two proposals. Thus *any* specific content will do, as long as it happens to have the payoffs we shall specify.

In determining the new payoff matrix, we note that C and D lie on the same straight line as did the original proposals A (German reunification) and B (Britain's entry; see Figure 13.1). Thus the line has to go through points A and B where

$$A: \quad (3.75, -1.70)$$
$$B: \quad (0.25, 2.50)$$

Since $\overline{CD}$ is a *straight* line, it has to obey the equation

$$Y = aX + b$$

Substituting the coordinates of A for X and Y, we write

$$-1.70 = 3.75a + b$$

Substituting the coordinates of B, we write

$$2.50 = 0.25a + b$$

Solving these two equations, we obtain

$$a = -\tfrac{42}{35}, \qquad b = \tfrac{98}{35}$$

Hence the equation of the line $\overline{CD}$ of Figure 13.2 is

(13.4) $$v_2 = -\tfrac{42}{35}v_1 + \tfrac{98}{35}$$

where v_1 is the expected payoff for Germany and v_2 the expected payoff for Britain.

We now obtain the coordinates of the points C and D. Starting with point C, we note that it must satisfy eq. 13.4 since it lies on the line $\overline{CD}$. Hence we can substitute the coordinates of C into (13.4) by setting $v_1 = c_1$ and $v_2 = c_2$. But, as Figure 13.2 shows, C lies on the horizontal axis, which means that $c_2 = 0$. Setting $v_2 = c_2 = 0$, we obtain from (13.4) that $c_1 = 2.33\ldots$ and write the payoffs for C:

$$C: \quad (2.33, 0)$$

We use the same procedure with point D. D lies on the vertical axis and hence $d_1 = 0$. Letting $v_1 = d_1 = 0$ and $v_2 = d_2$, we obtain from (13.4) that $d_2 = 2.80$ and write

$$D: \quad (0, 2.80)$$

And, since the line $\overline{CD}$ describes our simplified game completely, we can write the payoff matrix of the new game V' as follows:

	Germany	Britain
Proposal C	2.33	0
Proposal D	0	2.80

(13.5) $V' = $

Standardization of Utilities

The stage is now set for the crucial step, the determination of a *unique* utility function for each player. It would be easy to find a point on the line $\overline{CD}$ which gives both players equal payoff, but we have argued that this solution would start a never-ending series of arguments as to who is getting a better deal, more subjective satisfaction. To end this discussion, we shall now consider cases in which the players agree (explicitly or implicitly) that the game gives them both equal satisfaction if it is completely symmetrical. In other words, if we can transform V' into a utility matrix which is symmetrical in the sense described earlier, then this matrix will represent the players' unique utility functions, u_1^* and u_2^*.

A glance at (13.5) shows that it is easy to find the constants a_1 and a_2 which transform V' into a symmetrical game. In fact, there is an infinite number of such transformation constants. To eliminate this surplus of possible constants, it is customary to choose those that yield "0, 1 standardization," that is, constants a_1^* and a_2^* which give each player the payoff of 1 for his best outcome, 0 for his worst outcome. In other words, we wish to find a_1^* and a_2^* that transform V' of (13.5) into

$$
\begin{array}{cc}
 & \text{Germany} \quad \text{Britain} \\
\end{array}
$$

(13.6) $\qquad U = \begin{array}{c} \text{Proposal } C \\ \text{Proposal } D \end{array} \begin{bmatrix} 1 & 0 \\ 0 & 1 \end{bmatrix}$

It is not difficult to see that in order to transform V' into U, we multiply the first column of V' by $1/2.33$, the second column by $1/2.80$; hence

(13.7) $\qquad a_1^* = \dfrac{1}{2.33}, \qquad a_2^* = \dfrac{1}{2.80}$

Note that the game (13.6) is indeed symmetrical. It holds that for a proposal with utilities (a, b) there is another proposal with utilities (b, a). The graphic representation of the game in Figure 13.4 shows that symmetry has the following geometric meaning: To every outcome to the right of the axis of symmetry $\overline{OS}$ (a line that forms a 45° angle with the horizontal axis and goes through the original) there is a "corresponding" outcome to the left of the axis. When we

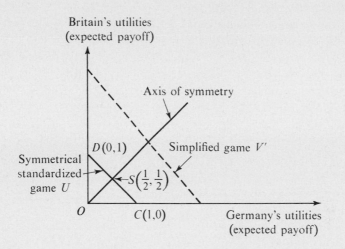

Figure 13.4. Associating standardized utilities U with the simplified game V'.

say that two outcomes "correspond" to each other we mean that, if we folded the graphic representation of a symmetric game along the line of symmetry, the two halves of the game would overlap exactly.

Solution

Only one further major step separates us from a solution of the bargaining game. The two players must be willing to agree that an outcome is fair if it gives them equal satisfaction, that is, equal subjective utility. Once this is agreed to, it remains to identify such an outcome and to determine the payoffs associated with it and the joint strategy which yields it.

An inspection of Figure 13.4 suggests that the recommended outcome must have the following properties:

1. It must lie on the axis of symmetry (because only then does it give equal utility to both players).
2. It must lie on the line $\overline{CD}$ (because the points on that line represent the only outcomes the players will consider).

And the intersect S of the line of symmetry and the line $\overline{CD}$ is the only point which satisfies both requirements; hence S is the outcome the two players should agree on.

Once the recommended outcome S is identified, it remains to determine the payoffs associated with it and the strategy which yields it. To be sure, it is easy to determine the *utilities* associated with S. Since the line of symmetry intersects the line $\overline{CD}$ at the midpoint, the utilities associated with S are $(\frac{1}{2}, \frac{1}{2})$. Similarly, since S is the midpoint of the line $\overline{CD}$, it follows that the joint strategy which yields S is $P = (\frac{1}{2}, \frac{1}{2})$, that is, a strategy assigning an equal probability to the two proposals C and D. However, we need to know the *payoffs* associated with S, not the utilities; and we need to know the joint strategy applicable to the original game V. Recall that the original game does not contain the proposals C and D and hence the strategy that specifies the probabilities associated with C and D is not applicable to V.

Turning to the determination of the payoffs from S, we note that we obtained the utilities from the simplified game V' by applying the transformation constants $a_1{}^*$ and $a_2{}^*$. We multiplied the first columns of V' by $a_1{}^* = 1/2.33$, the second column of V' by $a_2{}^* = 1/2.80$. We now reason as follows: Matrix U represents the utilities associated with the proposals C and D, and V' represents the payoffs associated with the very same proposals C and D. Furthermore, U and V' are related through the coefficients of proportionality $a_1{}^*$ and $a_2{}^*$ so that we can obtain not only U from V' but also V' from U. As the reader may verify for himself, V' of (13.5) is obtained from U of (13.6) if we (1) multiply Germany's utilities (the first columns of U) by $1/a_1{}^* = 2.33$, and (2) multiply Britain's utilities (the second column of U) by $1/a_2{}^* = 2.80$. Since this procedure can be applied to obtain the payoffs of any outcome, it can be applied also to determine the payoffs of the recommended outcome S. Recalling that the utilities of S are $u^* = (\frac{1}{2}, \frac{1}{2})$, we write that the payoffs associated with S, $v^* = (v_1{}^*, v_2{}^*)$ are

$$(v_1{}^*, v_2{}^*) = \left(\frac{u_1{}^*}{a_1{}^*}, \frac{u_2{}^*}{a_2{}^*} \right) = \left(\frac{2.33}{2}, \frac{2.80}{2} \right) = (1.17, 1.14)$$

At this point the reader may accept our results, but still wonder about one thing. Granted that it is plausible to say that the two players should agree on S in game U (after all, S does give both the same satisfaction), why should they agree to S in V' when v_1^* does *not* equal v_2^*, when Britain receives a higher payoff (1.40) than Germany does (1.17)? The answer, of course, is that v^* is the payoff which gives the two players equal satisfaction, equal utilities! Our reason for finding U in the first place was to define a unique utility matrix defined over the outcomes of the game V'. Since U is such a utility matrix, it follows that u_1^* is Germany's utility from the payoff $v_1^* = 1.17$, u_2^* is Britain's utility from $v_2^* = 1.40$. Since these utilities are equal, $u_1^* = u_2^* = \frac{1}{2}$, the two players should accept the payoffs v^*.

We now turn to the determination of the joint strategy yielding the recommended payoffs v_1^* and v_2^*. It could be shown that the same joint strategy $P = (\frac{1}{2}, \frac{1}{2})$ yields S both in the game V' of (13.4) and in the game U of (13.5). However, a different joint strategy is needed for the original game V of (13.1) since that game deals with proposals A and B rather than with proposals C and D (see Figures 13.1 and 13.3).

We start from the fact that, when a joint strategy P is used with any bargaining game V, the expected payoff $v = (v_1, v_2)$ is given by

$$v = PV$$

Our problem thus is to find P^* which yields the recommended (expected) payoffs $v^* = (1.17, 1.14)$ in the original game given by

		Germany's payoffs	Britain's payoffs
O:	No agreement	$\begin{bmatrix} 0 \\ 3.75 \\ 0.25 \end{bmatrix}$	$\begin{bmatrix} 0 \\ -1.70 \\ 2.50 \end{bmatrix}$
A:	German reunification		
B:	Britain's entry		

Using the definition of the expected payoff, $v = PV$, setting $v = v^*$, and letting V be the original game V, we can write that

$$(1.17, 1.14) = (P_O^*, P_A^*, P_B^*) \begin{bmatrix} 0 & 0 \\ 3.75 & -1.70 \\ 0.25 & 2.50 \end{bmatrix}$$

$$= (3.75P_A^* + 0.25P_B^*, \; -1.70P_A^* + 2.50P_B^*)$$

Recalling that when two matrices are equal the corresponding components must be equal, we write this result as two equations:

$$1.17 = 3.75P_A^* + 0.25P_B^*$$
$$1.14 = -1.70P_A^* + 2.50P_B^*$$

Using the customary procedure to solve these equations, we obtain that

$$P_A^* = .26, \qquad P_B^* = .74$$

and, that, therefore, $P_O^* = 0$.

Thus we have reached the end of our long argument: Germany and Great Britain should decide between German reunification (proposal A) and British entry into the Common Market (proposal B) by using a random device which assigns the probability of .26 to proposal A, probability of .74 to proposal B. An alternative interpretation is that Germany should exercise considerable diplomatic pressure to secure Britain's acceptance to the Common Market (this pressure, measured on a 0–1 scale, amounting to .74 points), while Great Britain should exercise moderate pressure (.26 points on a 0–1 scale) to secure German reunification. In either case, Great Britain would receive a somewhat larger (expected) payoff than Germany, 1.40 points versus Germany's 1.17 points.

Nash Solution

So far we have discussed the logical reasoning leading to the Nash solution. It is possible, however, to define the solution in a different and more concise fashion. Since we have discussed the assumptions in sufficient detail, we can now state them compactly. Let us focus our attention on a player in a bargaining game (defined in Chapter 12) who satisfies the following requirements:

1. His utility function is proportional to his payoff.
2. He is rational in the sense that he prefers a high expected payoff to a low expected payoff.
3. He is willing to add or discard proposals, as long as any outcome that is thereby added or discarded is not the solution of the game.

4. He is willing to agree that his subjective utilities are uniquely defined when the game is completely symmetrical; moreover, he agrees to an outcome which gives him the same standardized utility as it gives to his opponent.[3]

Nash (1950) proves not only that his solution satisfies these four requirements, but also that it is the only solution that does. Furthermore, he proves that this solution has the property of maximizing the product of the two players' expected payoffs.

To clarify this last result, let us associate with each outcome of the game, O, its *Nash product*. If the (expected) payoffs from O are $v_O = (v_{O1}, v_{O2})$, then the Nash product, $\prod v_O$, is

$$(13.8) \qquad \prod v_O = v_{O1} v_{O2}$$

Nash's theorem states that the solution we have described on the preceding pages satisfies the four requirements, and also has always the property of maximizing the Nash product. Let the outcome that satisfies the four conditions be $O = S$, then

$$(13.9) \qquad \prod v_S \geq \prod v_O \qquad \text{for all outcomes } O$$

We shall not prove the Nash theorem here; but the fact that the Nash solution maximizes the Nash product is quite useful, both when we wish to identify the solution and when we discuss some of its mathematical properties.

Procedure

We shall now outline a procedure for finding a Nash solution to any two-person bargaining game with a finite number of proposals. It can be demonstrated[4] that such a game will always be represented by a convex polygon similar to the one in Figure 13.5. The proposals of the game will be represented by the corners of the polygon (A, B, C, D, E, F, and G), the probability mixtures of any two proposals (such as A and B) will be represented by the line segment connecting the two corners (such as line $\overline{AB}$ in Figure 13.5).

---

[3] These four assumptions are customarily referred to as the assumptions of (1) invariance with respect to utility transformations, (2) Pareto optimality, (3) independence from irrelevant alternatives, and (4) symmetry. See Luce and Raiffa (1958), pp. 124–28.

[4] For example, *ibid.*, p. 401.

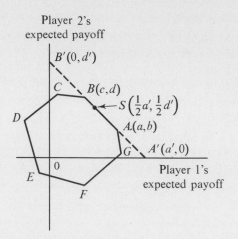

Figure 13.5. Finding Nash solution graphically.

As a first step toward finding the Nash solution, we identify the Pareto optimal set of the game, that is the upper right boundary of the polygon (*GABC* in Figure 13.5).[5] As a second step, we identify graphically that segment of the Pareto optimal set which must contain the Nash solution. We do this by making use of the following corollary to the Nash theorem.

Corollary. If the Pareto optimal set is a straight line that intersects the horizontal axis at a point $A(a, 0)$ and the vertical axis at a point $(0, d)$, then the Nash solution lies at the midpoint between A and B, i.e.,

$$P^* = (\tfrac{1}{2}, \tfrac{1}{2})$$

$$v^* = (\tfrac{1}{2}a, \tfrac{1}{2}d)$$

This corollary is easily proven.[6] We make use of it by drawing straight lines which pass through the adjacent corner points of the

[5] That is to say, we exclude from consideration all boundary segments with a *positive* slope.

[6] The payoffs associated with the Nash solution, v^*, are as given in (13.11). It follows directly from (13.10) and (13.11) that, if $a,d \neq 0$ while $b,c = 0$, then

$$v^* = \left(\frac{ad}{2d}, \frac{-ad}{-2a} \right) = (\tfrac{1}{2}a, \tfrac{1}{2}d).$$

Pareto optimal set (such as $\overline{A'B'}$ in Figure 13.5), identifying the points at which these lines intersect the axes of the graph, and finding the midpoint of each extended line segment (such as the midpoint of $\overline{A'B'}$ in Figure 13.5). If the midpoint falls within the unextended line under consideration (in Figure 13.5, if it falls within the segment $\overline{AB}$, as it does), then this midpoint is the Nash solution S, and we proceed to compute v^* algebraically; if the midpoint does not fall within the unextended segment, we examine another segment of the negotiation set. If none of the line segments contains the midpoint S, then one of the proposals (corners) is the Nash solution.

The third step involves algebraic computations yielding v^*. If the second step fails to identify a segment of the negotiation set within which the solution must lie, we compute the Nash product for each proposal, and the proposal with the highest Nash product is the Nash solution. If a segment is identified, we designate the end points of that segment as A (for the lower right end point) and B (for the upper right point) and define the coordinates as shown in Figure 13.5:

(13.10)
$$\text{Point } A: \quad (a, b)$$
$$\text{Point } B: \quad (c, d)$$

The Nash solution then is as follows:

$$v^* = \left(\frac{ad - bc}{2(d - b)}, \frac{bc - ad}{2(c - a)} \right)$$

(13.11)
$$P_A^* = \frac{ad + bc - 2cd}{2(a - c)(d - b)}$$

$$P_B^* = \frac{ad + bc - 2ab}{2(a - c)(d - b)}$$

where P_A^* is the probability assigned to proposal A, P_B^* the probability assigned to proposal B. If application of eq. 13.11 yields $P_A^* \geq 1$, then A is the solution; if it yields $P_B^* \geq 1$, then B is.

13.2 THE MEANING OF THE NASH SOLUTION

Since the Nash solution is the recommended solution for the bargaining games, it is of considerable interest to explore further the grounds on which it rests. Just why should the players agree to an outcome that maximizes the product of their payoffs? We shall now attempt to answer this question by citing arguments both for and against the solution, and by considering what accepting it as *the* solution may mean for a society.

Assumptions

The purely mathematical argument for accepting the Nash solution is that it is the only solution that satisfies certain assumptions and that a unique solution exists for every bargaining game, no matter how many persons participate in it. The Nash product for the solution S will always be the largest of the product associated with any outcome O,

$$\prod_{j=1}^{n} v_{js} \geq \prod_{j=1}^{n} v_{jO} \qquad \text{for all outcomes } O$$

no matter how large n is.

However, it is always true that a house is only as good as the foundation on which it rests—if the foundation is shaky, so is the house. Thus we are ultimately forced to ask whether the four assumptions (as stated in note 3, this chapter) that form the foundation of Nash solution are sufficiently solid to withstand criticism. We shall not consider here the possible criticisms, since they have been treated very well elsewhere.[7] Suffice it to say that the basis of these criticisms is always the same. The critic cites a plausible case in which one or the other assumption is clearly violated. Thus one cites examples when the utility of the "no agreement" is *not* zero, when men do *not* choose the outcome that maximizes their expected payoff, when adding "irrelevant" *does* change the location of the solution, when men playing a symmetrical game do *not* agree on an outcome that gives them equal payoffs (utilities).

There is one defense which, in our opinion, is best against such criticisms. If it can be shown that Nash's assumptions are satisfied in many (although not necessarily all) bargaining situations, then the theory of Nash is sufficiently vindicated to justify its existence.

---

[7] See Luce and Raiffa (1958), pp. 128–34.

We shall discuss some experiments in Chapter 14 which permit such an evaluation of the theory of bargaining games.

Psychological and Sociological Interpretation

In many cases the Nash solution yields unequal payoffs, and we have argued that a rational player should accept this inequality. We shall now present some arguments which, in our opinion, support the claim that unequality can, under certain circumstances, be fair and just.

We shall limit our arguments to a very simple bargaining game, shown in Figure 13.6. The game is represented by a triangle, two sides of which are parts of the two coordinate axes. In this game, A and B represent the two most extreme proposals; A has the highest possible payoff, a, for player 1 and 0 payoff for player 2, while B has the highest payoff, d, for player 2 and 0 payoff for player 1. In its simplest form this game is a two-proposal bargaining game:

$$(13.12) \qquad V = \begin{matrix} 0 \\ 1 \\ 2 \end{matrix} \begin{bmatrix} 0 & 0 \\ a & 0 \\ 0 & d \end{bmatrix}$$

Note in Figure 13.6 that this game is unfair to player 2 in the sense that his highest possible payoff is smaller than player 1's highest possible payoff; $d < a$.

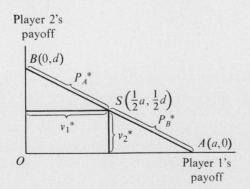

Player 2's payoff

Player 1's payoff

Figure 13.6. A simple bargaining game.

The game represented by Figure 13.6 is the one referred to in the Corollary of this chapter. By this Corollary we obtain the solution

$$v^* = (\tfrac{1}{2}a, \tfrac{1}{2}d)$$
$$P^* = (\tfrac{1}{2}, \tfrac{1}{2})$$

Notice that this solution contains elements of both equality and inequality. The equality stems from the fact that both players are supposed to make equal concessions, since, as indicated by the fact that $P^* = (\tfrac{1}{2}, \tfrac{1}{2})$, the solution P lies at a midpoint between A and B; the unequality stems from the fact that if $a > d$, the recommended payoff $v^* = (\tfrac{1}{2}a, \tfrac{1}{2}d)$ is unfavorable to player 2 since $v_1^* = \tfrac{1}{2}a > \tfrac{1}{2}d = v_2^*$. This dual nature of the solution is a key to the argument that the Nash solution is fair even when it gives unequal payoffs to the two players. We shall offer a psychological and a sociological interpretation and justification of the Nash theory.

A *psychological* interpretation of the rule is obtained when we identify the largest possible payoffs, a and d, as the realistic levels of aspiration of the two players.[8] In other words, we propose to assume that the game (13.8) affects the two players psychologically, causing player 1 to expect payoff a, player 2 to expect payoff d. As a result, player 1 requests proposal A as his first demand; player 2 advocates proposal B. Now the level-of-aspiration theory holds in general that success raises one's level of aspiration, and failure lowers it.[9] Both players experience failure in their first round of negotiation, since the opponent urges acceptance of a proposal that has for each player 0 payoff. But note that player 1's failure is larger than player 2's failure precisely because the "distance" between player 1's demand (payoff a) and his opponent's offer (0 payoff) is greater than the "distance" between player 2's demand (payoff d) and his opponent's offer (0 payoff).[10] Thus one would expect that player 1 has reduced his level of aspiration more than has player 2. To the extent to which reduction in the level of aspiration is proportional to the size

[8] The highest negotiable payoff for *any* bargaining game may be obtained by identifying the side of the polygon that contains the Nash solution, and by extending this side until it intersects both coordinate axes. The intersects with the axes are the two highest negotiable payoffs.

[9] See, for example, Thibaut and Kelley (1959), Chapter 6, especially p. 98.

[10] The "distance" is a for player 1 and d for player 2, and we are assuming that $a > d$.

of failure, the two players' levels of aspiration will ultimately meet at the point of the Nash solution, S.

Thus, the level-of-aspiration theory suggests that the two players' demands will in fact meet at the point S. One could argue that the Nash solution is fair and just precisely because it is in harmony with "human nature." But the justification can be made even stronger by emphasizing the fact that, in accepting the solution S, both players have in fact made equal concessions: Both players have cut their original levels of aspiration by one-half. To the extent that equality is held as an ultimate goal of justice, this aspect of the solution further supports its claim to moral superiority.

A *sociological* interpretation of the rule may be obtained by linking it with the principles of "distributive justice" as stated by Homans (1961). According to Homans, men have always felt that rewards should be distributed according to merit, that rewards should be proportional to, among other things, a member's "investment" in the group and his "costs."[11] The main reason why men disagree over what is just in a particular instance is not that their principles of justice differ, but rather that their evaluation of "investments" may differ. Thus, for example, most men will agree that seniority is important, that is, that time spent as a member of the group is itself an important investment, and hence that members with senior standing should receive greater rewards (e.g., higher pay) than newcomers. But the trouble arises when social attributes such as sex, race, or religion are also viewed as investments. Some Americans, for example, feel that men in general are more useful as group members than women, and that "being a man" constitutes a higher investment than "being a woman." Consequently, they believe that men should receive higher rewards (such as salary) than women. Other Americans feel that such attributes as sex, race, and religions should not be viewed as constituting differential investment, that when a woman joins a group she brings with her just as valuable an investment as does a man. It is this difference in evaluating investment that causes many of the social conflicts—not a difference in abstract principles of justice.

It may seem that Homans' theory is too far removed from Nash's to allow us to link the two, but this is not so. Let us assume that the

[11] Homans (1961), pp. 232–64.

highest possible payoffs, a and d, are always proportional to investment, that the higher a member's investment, the higher is his
highest possible payoff in the games he plays. The Homans principle
of distributive justice follows from the Nash theory. Since $v_1{}^*$ is
always proportional to a (and $v_2{}^*$ is always proportional to d),[12]
the payoff "recommended" by Nash will always be proportional
to investment.

Let us be clear about the assumption which links Nash with
Homans. We are not assuming simply that a member with high
investment will have a higher level of aspiration, although this
proposition does follow from the present assumption. We are
assuming that it is considered just that members with high investment be allowed to play games that are more favorable to them
(have a higher a or d for them) than to the members with low
investment. Since the proposals A and B constitute the agenda of
the bargaining game, we are in effect stating that the Homans theory
of distributive justice coincides with the Nash theory if we assume
that members with high investment always succeed in arranging
agendas that are more favorable to them than to the members with
low investment.

The sociological interpretation of Nash's theory can be used to
support the moral claims of that theory if it can be shown that it is
"in the nature" of society that agendas will always be more favorable
to those members with high investment. One possible argument
is this: To the extent to which members with high investment come
closer to the group's image of an ideal member, their interests will
tend to coincide more nearly with those of the group than will the
interests of members with low investment.[13] Thus, agendas reflecting
group interests and group problems are bound to be more favorable
to those with high investment than to those with low investment.
This is perhaps the justification for the often-heard complaint that
one cannot "beat the system," as well as for a cynic's assertion that
the "game" is always rigged to favor the rich.

---

[12] Since $v^* = (\frac{1}{2}a, \frac{1}{2}d)$ in this game.

[13] This proposition may be true in the sense that men who possess certain desirable
characteristics (such as "being white") are automatically seen as bringing high
investment, such characteristics being desirable precisely because they are those of an
ideal member. Or, it may be true in the sense that men with high investment strive
to conform to the group's norms more than those with low investment.

Misrepresentation of Payoffs

The preceding section suggests that, when playing a game whose Pareto optimal set is a straight line intersecting the coordinate axes, it may be in the interest of each player to work toward an agenda that gives him a higher "highest possible payoff," a (or d) than it does his opponent. This has some disturbing consequences for practical applications of the Nash theory. If it should ever happen that the players do not know their opponents' payoffs,[14] then it may be to the advantage of each player to misrepresent his true interests.

To illustrate, let us consider the following simple game:

$$(13.13) \qquad\qquad V = \begin{bmatrix} 0 & 0 \\ 8 & 3 \\ 2 & 6 \end{bmatrix}$$

Suppose that these are the true preferences of the two players, but that each player knows only his own payoffs. Suppose, furthermore that the dispute represented by (13.13) goes before an arbitrator who is bound to use the Nash solution as the arbitrated agreement. In order to make the computation of the Nash solution possible, he has to know the two players' payoffs; thus he asks them to assign to each proposal a payoff to represent their own interests. He specifies that only *non-negative* payoffs may be used.[15]

Let us consider the task of "revealing" one's own interest from the point of view of the first player. He knows that the arbitrator, being constrained to use the Nash solution, will have to decide on a joint strategy that assigns probability $P_1{}^*$ to the first proposal, probability $P_2{}^*$ to the second proposal. Since the first proposal has for player 1 a higher payoff (8 points) than the second proposal

---

[14] In this section we shall assume that the player is completely ignorant of his opponent's payoffs and hence he does not know his opponent's utilities even in the proportional sense (knowledge he is normally assumed to have in bargaining games).

[15] This restriction is made primarily to make our illustration simpler. However, one may see this rule as applying to cases in which the proposals on the agenda have higher utility for both parties than no agreement at all. Such conditions might prevail if the two parties could choose whether or not to submit their dispute to arbitration: if they decide to do so, one may assume that all possible outcomes are preferable to the "no agreement" outcome.

(2 points), it is in his interest to see to it that P_1* is as large as possible. What can he do to maximize P_1*?

Remember that player 1 is the only person who knows his own true interests. Since the rules set down by the arbitrator do not require that he reveal his true interests,[16] the player is free to choose any non-negative payoff he wishes. Let us call the payoffs he gives to the arbitrator his "revealed" payoffs x and z, and let us agree to call his opponent's revealed payoffs y and w. Thus we obtain the revealed matrix V'

$$(13.14) \qquad V' = \begin{bmatrix} 0 & 0 \\ x & y \\ z & w \end{bmatrix}$$

This revealed matrix will become available to the arbitrator and he will decide on a "fair" joint strategy such that, according to (13.11),

$$(13.15) \qquad P_1{}^* = \frac{xw + yz - 2zw}{2(x - z)(w - y)}$$

Thus the problem for player 1 is to choose x and z so that P_1* is maximized.

Player 1 may consider first whether by letting $z = 0$ he is maximizing P_1*. Intuitively, this would seem to be to his advantage, since z is the revealed payoff corresponding to his lowest *true* payoff of 2 points. It would seem reasonable to assign the lowest possible payoff (0 points) to the proposal which in fact has the lowest payoff. To test whether intuition is correct, we substitute $z = 0$ into (13.15) and obtain

$$(13.16) \qquad P_1^{**} = \frac{xw}{2x(w - y)} = \frac{w}{2(w - y)}$$

Is P_1^{**} larger than P_1* of (13.11), i.e., is $P_1^{**}/P_1{}^* > 1$?

$$\frac{P_1^{**}}{P_1{}^*} = \frac{w}{2x(w - y)} \frac{2(x - z)(w - z)}{xw - yz - 2zw} = \frac{x - z}{x - z - z[1 - (y/w)]}$$

---

[16] It would be futile to make such a requirement, since one cannot possibly enforce it. Only the player who reveals his interests knows whether the requirement has been violated.

It is not difficult to see that as long as $w > y$ (and as long as $x > z$) the above expression will be larger than 1. Since $w > y$ describes the opponent's revealed payoffs which preserve the ranking of his true preferences, we conclude that $z = 0$ is a good strategy as long as the opponent maintains the true order of his preferences. But note that it would be completely irrational for player 2 to misrepresent the *order* of his preferences; that is, he would be foolish to set $w < y$ whenever player 1 preserves the order of his true preferences, $x > z$. The reason is that when $y > w$ and $x > z$, then proposal 1 (the revealed payoffs of which are x and y) jointly dominates proposal 2, and hence proposal 1 becomes the arbitrated solution. This, of course, is the worst possible result for player 1, and thus he should never set $y > w$. We conclude that to set $z = 0$ is always a good strategy for player 1.

But note that when $z = 0$, the arbitrated joint strategy becomes P_1^{**} of (13.16), and that P_1^{**} does not depend on x at all, which means that player 1 can choose x as large or as small (as long as $x > 0$) as he wishes; his choice of x has no effect upon P_1^{**}. Furthermore, it is easily seen that when $z = 0$, it is in player 2's interest to set $y = 0$. P_1^{**} will be smallest when $y = 0$, and player 2 wishes to minimize P_1^{**} (because proposal 1 has the lowest payoff for him, -3 points). But when $z = 0$ and $y = 0$, it follows from (13.15) that $P_1^* = \frac{1}{2}$!

Thus we have arrived at the optimal strategy for assigning revealed payoffs: *each player should assign 0 payoff to the proposal which has for him the lowest payoff*. The result of this strategy is $P = (0, \frac{1}{2}, \frac{1}{2})$; that is, the arbitrated solution will assign equal probability to the two proposals on the agenda.

Let us investigate some consequences of this conclusion. Of particular interest is the situation in which each player is given a choice either of representing his utilities truthfully or of misrepresenting them optimally (that is, player 1 setting $z = 0$, player 2 setting $y = 0$). This situation can be conceptualized as another game the strategies of which are "to represent payoffs truthfully" and "to misrepresent payoffs optimally," and the payoffs of which are the true payoffs of the two players.

For example, consider what happens in game (13.13) when both players represent their payoffs truthfully. In this case the payoffs are the Nash solution to (13.13) which, according to (13.11), is

$v^* = (7.0, 3.5)$. If both players misrepresent their payoffs optimally, the arbitrated joint strategy will be, as shown above, $P = (0, \frac{1}{2}, \frac{1}{2})$, and the payoff from this strategy will be $v = (5.0, 4.5)$. What happens if, say, player 1 reveals his payoffs truthfully while player 2 misrepresents them optimally, i.e., when the revealed payoffs are

$$V' = \begin{bmatrix} 0 & 0 \\ 8 & 0 \\ 2 & w \end{bmatrix}$$

where w is any positive number? Using (13.14) and (13.15), we obtain $P = (0, \frac{1}{3}, \frac{2}{3})$ with the resulting true payoffs $v = (4, 5)$. Similarly, when player 1 misrepresents his payoffs optimally and player 2 represents them truthfully, the arbitrated joint strategy is $P = (0, 1, 0)$ with the associated true payoffs of $v = (8, 3)$.

We can now represent the resulting game in matrix form:

Player 2's strategies

		Reveal true payoffs	Misrepresent optimally
(13.17) Player 1's strategies	Reveal true payoffs	(7.0, 3.5)	(4, 5)
	Misrepresent optimally	(8, 3)	(5.0, 4.5)

Several observations can be made about this game. First of all, note that for both players the "misrepresent optimally" strategy strongly dominates the "reveal true payoffs" strategy.[17] Consequently, two rational players will in fact choose to misrepresent their payoffs optimally. In the second place, the payoff from rational behavior is, in some ways, inferior to the payoff from "truthful" behavior.

The most obvious deficiency of the payoff (5.0, 4.5) is that, while it gives higher payoff to player 2 than the jointly truthful behavior would (4.5 instead of 3.5 points), it gives player 2 a lower payoff

---

[17] For a given player, the payoffs from the "misrepresent" strategy are always higher than the corresponding payoffs from the "reveal true payoffs" strategy.

(5 points instead of 7). Less obvious but in some respects more important is the fact that player 2's gain is purchased at a high price. Player 1's gain is smaller than player 2's loss. This can be seen by considering the two players' *joint payoff*, that is, the sum of their individual payoffs. When both players are truthful, their joint payoff is $7 + 3.5 = 10.5$, when both misrepresent their interests, their joint payoff is only $5 + 4.5 = 9.5$.

This decrease in joint payoff as both players behave "rationally" may be of considerable practical interest. Imagine, for example that the two players are representatives in a labor-management dispute, and that the payoffs are profits in the case of management, wages in the case of the workers. The fact that it is rational for the two parties to misrepresent their true interests, and that this joint rationality leads to a smaller joint payoff than would joint truthfulness means that the nation's economy is the loser. Had both been truthful rather than "rational," more money would have flowed into the economy. In the next chapter we shall explore further the implications of this anomaly.

EXERCISES

1. Represent the following game graphically:

$$V = \begin{bmatrix} 0 & 0 \\ 5 & 2 \\ 1 & 7 \end{bmatrix}$$

Locate the Nash solution on the graph.

2. Solve the game of exercise 1 algebraically using eq. 13.11.

3. Represent the following game graphically:

$$V = \begin{bmatrix} 0 & 0 \\ 5 & 2 \\ 1 & 3 \end{bmatrix}$$

Locate the Nash solution on the graph (*Ans.:* The solution is point A). What happens when eq. 13.11 is used to compute the solution algebraically? Why?

4. Represent graphically the following bargaining game:

$$V = \begin{bmatrix} 0 & 0 \\ 10 & 2 \\ 3 & 9 \\ 4 & 1 \\ 2 & 8 \end{bmatrix}$$

Find the Nash solution graphically and then algebraically.

5. Multiply the first column of the game given in exercise 1 by 5, the second by 2 and identify the Nash solution. Is the recommended joint strategy P^* different than it was for the original game? Why?

6. Add 3 to every cell of V in exercise 1, and represent the new game graphically. Does it have a Nash solution? (*Ans.:* No.) Why?

CHAPTER 14

Application of the Nonzero–Sum Games Theory

Nonzero-sum games are the *enfants terribles* of the theory of games: full of promise but very unmanageable. Their promise stems from the ease with which they can be applied to real-life situations, their unmanageability from the fact that most of them lack the well-behaved solutions that characterize the zero-sum games. Application of these games has been correspondingly varied. Some researchers have all but discarded game-theoretical considerations and have started from scratch, studying the behavior of subjects playing a game as if it were any other laboratory behavior. Others have dealt with those games for which a solution is available and proceeded to determine whether these solutions can be obtained under experimental conditions.

We shall discuss three applications of the nonzero-sum games. The first one attempts to show that many segments of everyday behavior can be profitably conceptualized as a sequence of nonzero-sum games. The second example involves experiments with bargaining games, investigating whether subjects playing such games do in fact reach the Nash solution. The third illustration deals with the Prisoner's Dilemma game, presenting some findings on the manner in which subjects tend to resolve this dilemma in repeated plays of the game.

14.1   DILEMMAS OF ANTAGONISTIC COOPERATION

Walton and McKersie (1965) use the framework of the nonzero-sum games with considerable success to capture the flavor of antagonistic cooperation. By arguing that many social relationships involve two consecutive "games," and that the strategy which is optimal for the first game played by itself is often not optimal when the second game is also taken into consideration, the authors expose the basis of many of the problems that beset human relations.

Stated most simply, Walton and McKersie maintain that many social relationships have a dual nature. On one hand, there is the "getting to know you" process, in which the participants reveal to each other their innermost selves, their true interests and values. On the other hand, there is the "taking advantage of you" process, a process in which each participant struggles to capture as large a share of a common payoff as possible. The basic dilemma stems from the fact that the person who cooperates in the "getting to know you" process, who through revealing his true interests is helping to assure a high payoff for all concerned, often thereby seriously handicaps himself in the second process. Revelation of his true interests hampers his ability to bargain for a large share of the common payoff.

We have already shown that there are bargaining games in which the truthful player is handicapped when pitted against a canny opponent who misrepresents his interests. We have also shown that in these games the joint payoff is indeed larger when both players state their preferences truthfully than it is when both misrepresent them. Walton and McKersie go beyond our analysis by spelling out additional dilemmas and suggesting ways in which remedies may be applied.

According to Walton and McKersie, the "getting to know you" process, which they call the *problem-solving phase*, usually occurs before the actual *bargaining phase*. The question of whether or not to be truthful about one's preferences is viewed as a dilemma besetting the first, problem-solving, phase. But the second, bargaining, phase has a dilemma of its own. Here one must decide whether to be a hard bargainer (making almost no concessions) or a soft bargainer (making many concessions). Notice that this conceptualization is different from the one we employed in our discussion of bargaining games. There we were concerned only with the behavior of rational players, thus bypassing the problem of differential concession making.[1]

Once we admit the possibility of a choice between being hard or being soft, we encounter problems of the Prisoner's Dilemma variety. It is plausible to assume that if one player is hard while the other is soft, the hard bargainer will receive a greater payoff than will the soft bargainer. If, however, both happen to be tough, then it is likely that they will fail altogether to reach an agreement, both receiving a 0 payoff. Let us return for a moment to the game we discussed in Chapter 13:

$$(13.9) \qquad V = \begin{bmatrix} 0 & 0 \\ 8 & 3 \\ 2 & 6 \end{bmatrix}$$

We have shown that when the players of a game are allowed to misrepresent their payoffs by any non-negative number, they may be considered to have as alternatives either a true representation of payoffs or an optimal misrepresentation. This led to the following game:

$$(13.13) \qquad \begin{array}{c} \\ \text{Truthful} \\ \text{Untruthful} \end{array} \begin{bmatrix} \overset{\text{Truthful}}{(7.0, 3.5)} & \overset{\text{Untruthful}}{(4, 5)} \\ (8, 3) & (5.0, 4.5) \end{bmatrix}$$

We have also shown the arbitrated joint strategies P corresponding to each outcome of the game:

$$(14.1) \qquad \begin{array}{c} \\ \text{Truthful} \\ \text{Untruthful} \end{array} \begin{bmatrix} \overset{\text{Truthful}}{P = (0, \frac{5}{6}, \frac{1}{6})} & \overset{\text{Untruthful}}{P = (0, \frac{1}{3}, \frac{2}{3})} \\ P = (0, 1, 0) & P = (0, \frac{1}{2}, \frac{1}{2}) \end{bmatrix}$$

---

[1] Nash theory is concerned only with rational players, thus treating all players as being identical. Consequently, the idea that some negotiators have an invariant tendency to be tougher than others is foreign to that theory.

We can now take into account the possibility of hard bargaining by making the following arbitrary but illustrative assumption. When a player is hard while his opponent is soft, he will make only two-thirds of the concessions he would have to make in order to arrive at the "fair" agreement. This means, for example, that when player 1 is soft while player 2 is hard, P_2 has two-thirds of the value it had in (14.1). For instance, when both players are truthful and player 1 is soft while player 2 is hard, the joint strategy $P = (0, \frac{2}{3}, \frac{1}{3})$ of (14.1) is changed into $P = (0, \frac{4}{9}, \frac{5}{9})$.[2] We shall assume, furthermore, that when both players are soft, they reach the fair agreement represented by (14.1) and (13.13). Finally, when both are hard, their payoff is always (0, 0).

Applying these assumptions to our games requires a considerable amount of computation, but the result is the game that represents both dilemmas—that of the first phase (the problem of truthfulness) and that of the second phase (the problem of toughness). It also shows the (expected) payoff corresponding to each of the 16 ways in which the dilemmas may be resolved:[3]

		Truthful		Untruthful	
		Soft	Hard	Soft	Hard
Truthful	Soft	(7.0, 3.5)	(5.3, 4.3)	(4, 5)	(3.3, 5.3)
	Hard	(7.3, 3.3)	(0, 0)	(5.3, 4.3)	(0, 0)
Untruthful	Soft	(8, 3)	(6, 4)	(5, 4.5)	(4, 5)
	Hard	(8, 3)	(0, 0)	(6, 4)	(0, 0)

Comparing the payoffs for each strategy, we note that the "truthful" strategies are always dominated by the "untruthful" strategies.[4] This is hardly surprising, in view of the fact (as we have already

---

[2] This change is brought about by multiplying P_1 by $\frac{2}{3}$. Probability P_1 is chosen because proposal 1 is the proposal most advantageous to player 1, and player 1 is assumed to be "soft." Hence we are decreasing the probability that proposal 1 will be adopted.

[3] Walton and McKersie use a different example, one that has somewhat different properties than ours. We made our choice in order to follow a single case, the game (13.9), all the way through the discussion.

[4] As stated before, a strategy s' is dominated by a strategy s'' if the (expected) payoffs from s', $v' = (v_1', v_2', \ldots, v_j', \ldots)$, are always smaller than the corresponding (expected) payoffs from s'', $v'' = (v_1'', v_2'', \ldots, v_j'', \ldots)$, that is, when $v_j' < v_j''$ for all j.

shown) that, given the rules of our game, the rational choice in the first phase is for both players to choose to misrepresent their payoffs optimally (Section 13.2, "Misrepresentation of Payoffs"). In postulating that hard bargaining alters the joint strategy by a fixed factor of two-thirds, we have in effect preserved the superiority of the "untruthful" strategies.

Since, for both players, being rational means to misrepresent own payoffs, the above two-phase game can be reduced to the 2×2 game which results if both players make their rational choices during the first phase:

$$
\begin{array}{cc}
 & \text{Soft} \quad \text{Hard} \\
\begin{array}{c} \text{Soft} \\ \text{Hard} \end{array} &
\left[\begin{array}{cc} (5, 4.5) & (4, 5) \\ (6, 4) & (0, 0) \end{array} \right]
\end{array}
$$

Recalling (12.4), we note that it holds for both players that $P < R < T$, but not that $S < P$. Hence the above game is not exactly the Prisoner's Dilemma, "hard" bargaining does not dominate "soft" bargaining, and hence there is no "rational" solution for this game. But the game is similar to the Prisoner's Dilemma game in that a temptation to hard bargaining exists (this strategy being advantageous when the opponent is a soft bargainer), and that to yield to this temptation can backfire (when the opponent also is a tough bargainer).

Let us recapitulate. It is possible to formulate games played in two phases, the problem-solving phase and the bargaining phase. The dilemma plaguing the problem-solving phase is that to reveal one's own payoffs truthfully is jointly profitable but, if not reciprocated, it seriously handicaps the truthful player in the second phase. The dilemma of the second phase is whether or not to be a hard bargainer, since toughness is profitable only if the opponent is a soft bargainer.

Walton and McKersie identify many real-life situations which resemble these games. For example, friendship presupposes intimate knowledge, but intimacy makes one person vulnerable to exploitation by the other, precisely because the individual who is known intimately is unable to defend himself by pretending and misleading his partner, should the partner try to take advantage of him. Or consider the situation when sales and production managers meet to discuss common problems, such as the scheduling of production. They could perform a real service to their *company* if both discussed with complete candor the needs of their respective departments, but the manager who is truthful while his colleague is not may be doing a disservice to *his department*, for when it comes to agreeing on a schedule of production, the manager who misrepresents the needs of his department so as to be in a favorable bargaining position may get a better deal for his department than does his truthful colleague.

14.2   EXPERIMENTS WITH BARGAINING GAMES

We have already alluded to the difficulty involved in creating experimental conditions which satisfy the assumptions of bargaining games. Prominent among these is the problem of making certain that the players know their opponents' utilities only in a proportional sense, which assures, above all, that they cannot compare payoffs. The common practice of revealing the entire payoff matrix (one which shows everybody's payoffs) is particularly likely to violate this assumption. No matter how carefully the subjects are instructed not to equate the payoffs with the utilities, they very often will do so. Experience shows that when the subjects are shown the entire matrix and are allowed to communicate, they will search for a solution which gives everyone equal payoffs.[5]

We shall report here on a series of experiments conducted by the author.[6] In these experiments each subject was provided with only his own payoffs and never given authoritative information about his opponent's payoffs. He did gain some information, however, since the game progressed through a series of offers and counteroffers. By noting the proposals suggested by his opponent, he could get a fairly good idea of which proposals had a negative payoff

---

[5] For example, Schelling (1957) argues that an agreement between two parties is often influenced by a "cultural prominence" of certain outcomes. In our culture, the fifty-fifty split of rewards is a very powerful social norm, one that is likely to be applied whenever possible. When the payoffs are actually displayed, the subjects can apply the norm; when they are not displayed, there is no basis for comparing each other's payoffs, and hence the norm cannot be applied.

[6] The basic design of these experiments is described in Bartos (1966).

and which had a positive payoff for the opponent; he could also estimate how much more his opponent preferred one proposal to another. In short, he could discover the utility function of his opponent.[7]

Design

A total of 86 subjects, all of them students at the University of Hawaii, participated in the experiments. Each of these volunteers was assigned to a four-man experimental group, and in a training session he became thoroughly acquainted with the games he was to play later.

In playing the games, pairs of two-members teams opposed each other. Two different bargaining games (A and B) were used. In each the opposing teams could agree on any one of a number of proposals and every such agreement yielded a definite payoff for each team. In Game A the participants were trained to act as the representatives of two nations, the United States and Communist China, meeting to discuss a five-proposal agenda.[8] The agenda and the corresponding payoffs for the two teams were as follows:

	China	United States
0. No agreement	0	0
1. Total disarmament	12	−9
2. Nuclear test ban	−1	4
3. Inspection stations	−2	5
4. UN police force	−10	13
5. Destruction of nuclear weapons	20	17

The participants knew the specific provisions of each proposal as well as arguments which could be used to support or to attack them.

---

[7] We shall argue later that the subjects were able to discover their opponents' utility functions only in a probabilistic sense.

[8] The training consisted of giving each subject a dossier that described the interests of the government he was to represent as well as some arguments that could be used to defend these interests. In addition, of course, each subject went through a training session before playing Game A and B.

Each team also knew its own payoffs but was totally ignorant of those of the opposing team, although, since the payoffs represented fairly realistically the interests of the two nations, it was easy to make pretty accurate guesses.

The payoffs were expressed as dollars to be won or lost if a particular proposal was agreed upon. For example, if both teams agreed to the first proposal, China would gain $12, the United States would lose $9. The participants were allowed to agree on as many of the five proposals as they wished. The payoff from a package deal involving several proposals was the simple sum of the payoffs attached to the individual proposals. Table 14.1 shows all the agreements the participants could reach.

The second version, Game *B*, was quite similar to Game *A*, the major difference being that now the subjects played the roles of U. S. Senators meeting as a committee to approve or disapprove five legislative proposals. The five proposals and the associated payoffs were as follows:

	Senator from	
	New York	Oklahoma
0. No agreement	0	0
1. Funds to investigate Ku Klux Klan	16	− 17
2. Department of Housing and Urban Development	12	− 7
3. Labeling cigarettes as health hazard	− 1	4
4. Federal lie detector tests	− 2	5
5. Elementary-secondary education bill	− 10	13

Again the payoffs were in dollars, and again the participants could accept as many proposals as they wished. All the possible outcomes are listed, with their payoffs, in Table 14.2.

The training session consisted of playing a game in which the two sides were U. S. Senators (one from Massachusetts, the other from Vermont) dealing with five proposals (different from those of Game *B*). The subjects were allowed to ask the experimenter any questions

Table 14.1. Bargaining Game *A*

Outcome	Proposals Included	Payoff to		Number of Experiments Ending in the Outcome
		China	United States	
0	—	0	0	0
1	1	12	−9	0
2	2	−1	4	0
3	3	−2	5	0
4	4	−10	13	0
5	5	20	−17	0
6	1, 2	11	−5	0
7	1, 3	10	−4	0
8	1, 4	2	4	0
9	1, 5	22	−26	0
10	2, 3	−3	9	0
11	2, 4	−11	17	0
12	2, 5	19	−13	0
13	3, 4	−12	18	0
14	3, 5	18	−12	0
15	4, 5	10	−4	0
16	1, 2, 3	9	0	0
17	1, 3, 4	0	9	0
18	1, 4, 5	2	−13	0
19	1, 2, 4	1	9	2
20	1, 2, 5	31	−22	0
21	1, 3, 5	30	−21	0
22	2, 3, 4	−13	22	0
23	2, 3, 5	17	−8	0
24	2, 4, 5	9	0	0
25	3, 4, 5	8	1	5
26	1, 2, 3, 4	−1	13	0
27	1, 2, 4, 5	21	−9	0
28	1, 3, 4, 5	20	−8	0
29	2, 3, 4, 5	7	5	15
30	1, 2, 3, 5	29	−17	0
31	1, 2, 3, 4, 5	19	−4	0

Table 14.2. Bargaining Game *B*

Outcome	Proposals Included	Payoff to		Number of Experiments Ending in the Outcome
		New York	Oklahoma	
0	—	0	0	2
1	1	16	−17	0
2	2	12	−7	0
3	3	−1	4	0
4	4	−2	5	0
5	5	−10	13	0
6	1, 2	28	−24	0
7	1, 3	15	−13	0
8	1, 4	14	−12	0
9	1, 5	6	−4	0
10	2, 3	11	−3	0
11	2, 4	10	−2	0
12	2, 5	2	6	2
13	3, 4	−3	9	0
14	3, 5	−11	17	0
15	4, 5	−12	18	0
16	1, 2, 3	27	−20	0
17	1, 3, 4	13	−8	0
18	1, 4, 5	4	1	0
19	1, 2, 4	26	−19	0
20	1, 2, 5	18	−11	0
21	1, 3, 5	5	0	0
22	2, 3, 4	9	2	11
23	2, 3, 5	1	10	0
24	2, 4, 5	0	11	0
25	3, 4, 5	−13	22	0
26	1, 2, 3, 4	25	−15	0
27	1, 2, 4, 5	16	−6	0
28	1, 3, 4, 5	3	5	7
29	2, 3, 4, 5	−1	15	0
30	1, 2, 3, 5	17	−7	0
31	1, 2, 3, 4, 5	15	−2	0

during the training session and thus became thoroughly familiar with the game.[9]

After this training period, half of the subjects played Game *A* first, the others played Game *B* first. The play followed this procedure:

1. The United States spoke first in Game *A*, New York in Game *B*.
2. Each team was allowed to make a total of 12 speeches.
3. After each team had made three speeches, they went into separate caucus rooms to plan their strategy. A caucus lasted about three minutes.[10]
4. The two members of a team alternated in representing the team, the switch taking place after each caucus.
5. After the last "scheduled" (twelfth) speech was delivered, the participants were allowed three minutes to arrive at an agreement. During this three-minute "free-for-all," all four subjects participated, speaking in any order they wished.
6. If no agreement was reached by the end of the "free-for-all," the session ended in "no agreement" and everybody received zero payoff. If an agreement was reached, the teams received the appropriate payoffs.
7. At no time were the subjects permitted to reveal their own payoffs to the opponent.

All of the caucus meetings were tape recorded. The transcripts indicate that the subjects took their job quite seriously, trying to determine the course of action which would secure for themselves as high a payoff as possible.

Findings: Nash Solution

In order to determine the Nash solution, we represent the game graphically. By placing the payoffs of China along the horizontal axis and the payoffs of the United States along the vertical axis, and by representing each proposal by a dot and each mixed joint strategy (involving two proposals) by a straight line between two dots, we

[9] The experimenter sat in the same room where the negotiation took place. His role was to explain the rules whenever asked, and to record the interaction.

[10] Subjects were urged to limit their caucuses to three minutes. However, more time was allowed whenever needed.

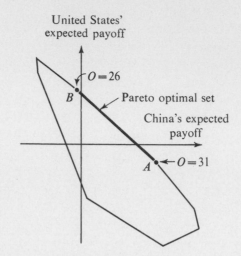

Figure 14.1. Expected payoffs of Game *A*.

obtain the convex polygon of Figure 14.1 as the representation of Game *A*. All possible outcomes of the game lie inside that polygon.

We know (from the arguments advanced in Chapter 13) that the Nash solution has to lie on the Pareto optimal segment $\overline{AB}$ of Figure 14.1. Since point *A* corresponds to the acceptance of all five proposals (outcome $O = 31$ of Table 14.1) and point *B* to the acceptance of the first four proposals (outcome $O = 26$ of Table 14.1), it follows that the players of Game *A* should have agreed on either of the two package deals. Using (13.11) we could determine the proportion of experiments which should have ended in the acceptance of all five proposals, P_A^*, and the proportion that should have ended in the acceptance of the first four proposals, P_B^*. However, we shall not do this for a simple reason: None of the 22 groups playing Game *A* reached either one of the two recommended outcomes.

Figure 14.2 represents graphically Game *B*. We again observe that the Pareto optimal set is represented by the line $\overline{AB}$ and that, therefore, the Nash solution must lie on that line. Point *A* again corresponds to approval of all five proposals; point *B*, however, is different than in Game *A*. It corresponds to approval of the last four proposals (outcome $O = 29$ in Table 14.2). Thus the subjects

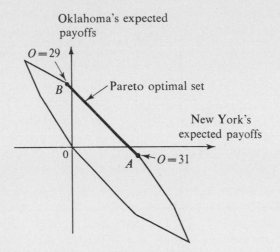

Figure 14.2. Expected payoffs of Game B.

should have arrived at these two outcomes, but they did not. None of the 22 groups playing Game B agreed to either one of the two recommended proposals.

Rationality Reconsidered

There could hardly be a more definite refutation of a theory than that suggested by our findings. Not even one of our experiments supports it. Before we reject the theory in toto, however, let us consider which assumption appears to be most clearly violated in our experiments. Perhaps we can salvage enough of the theory to give it some validity.

First of all, let us point out that the two objections we raised against Lieberman's (1965) experiments with zero-sum games apply in full force to our work. Strictly speaking, we have no business testing empirically a normative theory such as Nash's; furthermore, it is unreasonable to expect subjects to use mixed strategies without giving them any means for doing so. The first objection is routine and we shall not give it full attention until the next chapter. The second objection, however, can and should be considered now.

We questioned in Chapter 10 whether it is reasonable to postulate that one should try to maximize expected payoff. We argued that this requirement makes considerable sense when a game is to be played many times, but much less so when the game is played only once. Now it is true that each subject in the experiments under discussion played two games, Game A and Game B, and that he could have played a de facto mixed strategy. For example, if all five proposals were accepted in both games, and if the team which played China in Game A played Oklahoma in Game B, then the total payoff of the two teams ($17 and $11) would have been close to the payoff resulting from the Nash solution. However, to agree on such a procedure was difficult for the players since they were not certain whether they would play their second game against the same opponents and thus be able to enforce this agreement. Given this difficulty in playing a de facto mixed strategy, and given the fact that the subjects had no means for playing a "true" mixed strategy—no random device was given to them—we conclude that our experiments did not create the conditions required for the use of mixed strategies. Consequently, we have to modify the rationality assumption from "the player always maximizes his *expected* payoff" to "the player always maximizes his payoff."

Let us inspect the findings to see whether this assumption is supported. Since no mixed strategies are now permitted, the representation of the game is not a compact polygon but rather a number of separate dots; since the players can secure for themselves zero payoff by refusing to come to an agreement, we need be concerned only with outcomes having non-negative payoff for both teams. Figures 14.3 and 14.4 show the appropriate representation of the two games.

As was noted in Chapter 10, the assumption of individual rationality implies that the players will never agree on a "dominated" outcome, that is, an outcome which is graphically represented by a dot lying to the left and below another outcome (see Figure 13.2). Inspection of Figure 14.3 shows that there was one such outcome in Game A, outcome $O = 8$ of Table 14.1 (agreement on proposals 1 and 4). Outcome $O = 29$ with payoffs $(7, 5)$ dominates outcome $O = 8$ with payoffs $(2, 4)$ because both players receive more from $O = 29$ than from $O = 8$. Thus, if the players were rational, none of the experiments should have ended in an agreement on proposal 8. And we see from Table 14.1 that this expectation is met, since none

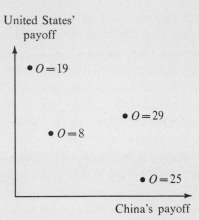

Figure 14.3. Outcomes with positive payoffs, Game *A*.

of the 22 groups playing Game *A* agreed on proposal 8 (although proposal 29 was agreed to by 15 groups).

As Figure 14.4 shows, Game *B* also had one dominated outcome, $O = 18$ (agreement on proposals 1, 4, and 5). This proposal with payoffs (4, 1) was dominated by $O = 22$ with payoffs (9, 2). And again we find (from Table 14.2) that the dominated outcome $O = 18$ did not occur at all, while the dominating outcome, $O = 22$, occurred in 11 of the 22 experiments using Game *B*.

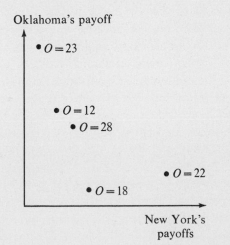

Figure 14.4. Outcomes with positive payoffs, Game *B*.

One more observation should be made about Game *B*, however. As shown in Figure 14.4, the "no agreement" outcome $O = 0$ with payoffs (0, 0) is dominated by a number of outcomes and hence should never have occurred. Nevertheless, two groups playing Game *A* did actually end without reaching an agreement, thus contradicting the assumption of rationality. However, this evidence is not too damaging. The subjects did not *choose* the "no agreement" outcome in the same sense as they chose to agree on a particular proposal—the no agreement outcome just "happened" when, at the end of the three-minute free-for-all, no agreement had been reached. Thus one cannot hold a failure to agree as evidence against the assumption that the players will choose the outcome which maximizes their payoff. And we conclude that the assumption of individual rationality (postulating maximization of payoffs rather than of expected payoffs) is supported by the data.

Nash's Theory Revised

Since our findings indicate that the rationality assumption should be revised by eliminating expected payoffs, it is of considerable interest to investigate whether Nash's theory predicts the findings when the rationality assumption is the only assumption revised. We shall argue that, when mixed strategies are not allowed, it is plausible to postulate that the players should agree on that one proposal which maximizes the Nash product of their payoffs. This new solution differs from the old in that it refers to *one* proposal (thus implicitly excluding "probability mixtures" of several proposals) and to *payoff* (thus excluding expected payoff). To use Game *A* as an illustration, we select (from Table 14.1) the proposals having positive payoff for both players:

	Payoff to		
Outcome	China	United States	Nash Product
8	2	4	8
19	1	8	8
25	8	1	8
29	7	5	35

Since outcome $O = 29$ has the highest Nash product, we postulate that the players should agree on proposal 29.

Before we note whether this happens, let us consider a justification for our recommendation. Suppose that we have two proposals, A and B, with payoffs

$$A: \quad (a, b)$$
$$B: \quad (c, d)$$

Now let us assume for a moment that it is possible to use a mixed strategy; then (13.11) states that the two players should use the joint strategy

$$P^* = \left(\frac{ad + bc - 2cd}{2(a - c)(d - b)}, \frac{ad + bc - 2ab}{2(a - c)(d - b)} \right)$$

Note that the expressions for P_A^* and P_B^* are identical except for the terms $-2cd$ and $-2ab$; and that, therefore, P_A^* must be larger than P_B^* whenever ab is larger than cd. But note that ab is the Nash product for proposal A, cd the Nash product for proposal B. Hence it follows that the Nash solution (in mixed strategies) always assigns the largest probability to the proposal with the largest Nash product. And our assumption that rational players who cannot use mixed strategies will turn to the proposal with the highest Nash product may thus be seen as equivalent to the assumption that players will choose that pure strategy which is assigned the highest probability by the mixed strategy. To the extent to which this assumption is justified, our modification of the Nash theory is justified as well.

We have shown above that proposal 29 has the highest Nash product. And the experimental results confirm our modified theory in that proposal 29 was the one most frequently agreed upon, by 15 of the 22 groups playing Game A. Table 14.2 may be used to compute the Nash products for Game B. Here proposal 22 has the highest Nash product and again the data confirm the theory in that this proposal was the most popular; 11 of the 20 groups that reached an agreement chose proposal 22.

Further Modifications of Nash's Theory

We noted that the proposal with the highest Nash product was agreed to by a total of 26 out of 42 groups, that is, in about 42%

of the experiments. This result is certainly more encouraging than that obtained using the original theory (which was not supported in even a single case); still, the discrepancy between theory and actual behavior is substantial. We shall therefore inquire whether the Nash theory could not be modified further to increase the goodness of fit.

We have argued earlier that it is not permissible to inspect a set of data to find what theory fits it best and then turn around and claim that the theory is supported by the data since it fits it well. However, the modification we shall now propose was suggested to us by data other than those presented here, and hence our data can be used to test it.[11]

Instead of stating which assumption is to be modified, we start by stating the implication of such a modification. We shall hypothesize that the probability that players of a bargaining game will agree on a proposal is proportional with the Nash product associated with that proposal. To test this hypothesis, we use the entries of Table 14.1 to construct the following table for Game A:

		Number of Groups Agreeing	
Outcome	Nash Product	Predicted	Actual
8	8	3	0
19	8	3	2
25	8	3	5
29	35	13	15
Total	59	22	22

It should be explained that the predicted frequencies are obtained by multiplying the Nash product column by $\frac{22}{59}$.[12] The chi-square for the difference between the predicted and the actual frequencies is 1.58, which means that the discrepancy between prediction and observation would occur by chance in about 70% of cases. Thus the modified theory is supported fairly well by our data.

---

[11] This modification was suggested by the data gathered in experiments described in Bartos (1966).

[12] Note that 22 is the total for the fourth column, 59 the total for the second column. Hence multiplying the second column by 22/59 yields the entries in the third column.

Turning to Game *B*, we construct a similar table from the entries of Table 14.2:

		Number of Groups Agreeing	
Outcome	Nash Product	Predicted	Actual
12	12	4.0	2
18	4	1.3	0
22	18	6.0	11
23	10	3.3	0
28	15	5.0	7
Total	59	19.6	20

The chi-square for the last two columns is 3.00, suggesting that the discrepancy between prediction and observation of this magnitude will occur by pure chance in about 56% of cases. Thus the data fit the predictions less closely than in Game *A*. Still, the fit is about as good as that displayed by the model of conformity discussed in Chapter 7, and therefore we shall be satisfied with it.

Granting that this hypothesis (that the frequency with which a proposal is accepted is proportional with its Nash product) is supported by the data as well as one may expect when using a simple model, we now consider which assumptions yield such a hypothesis.

It seems to us reasonable to maintain that our experiments violated the assumption that each player knows his opponent's utilities in a proportionate sense. This assumption, we now believe, is far too strong; the subjects could never be certain about even a proportionate knowledge of their opponents' utilities. A much more plausible assumption would be that the subjects acquired only a probabilistic knowledge of their opponents' payoffs. But what sort of probabilistic knowledge?

A variety of assumptions could be made. For example, we could assume that each participant knew only the probability that a given proposal has a positive payoff. Or we could assume that he knew only the probability that a given proposal has, for the opponent, the highest[13] payoff of all proposals. But, in view of the particular

---

[13] Luce and Raiffa (1958) suggest a probabilistic utility function of this kind in their Appendix A.

problem we are discussing, it is convenient to assume that each subject acquired (through participation in the experiments) an estimate of how likely it is that a particular proposal has the same subjective utility for the opponent as it has for himself. Furthermore, it seems plausible to assume that this estimated probability P is proportional with the Nash product so that

$$P_O = bv_{o1}v_{o2} \quad \text{for} \quad v_{o1}, v_{o2} > 0$$

where b is a constant of proportionality that causes all P_O to sum up to 1.

Is this assumption plausible? We certainly can assume that the player knows his own utilities since, in the experiments, he knows his own payoffs. Now it seems to us that if we are willing to assume that the players can agree on that proposal which gives them equal satisfaction (utility) when they know the utilities in a proportional fashion, as we have assumed in Chapter 13, then under conditions of lesser information the subjects will acquire the same knowledge with a certain margin of error. In some cases they will think that the proposal has equal (standardized) utilities for them when, in fact, it does not. We are assuming that this margin of error is related to the utility indices. The error is least likely to occur when the (standardized) utilities are in fact identical, that is, the closer the utility indices are to being equal, the more likely it is that the two players will in fact view them as being equal.

Thus our modification of Nash's theory continues to assume that the players want to agree on the proposal which has the highest Nash product and which therefore should be preferred when mixed strategies are not permitted. If the players knew accurately their opponents' payoffs (although knowing their utilities only proportionately), they would all agree on the proposal with the highest Nash product, just as hypothesized in the preceding section. However, since they cannot attain such accurate knowledge, they choose also proposals which do not have the highest Nash product, in the mistaken belief that they do.

Conclusions

We have seen that it is possible to bring about a convergence between Nash's theory and experimental findings if one investigates systematically whether the assumptions of the theory are satisfied. Although Nash's theory was not supported in even a single case, a progressive modification of the assumptions led to a fit that is reasonable for a simple model. Undoubtedly, the modification could proceed even further. For example, we could specify that the players, although having only a probabilistic knowledge of opponents' payoffs, were able to discover with certainty which outcomes were strongly dominated, thus assigning the probability of zero to such dominated outcomes. It is not difficult to see that such a modification would improve the fit even further. However, even the modifications we introduced were perhaps sufficient to outline one of the ways in which the theory of games and empirical research can be reconciled. We shall return to this topic in the next chapter.

14.3   EXPERIMENTS WITH PRISONER'S DILEMMA GAMES

The main objective of the experiments using bargaining games was to discover whether the Nash solution for these games is in fact the solution most frequently chosen by players. The objective of the experiments to be described now was to observe the behavior of the subjects under the perplexing conditions of Prisoner's Dilemma games.

The literature dealing with experimental applications of the Prisoner's Dilemma is extensive. Some studies are concerned with the impact of personality variables upon the manner in which the game is played; others focus upon the effect of varying the payoffs, or varying the degree of "cooperativeness" of one of the players. But we shall consider here only the recent work by Rapoport and Chammah (1965), because their work studies systematically the game itself, searching for basic links between the inherent properties of the game and the actual behavior of the players.

Design

As in most experiments using the Prisoner's Dilemma, Rapoport and Chammah use repeated plays of the same game. Typically, a pair of students was shown a payoff matrix such as

$$(14.2) \qquad V = \begin{array}{c} \\ C_1 \\ D_1 \end{array} \overset{\begin{array}{cc} C_2 \qquad\quad D_2 \end{array}}{\begin{bmatrix} (1, 1) & (-10, 10) \\ (10, -10) & (-5, -5) \end{bmatrix}}$$

After the meaning of the matrix has been explained, the students were asked to start playing the game. Each subject was instructed to select one of the two possible strategies without knowing his opponent's choice. After both choices had been made, the outcome was announced, and the game was repeated. Each pair of subjects played the same game 300 or more times in succession.

There were two main variations in the design, the first being variation of the payoff. Matrix 14.2 represents only one of seven different matrices used in these experiments; in the other matrices payoff was varied systematically so that the effect of increasing the payoff in some but not all cells of the matrix could be studied.

The second variation had to do with repeated plays of the game. In ten experiments the pairs of subjects played the same game 300 times (the "pure matrix" condition; in ten other experiments each pair played all seven matrices, switching to a new matrix after 50 consecutive plays (the "block matrix" condition); in ten experiments each pair also played all seven matrices, but the switches from one matrix to the next were *random* (the "mixed matrix" condition). The last two variants of the game were the same as the pure matrix and the mixed matrix conditions, except that in these experiments the payoff matrix was not actually displayed for the subjects to see (although the payoffs were announced after each play, so that the subjects soon knew the entire matrix). These last two variants were called the "pure no matrix" and the "mixed no matrix" conditions. Again each was played with ten different pairs of subjects.

Findings

The bulk of the findings has to do with the "cooperative" responses C_1 [the first row in (14.2)] and C_2 [the first column in (14.2)]. An attempt was made to investigate systematically which properties of the game induce cooperation and which ones hamper cooperation. Among these properties two are of particular interest. These are the absolute as well as the relative size of the payoffs, and experience.

Even though repeated playing of the Prisoner's Dilemma makes the choice of noncooperative strategies D_1 and D_2 less clearly "rational" than when the game is played only once, a fairly strong argument can still be made that rational players should stick to those strategies.[14] Furthermore, the relative size of the payoffs should make no difference, as long as the game remains a Prisoner's Dilemma, that is, as long as $S < P < R < T$, where

$$
\begin{array}{cc}
& \begin{array}{cc} C_2 & D_2 \end{array} \\
\begin{array}{c} C_1 \\ D_1 \end{array} & \left[\begin{array}{cc} (R, R) & (S, T) \\ (T, S) & (P, P) \end{array} \right]
\end{array}
$$

The variation in payoff, described earlier, increased the relative size of the payoffs, but it never violated the principle of inequality that identifies the game as a Prisoner's Dilemma. Therefore, the variation in payoffs should not have made any difference, if indeed the subjects were rational.

But difference it did make. The incidence of cooperative responses C was found to depend on all four types of payoff, S, P, R, and T. When the "reward" R or the "sucker's payoff" S are increased (while the remaining payoffs are kept unchanged), the subjects are more likely to cooperate (choose C); when the "temptation" T or "punishment" P payoffs are increased, the subjects are less likely to cooperate. This boils down to a fairly simple proposition: *Increasing the payoffs associated with a given strategy makes its choice more likely.* Thus it would seem that the subjects not only engage in the fine logical analysis prescribed by the theory of games, but are also influenced by the gross gestalt of the game.

The design of the experiments permitted the authors to consider another aspect of the payoff matrix—its "visibility." The reason for including the "no matrix" conditions into the design, as Rapoport and Chammah confess, was their expectation that permanent display of the matrix would *inhibit* cooperation among the subjects. But exactly the opposite occurred. When the matrix was permanently displayed the incidence of cooperation was far greater than when it was concealed from the subjects. Apparently the visible matrix served to remind the subjects of the possibility of cooperative

[14] See Rapoport et al. (1964), pp. 27–30.

collusion (outcome C_1C_2) rather than a double cross (C_1D_2 or D_1C_2). We may add that this finding is in line with our insistence that displaying the entire matrix tends to alter the game substantially.

Let us turn now to a consideration of the findings which deal with the broad category of "experience"—the impact upon cooperation

Table 14.3.

Condition	r_0	r_1	r_2	r_3	r_4	r_5	r_6
Pure matrix	.46	.51*	.46	.42	.40	.38	.36
Block matrix	.56	.59*	.56	.52	.51	.49	.46
Mixed matrix	.47*	.34	.31	.30	.31	.30	.29
Pure, no matrix	.37	.47*	.40	.33	.32	.32	.32
Mixed, no matrix	.34*	.22	.22	.23	.21	.21	.20

* Largest coefficient in the row.

of previously received payoffs and of the cooperativeness of the opponent. Of fundamental significance in this connection is the question as to whether cooperation encourages cooperation or, inversely, whether it invites a double cross. This problem is particularly important because certain sociological theories support the first possibility, while some social psychological theories support the second.[15]

In order to examine this problem, Rapoport and Chammah assigned the arbitrary value 1 to the cooperative choice C, and 0 to choice D. They then correlated the choice of player 1 with the choice of player 2 for differing time lags. For time lag 0 they computed the coefficient r_0 which paired the two simultaneous choices of the two players; for time lag 1 they computed r_1 by pairing player i's choice at time t with player j's choice at time $t + 1$, and so on.[16] Table 14.3 show the results.

[15] See, for example, Bartos (1966).
[16] The measure used was a biserial coefficient of correlation. It is perhaps clear that a positive coefficient indicates that the players tended to reciprocate (that C from one player was followed by C from the other player and D was followed by D), while a negative coefficient would indicate that the players tended to respond unilaterally (that a C followed a D or a D followed a C).

Two aspects of Table 14.3 are of particular interest. First, note that all coefficients are positive. This means that in all cases there was a strong tendency to reciprocate, to play cooperatively by choosing C when the opponent chose C, playing D when the opponent chose D. In the second place, note that, with two exceptions,[17] the coefficients r_1 are higher than any other coefficients, and that as we read from left to right, the coefficients r_t tend to decrease in size for $t > 1$. This indicates that the immediately preceding choice made by the opponent exercised the strongest influence upon the player's "present" choice. As we shall show below, the subjects had a tendency to "lock in" either the cooperative collusion C_1C_2 or the punishing collusions D_1D_2. But Rapoport's findings suggest that the response to a unilateral breaking of the collusion was likely to follow immediately. If one player suddenly stopped cooperating after a sequence of cooperative moves, the other player tended to reciprocate immediately; if one player stopped choosing D, the other tended to follow suit immediately by also playing C.

The "lock-in" effect was one of the most pronounced features of the Prisoner's Dilemma. Typically, there were long stretches of choices which were both either cooperative C_1C_2 or punishing D_1D_2, but very few stretches of the unilateral choices C_1D_2 or D_1C_2. In this respect the game-theoretical analysis of the Prisoner's Dilemma is supported, since there was a very distinct tendency for the subjects to fall into the D_1D_2 trap and not escape for a long time. Furthermore, the early tendency is to become locked in the punishing outcome D_1D_2, as is clearly shown by Figure 14.5.

Thus it would seem that the effect of the early plays of the game was to teach the subjects the hard realities of the Prisoner's Dilemma as reflected in the game-theoretical "solution" D_1D_2. As the game proceeded, however, the players began to understand that *trust* is the only way out of the trap, irrational as it may be. And, as Figure 14.5 shows, after some time the frequency of the cooperative lock-in C_1C_2 began to rise, ultimately lowering the frequency of the "rational" lock-in D_1D_2.

But—and this is an important "but"—this escape from the D_1D_2 trap occurred mainly when the matrix was permanently displayed. When the matrix was concealed from the subjects, the tendency

[17] For the explanation of the two exceptions see Rapoport, *op. cit.*

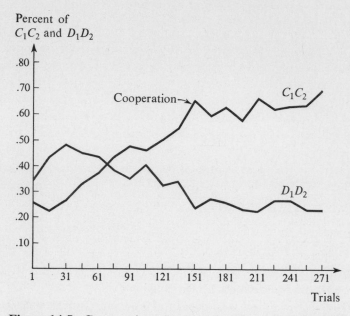

Figure 14.5. Cooperation when the payoff matrix is displayed.

to escape from the trap was much weaker. As shown in Figure 14.6, the number of pairs locked in $D_1 D_2$ tended to remain almost constant after about the first 50 plays of the game. Again, apparently, the assumptions of the theory of games, and its conclusions as well, are more nearly satisfied when the payoff matrix is not displayed in its entirety.

Conclusions

The experiments reported by Rapoport et al. have significance both for the theory of games and for the study of antagonistic cooperation. They suggest that, punishing as the noncooperative choices $D_1 D_2$ may be, the theory is correct in drawing attention to its inescapable logic: The first thing subjects learned about the game was that response D was the safe way of playing, and many were trapped by it.

But the theory was shown also to be far from 100% correct. Even in the early plays of the game, many subjects managed to lock in the cooperative outcome C_1C_2, inspite of the fact that this outcome invited a double cross and hence was unstable when compared with the D_1D_2 trap. Furthermore, the frequency of the cooperative choices C was shown to depend on the payoffs associated with that strategy, a finding contrary to the notion that the outcome D_1D_2 is the solution of the game. Finally, it was shown that as the game progresses beyond, say, the first 50 plays, subjects tend to shift from the D_1D_2 trap into the mutually beneficial outcome C_1C_2.

The experiments suggest a valuable lesson in antagonistic cooperation. It takes time to develop mutual trust and thus escape the harsh "realities" implicit in many human relations. The development of trust, observed in the experiments, is something the theory of games

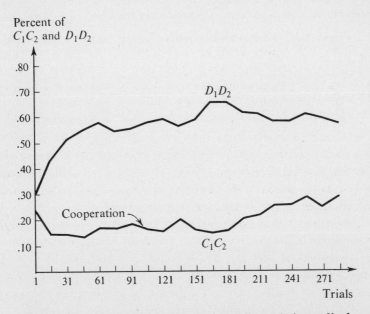

Figure 14.6. Cooperation when the payoff matrix is not displayed.

is ill prepared to handle at this time. Thus it behooves the game-theoretician either to reconsider the definition of rationality so as to permit trust to be rational under some circumstances, or else to admit that the theory of games cannot adequately cope with nonzero-sum games such as the Prisoner's Dilemma.

14.4   DISCUSSION

One of the most obvious contributions which the theory of nonzero-sum games can make to behavioral science is, again, in the area of *conceptualization*. As the work of Walton and McKersie (1965) suggests, it is possible to view a substantial segment of social interaction as possessing properties that are analogous to the problem inherent in games such as the Prisoner's Dilemma.

What are the virtues of such conceptualization? First, and perhaps most important, it encourages a systematic examination of the problem in a manner that is easily manageable, thereby making new insights possible. For example, in their article Walton and McKersie argue that there are some social situations in which truthfulness is mutually rewarding but may be dangerous in that it weakens future bargaining positions. Their discussion encouraged us to search for games having this property, and we found them (see Section 13.2). Furthermore, Walton and McKersie themselves benefited considerably from using the framework of the nonzero-sum games in their discussion. They were able to consider the question of optimal strategies within the constraints of the dilemma as well as the methods for resolving it. Once a problem is stated clearly and precisely, its solution becomes easier.

The second major contribution of the theory is that, through encouraging research of a new kind, it encourages acquisition of new knowledge about man and his behavior. For example, the experiments by Rapoport et al. (1964) have certainly added to our knowledge of social conflict and its resolution by showing that men can and do transcend the limited rationality of conflict by learning to trust. By continuing the investigation of the conditions under which such trust develops and is maintained, our understanding of social conflict will be increased substantially.

Rapoport and Chammah suggest several profitable avenues of research using the Prisoner's Dilemma. One of these would employ a "stooge" who is instructed in the use of a certain strategy. What will happen when he plays a tit-for-tat strategy, always playing C after opponent played C, D after opponent played D? Which strategy is most effective in causing the "naive" subject to cooperate? Another interesting variant would allow the subjects to announce publicly the choices they are about to make. Supposing that their announcements are not binding, under what conditions are they more likely to actually choose C—when both announce that they intend to choose C, or when both announce their intention of choosing D? The reader is urged to examine the alternative research designs discussed by these authors.

As a third major contribution, empirical research not only expands empirical knowledge but it also can contribute to the theory of games itself. For example, the research by Bartos suggests that in simulated negotiations the subjects do not choose the outcome with the highest Nash product, as Nash theory suggests they should, but instead they choose outcomes with a probability that is proportional to the Nash product. This finding in turn encourages the game-theoretician to consider games in which opponents' payoffs are known only in a probabilistic fashion, thus leading to a new branch of games. These new games would have the advantage of possessing a solid empirical base to which they can be applied.

PART FOUR

PROBLEMS OF MODEL CONSTRUCTION

Having surveyed the application of two distinct mathematical theories to group behavior, we may pause and take stock of our accomplishments. What have we learned about constructing models? In Chapter 15 we shall explore the challenge which the theory of games offers to the behavioral scientist—the source of the challenge, its problematic nature, and some of the ways in which it could be met. Chapter 16 will be devoted to the more general principles that apply to the enterprise of model building. We shall be concerned also with the advantages and possible dangers inherent in this enterprise.

CHAPTER 15

Descriptive and Normative Models

Throughout our discussion, we have pointed out the very important distinction between Markov chains models and game-theoretical models—the Markov chains models represent the approach which aims at describing how men actually behave, while the game-theoretical models exemplify the approach aiming at prescribing how men should behave. We shall now give more systematic attention to this distinction.

We admit freely that other important classifications of models are possible. In Chapter 7, for example, we noted that models which use behavioral theory to define their assumptions (the "theoretical-construct" models) can be distinguished from those which do not. However, we feel that the distinction between "descriptive" and "normative" models is of particular interest to the behavioral scientist. In the first place, many existing behavioral theories can be meaningfully characterized as either descriptive or normative. Indeed, it is even possible to characterize entire fields of inquiry as belonging predominantly to one or the other of the two categories. Present day psychology and sociology rely heavily on the descriptive mode of analysis, while economic and political science employ primarily the normative mode.

In the second place, we believe that neither approach alone can adequately answer all the questions we may want to ask about man and his society. As a result, we observe a considerable tension along the boundary separating the two approaches. Time and again, attempts are made to reconcile them. The development of the field of econometrics, attempts to make political science more "behavioralistic," the concern with human judgments and optimality in psychology—these are but a few of the contemporary manifestations of this tension. We shall now investigate the nature of the gap separating the two approaches, and some of the ways in which it might be narrowed.

15.1   THE GAP

It is not easy to characterize the gap that separates descriptive from normative models since there are no formal differences between the two. To be sure, normative models usually involve maximization of some evaluation function (e.g., the utility function), but there are descriptive models which also employ the operation of finding the maxima of a function. Important differences exist, however, in the manner in which mathematical theories are applied to human behavior. Descriptive models utilize mathematical theories in order to predict human behavior, normative models in order to shape it.

Thus the fundamental difference between the two types of models lies not in the models themselves but rather in the intent of the model builder. Does he wish to stand in the background, satisfied with observing behavior and simply reporting what he sees? Or does he prefer to become involved to the extent of suggesting how men should behave?

Intent and Its Consequences

Let us start from the premise that the difference between the descriptive and normative models is one of intent, that a model becomes descriptive when we use it to predict how men will behave, normative when we use it to prescribe how men should behave. What are the consequences of having one intent rather than the other?

One consequence, so obvious that it is difficult even to verbalize and yet is of paramount importance, is that to want to prescribe how men should behave is unreasonable without granting them the freedom to follow the advice. For example, what reasons could one possibly have for trying to determine the optimal strategies of a zero-sum game unless it is taken for granted that the players *can* play them? If we assume that a man's behavior is predetermined in the sense that there exist a priori probabilities (which specify how likely he is to play a given alternative), then the player can use the optimal strategy only when his a priori probabilities happen to coincide with the optimal strategy he should play! Thus the model builder who wishes to determine how men should behave is inevitably drawn to the fundamental assumption that men are free to make choices.

It is even more obvious that the theoretician who wishes to predict how men will behave has to assume that their behavior is (stochastically) determined in the sense that there exist a priori probabilities of choice.[1] It is difficult to offer much support for this contention, because it is true by definition. Scientific prediction (as opposed to crystal ball gazing) is possible only if the scientist has some grounds for defining such a priori probabilities. We have encountered this definition in considering Markov chains models. The grounds for predicting, for example, the proportion of subjects who will conform in the Asch-type experiments are the a priori probabilities of conforming at time t, $p_F^{(t)}$. These probabilities were predetermined (a priori) because they were deduced logically from the assumptions of the Markov chains model.

Thus we see that descriptive models are bound to be (stochastically) deterministic, normative models are bound to assume freedom of choice. But more than that, descriptive models are evaluated primarily against *empirical observations* (does the model fit the data?) while a normative model, when it is treated as a normative model, is evaluated primarily through *logical reasoning* (are the assumptions free from contradictions? are they plausible?). Why these criteria apply is again quite obvious—each approach should be evaluated in terms of its own objectives. Descriptive models aim at predicting actual behavior, and hence it is natural to evaluate them with respect

[1] When a priori probabilities of choice are given it is also customary to say that they are stochastically stable. We prefer to call such choices stochastically determined, but the notion behind both terminologies is the same, that is, the probabilities cannot be changed as the problem is being solved.

to their ability to do so; normative models do not have this objective and hence to judge them in terms of their predictive power is just as naturally inappropriate.[2] We have seen that the justification for game-theoretical solutions was quite formal. For instance, the optimal strategies were singled out for special attention because of their properties of stability, equivalence, and interchangeability. It seems fair, therefore, to judge normative models on their own terms, through logical reasoning alone.

Thus we see that the decision to use a descriptive (or a normative) mode of inquiry has some far-reaching consequences. If we decide to build a model that predicts how men will behave, we are forced to assume that behavior is stochastically determined and we have to give close attention to the problem of gathering and analyzing empirical data. If we decide to build a model that will prescribe how men should behave, we shall have to assume that man has freedom of choice, and our main effort will go into building a tight argument in support of our prescription.

A Dilemma

The differences between the two types of models put the behavioral scientist into a difficult situation. More likely than not, he believes that to be a scientist means to keep an objective attitude towards his subject matter, that he should let the facts speak for themselves. In short, he is likely to believe that he should study man and his society descriptively.

But what should he do if he finds that his results are useless in a practical sense? Can he afford to maintain his objectivity even then? Let us consider an arbitrary, although not altogether ficticious,[3] example, using a problem that has long been of interest to behavioral scientists: conflict and its resolution.

Imagine a scientist who decides to study negotiation in a descriptive fashion. As is customary, he wishes to relate a variety of background factors (such as age, sex, socioeconomic status, and

[2] It is true that we have considered whether men behave in accordance with the prescriptions of the theory of games. However, in so doing, we have implicitly transformed the theory into a descriptive theory.

[3] The example has some basis in the unpublished results using the experimental design described in Bartos (1966).

personality) to a crucial variable of negotiation, say concession-making. Let us suppose, furthermore, that this approach is successful and that he finds personality to be related to concession-making, that the "socially mature" negotiators make greater concessions than do "socially immature" negotiators.[4] And the researcher proceeds to publish his findings.

Now suppose that these results find their way into the hands of a professional negotiator who has considerable respect for science. He may think along the following lines: "Since in most negotiations an agreement must be reached by a rather definite deadline, I should prepare myself by finding out whether my opponent is socially mature. If he is, then he will make many concessions and I shall need to make only a few; if he is not, then he will make only few concessions and I will have to make many if an agreement is to be reached by the deadline. In other words, the more mature my opponent, the fewer concessions will I make."

It is clear perhaps that our negotiator is right, that the strategy just identified is indeed optimal against an opponent who behaves as the findings indicate most people do. But notice that this strategy prescribes behavior which is the exact opposite of the behavior one presumably has observed to be typical. One is advised to be guided by the *opponent's* personality, not by one's own personality. Thus as negotiators become more familiar with the empirical findings on negotiation, these findings become less valid.

But this is not all. How can it be assumed that one negotiator is familiar with the findings, but his opponent is not? If both men are familiar with the findings and if they both apply the above strategy, then the strategy is no longer optimal. Consider, for example, two socially mature negotiators. Since each assumes that his opponent will be guided by his personality, both adopt a tough attitude and, applying the presumably optimal strategy, both will be stubborn and make only moderate concessions. As a result, each negotiator's calculations will be all wrong, and, in all likelihood, an agreement will not be reached by the deadline.

It should not be too difficult for the reader to identify the source of trouble. The descriptive and normative modes of analysis are mixed in a totally unacceptable way. Our fictitious negotiator

[4] This indeed is true for Bartos (1966) experiments.

assumes that his opponent's behavior is predetermined in the sense that information about his personality yields a priori probabilities of his willingness to make concessions—but he acts as if his own behavior were free from personality influences. This implicit assumption that the "game" is asymmetrical (that one "player" is free while the other is not) when in fact it is symmetrical (either both are free, or neither is) leads to the above paradoxical results.

But to affix blame for creating a problem is not the same as solving it. What other use than the one we have just described could a real-life negotiator make of the finding that mature men tend to make concessions? If he cannot utilize this information to define his optimal strategy, then the information is useless to him. And we are back at the original dilemma. What should a behavioral scientist do when the results of his efforts are useless to his most likely "consumer"? When his findings about negotiation have no value for those who negotiate? Is it plausible to maintain that he should simply shrug his shoulders and leave it at that? We do not think so. This dilemma constitutes a challenge that should be met. We now turn to some avenues that seem promising in this respect.

15.2 NARROWING THE GAP

The descriptive and normative modes of inquiry are in one sense irreconcilable. The descriptive mode presupposes that behavior is stochastically determined, the normative approach requires that it be free. And yet it is imperative that we find a way to bridge the gap which separates the two modes. Not only can the normative approach be of great help in studying man and his society, but our negotiation example shows that the purely descriptive approach can be totally futile in some contexts.

Since we are interested primarily in the behavioral scientist, we shall view this dilemma from his point of view. Assuming that the value of the descriptive approach for him has been established beyond a shadow of doubt, we ask whether he can enlarge his repertoire of skills by incorporating those skills unique to the normative approach. Can he inquire how men should behave without compromising his fundamental claim to being a scientist?

Attempts at such an enlargement of the role of a behavioral scientist fall into three obvious categories. He can cope with the challenge presented by the normative approach by (1) keeping the descriptive mode dominant, (2) shifting his ground and endorsing the normative mode as the dominant approach, or (3) attempting, slowly and painfully, to create a new mode that is in some sense a mixture of the two. We shall consider briefly each of these three avenues.

Normative Mode Dominant

Perhaps the most outstanding example of a predominantly normative approach within the social sciences is the theory of formal organizations. Scientists trained in business administration, political science, and sociology have long been concerned with the problem of determining how large numbers of people should be organized in order to achieve some more or less specific goals. The end result of this concern has been the various organizational "blueprints" as well as occasional claims that *the* rational form of organization has been identified.[5]

Without going into detailed discussion of these past and present attempts, several comments nevertheless seem appropriate. In the first place, it should be noted that an inquiry into the "best" type of formal organization may be viewed as a highly *asymmetrical* problem of decision-making under uncertainty. The asymmetry is inherent in the fact that we ask how one decision maker should organize a large number of men.[6] As a result, it does make some sense to assume that the decision maker is free to make choices while the others (those to be organized) are not. Unless these others can organize themselves so as to confront the decision-maker with one spokesman, their freedom of choice is lost in their very multitude, and it is plausible to assume that their responses are predictable, that a priori probabilities over their response alternatives can

---

[5] A classical list of attributes a rational organization (a bureaucracy) should have is given by Weber (1946), pp. 196–204.

[6] It is true that decisions concerning organization are seldom made by a single individual, that whole management often participates in such decisions. However, given the hierarchical organization of management, it seems plausible to view this process of decision-making as involving a single individual.

always be defined. And we do not have to worry too much about the dilemma outlined in the preceding section.

The second point is that the purely normative approach to formal organizations, while essentially successful, nevertheless falls short of perfection. We believe that its shortcomings are due primarily to the fact that "those to be organized" behave on occasions as individuals who have freedom of choice rather than as anonymous members of a huge mass in which their freedom is lost. Not only do employees tend to form unions that represent their interests vis-à-vis management, but also individual employees soon learn how to circumvent the formal organizational structure. As a result, modern organization theory finds it necessary to deal with "informal organizations" within the framework of the formal structure.

Thus echoes of our dilemma are heard even in the area where the predominantly normative approach is at its best. Men do not behave as the theory of formal organizations says they should, and hence there is a problem of accounting for their actual behavior. Should we be satisfied with the normative theory and act so as to maximize employees' conformity to its prescriptions? Or should we discard the normative theory altogether and start from scratch, taking into account only how men behave in fact? But if we do so, if we discard the normative "superstructure," are we not abandoning the original and very urgent problem of how men should be organized?

Descriptive Mode Dominant

Some theoreticians feel that mathematical models have primarily heuristic value, that they serve to initiate new research rather than to solve a problem once and for all. Implicit in this point of view is the assumption that the descriptive approach should maintain its ascendancy over the normative whenever the two happen to conflict: If men do not behave the way they should, then one ought to study how they behave in fact.

We have discussed several instances of research in which the prescriptions of the theory of games were tested experimentally: Lieberman's experiments with zero-sum games, Bartos's with bargaining games, and Rapoport's with Prisoner's Dilemma games.

In all of these experiments, the descriptive mode was implicitly assumed to be dominant since a normative theory was tested empirically. Rapoport went further in this direction than any of the others. He not only tested whether men play the Prisoner's Dilemma as the theory says they should, but also attempted to formulate a descriptive model of the way men actually resolve the dilemma.

Rapoport's approach is a genuine attempt at bridging the gap between the normative and the descriptive modes of inquiry. A typical game-theoretical problem is treated in a descriptive fashion. It is clear, however, that in this approach the descriptive mode takes the upper hand, since the game-theoretical problem is emptied of its normative content. Rapoport's work being a good example of how the two modes of inquiry may be brought closer together, we shall discuss it in some detail.

As shown in Chapter 14, a typical Prisoner's Dilemma game played in experiments conducted by Rapoport et al. (1965) was

$$
(15.1) \qquad V = \begin{array}{c} \\ C_1 \\ D_1 \end{array} \begin{array}{cc} C_2 & D_2 \\ \left[\begin{array}{cc} (1,1) & (-10,-10) \\ (10,-10) & (-5,-5) \end{array} \right] \end{array}
$$

The authors applied a number of distinct mathematical models to describe the manner in which their subjects made choices in repeated plays of the game. We shall limit our discussion to only one model and we have chosen a Markov chains model because in this book we have dealt extensively with the theory of Markov chains.

After considering a regular Markov chains model, Rapoport et al. discard it as fitting the data poorly. They then turn to an absorbing chains model, using the conceptualization developed by Cohen. They assume that each subject either could be undecided about how the game ought to be played, or could have made up his mind. Thus a subject could, at time t, be in any one of four states with respect to the two alternatives (C and D) available to him:

State Γ: If the player is in this state, he will henceforth play only C.

State C: If the player is in this state, he will play C but may play D on succeeding plays.

State D: If the player is in this state, he will play D but may play C on succeeding plays.

State Δ: If the player is in this state, he will henceforth play only D.

It is clear from these definitions that states Γ and Δ correspond to absorbing states in which the subject has made up his mind "forever" to cooperate (to choose C) or to defect (to choose D), while states C and D correspond to nonabsorbing states:

$$
\begin{array}{c} \\ \Gamma \\ C \\ D \\ \Delta \end{array}
\begin{array}{cccc}
\Gamma & C & D & \Delta \\
\begin{bmatrix} 1 & 0 & 0 & 0 \\ p_{21} & p_{22} & p_{23} & 0 \\ 0 & p_{32} & p_{34} & p_{34} \\ 0 & 0 & 0 & 1 \end{bmatrix}
\end{array}
$$

Note that, except for the labeling of the states, this matrix is identical with Cohen's model as given in eq. 7.1, which means that the assumptions which made the construction of Cohen's model possible have to be made here also.

The above matrix represents the behavior of a single individual. However, the data indicate that a player's choice depends not only on his own previous choices, but also on his opponent's previous choices—hence we must search for an alternative representation. Rapoport et al. believe that it might be possible to represent the process adequately by two transition matrices, one applicable when the opponent's previous choice was D, the other when it was C. Furthermore, they assume that the player makes up his mind (reaches an absorbing state) only if the opponent's behavior is favorable to such a decision. He decides to cooperate "forever" only if his opponent's previous choice was C; he decides to defect "forever" only if his opponent's previous choice was D. In other words, the authors assume that

$$p_{21} = 0 \quad \text{if opponent chose } D \text{ at time } t$$
$$p_{24} = 0 \quad \text{if opponent chose } C \text{ at time } t$$

Using these assumptions, and estimating the transition probabilities by the trial-and-error method (mentioned in Chapter 7), Rapoport et al. arrived at the following two matrices:

(15.2)

$$P = \begin{array}{c} \\ \Gamma \\ C \\ D \\ \Delta \end{array} \begin{array}{cccc} \Gamma & C & D & \Delta \\ \begin{bmatrix} 1 & 0 & 0 & 0 \\ .018 & .60 & .382 & 0 \\ 0 & .35 & .65 & 0 \\ 0 & 0 & 0 & 1 \end{bmatrix} \end{array} \qquad Q = \begin{array}{c} \\ \Gamma \\ C \\ D \\ \Delta \end{array} \begin{array}{cccc} \Gamma & C & D & \Delta \\ \begin{bmatrix} 1 & 0 & 0 & 0 \\ 0 & .43 & .57 & 0 \\ 0 & .30 & .6976 & .0024 \\ 0 & 0 & 0 & 1 \end{bmatrix} \end{array}$$

if opponent chose C if opponent chose D

In order to test how well the two matrices fit the actual behavior of the subjects, the authors computed (for each t) the proportion of subjects who chose the C-response. Assuming that the starting probability vector is

(15.3) $P^{(0)} = (0, \frac{1}{2}, \frac{1}{2}, 0)$

and using the two matrices of (15.1), they obtained the probability that a player chooses a C-response at time t, which is $p_C^{(t)}$. Since this probability is the best estimate of the proportion of such responses, $p_C^{(t)}$ can be used to predict the proportion of C-responses. Figure 15.1 shows both the predictions and the actual behavior.

Rapoport and Chammah show that the model performs in a less satisfactory fashion when it comes to predicting the two choices made simultaneously by the two partners at time t. They therefore do not pursue further the application of the theory of Markov chains to their data. Instead, they switch to other types of models: equilibrium models with adjustable parameters, stochastic learning models, and classical learning models.[7] They conclude that the stochastic learning models fit the data best, and that the most promising approach is to combine the Markov chains and the stochastic learning models by assuming that the transition probabilities are being modified as a result of learning. In this respect, their experience seems to be similar to that discussed in Chapter 8,

[7] See Rapoport and Chammah (1965), for the description of these models.

Proportion of *C*-responses

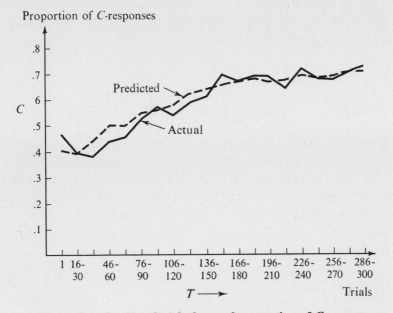

Figure 15.1. Predicted and observed proportion of *C*-responses.

that is, those who applied Markov chains to social mobility have found the current theory of Markov chains rather unsatisfactory and have proposed a number of modifications.

There is no question but that Rapoport's approach to his data increases our understanding of the way in which men solve the difficult problems of the Prisoner's Dilemma variety. However, as we shall now show, this method does not solve the fundamental dilemma confronting the researcher—the difficulty of gathering data relevant to the original problem.

To make our point, let us assume not only that the two matrices of (15.2) describe the manner in which the subjects actually play the game of (15.1), but also that both players know the two transition matrices P and Q of (15.2). Now consider that the game has been played t times and that both players chose C at time t; what choice should they make at time $t + 1$?

Let us begin by considering the game from the point of view of player 1, first by representing his payoffs only. From (15.1) we obtain player 1's payoffs as follows:

$$
\begin{array}{cc}
 & \begin{array}{cc} C_2 & D_2 \end{array} \\
\begin{array}{c} C_1 \\ D_1 \end{array} &
\begin{bmatrix} 1 & -10 \\ 10 & -5 \end{bmatrix}
\end{array}
$$

Since both players are assumed to have just played C, player 1 knows that his opponent was, at time t, in either state Γ or state C. If player 2 was in state Γ, then, as (15.2) shows, no matter what player 1 will do, player 2 will play C_2 at time $t + 1$. This being the case, it is rational for player 1 to choose D_1 at time $t + 1$ because this choice gives him the payoff of 10 points as opposed to 1 point if he chooses C_1.

It is possible, however, that player 1 has not made up his mind as yet, that he is in fact in state C. In that case, the probability that player 2 will choose to play C_2 at time $t + 1$ is given (since player 1 is assumed to have chosen C_1 at time t) by matrix P of (15.2) as $.018 + .60 = .618$; the probability that player 2 will choose D_2 is $.382$. Thus it is possible to assign a priori probabilities over the alternatives open to the opponent, $q = (.618, .382)$, and player 1's expected payoffs are given by multiplying his payoff matrix by q':

$$
v' = Vq' = \begin{bmatrix} 1 & -10 \\ 10 & -5 \end{bmatrix}\begin{bmatrix} .618 \\ .382 \end{bmatrix} = \begin{bmatrix} -3.102 \\ 4.270 \end{bmatrix}
$$

Since his expected payoff for his second alternative is larger (4.270) that his payoff from the first alternative (-3.102), he will choose D_1 if he is rational in the game-theoretical sense. Thus we see that, whether his opponent has made up his mind or not, player 1 should choose to defect, and so play D_1. Moreover, since the game is completely symmetrical, player 2 can go through exactly the same considerations, and he, too, should choose D_2 at time $t + 1$.

Thus we see that if both players chose C at time t and if they assume that the opponent will choose C with the empirically discovered probabilities of (15.2), then each should choose D. We could show that D is the recommended choice whether the choice at time t

was C or D. In fact, let us consider any probabilities q' and compute the expected payoff for the row player:

$$v' = Vq' = \begin{bmatrix} 1 & -10 \\ 10 & -5 \end{bmatrix} \begin{bmatrix} q_1 \\ q_2 \end{bmatrix} = \begin{bmatrix} q_1 & -10q_2 \\ 10q_1 & -5q_2 \end{bmatrix} = \begin{bmatrix} 11q_1 & -10 \\ 15q_1 & -5 \end{bmatrix}$$

It is clear that the row player should choose C if $v_1 > v_2$, that is, if $11q_1 - 10 > 15q_1 - 5$. However, no matter what values of q_1 we assign $(0 \leq q_1 \leq 1)$, v_1 will never be larger than v_2. Thus we see that information about the probability of opponent's choice q' is *completely irrelevant* to the problem, that each player should always choose D. Indeed, our analysis of the Prisoner's Dilemma game (see especially p. 231) would prove this to be the case: By definition, the defection strategy D always strongly dominates the cooperative strategy C, and hence D is the rational choice.

One could object by saying that we are putting the empirical findings to a wrong use. The transition matrices of (15.2) specify how men actually play the game of Prisoner's Dilemma, not how they should play it. But that is our point—the data gathered in the experiments, enlightening as they are, have no bearing on the original problem of how the game should be played. Investigations may ultimately lead to a definition of a game to which the actual behavior of the subjects, who are presumably playing the Prisoner's Dilemma game, is a solution. But that is clearly not the same thing as using empirical data to solve the original problem. Thus, ultimately, the predominantly descriptive approach solves our dilemma by avoiding it rather than by coming to grips with it.

Superimposing Normative Models upon Descriptive

The third avenue represents a true mixture of both modes of inquiry. In essence, this approach starts from the assumption that when man and his society are studied, the fundamental purpose is always to prescribe how man should behave; it incorporates the descriptive mode by sharply distinguishing those questions which can be answered through empirical research from those that can not.

Some of the game-theoretical próblems considered in earlier chapters may serve as examples. In all three types of games considered in detail (zero-sum games, Prisoner's Dilemma, bargaining games) it is possible to divide the assumptions into two categories: (1) assumptions about the *constraints* under which choices are made, and (2) assumptions about the *choice* itself. Prominent among the first of these categories were the assumptions that the game is completely described by a payoff matrix and that the players know the entire matrix; prominent choice assumptions were that players wish to maximize their expected payoff or their security level, or that they wish to agree to an outcome giving them equal standardized utility. As may be expected, this classification of categories serves to separate the two modes of inquiry by stipulating that empirical research should be limited to evaluation of the constraints; the assumptions about choice itself should be arrived at by purely logical reasoning.

It follows that "traditional" scientific research should be directed against the constraints of a decision problem. A moment's thought reveals that this limitation permits the scientist to pursue many of the objectives he has been pursuing in the past. A psychologist might wish to study the ways and means whereby an individual's true preferences should be ascertained; a sociologist may study how interaction with others alters (or helps to define) an individual's preferences; an anthropologist may be concerned with the way in which the norms of a given culture encourage or inhibit certain types of solutions to the problems; and so on. Any particular empirical study, however, is guided by a specific purpose—the purpose of discovering the constraints under which men make their decisions. In this sense the normative concern is superimposed upon the descriptive.

Exactly how this program for reconciling the two modes of inquiry can best be pursued, or whether it can be followed at all, is not clear at this time. Suffice it to say that there are some encouraging as well as some discouraging signs.

On the encouraging side, we note that the problems inherent in studying decision-making have been recognized and given serious attention by investigators in just about every field concerned with the study of man and his societies. For example, a collection of articles on human judgment and optimality by Shelly and Bryan (1964) contains contributions by mathematicians, statisticians, philosophers, psychologists, and economists. Their contributions range from a redefinition of the concept of probability to such "practical" considerations as how to simulate on a computer the relationship between a psychiatrist and his patient. Somehow or other, the gap between describing what men do and prescribing what they should do is in fact becoming narrower. Thus, even if we cannot quite anticipate how the dilemma can be resolved, perceptible progress is being made notwithstanding.

On the discouraging side is the ever-present possibility that we may be unable, in any realistic representation of a decision problem, to separate neatly the constraints from the process whereby choices are made. As we have argued in Chapter 11, it may not be possible to conceptualize a given problem as a payoff matrix in which an alternative is associated with a row of payoffs. For example, a military strategist may know the payoff for winning a major battle, but he may not know the payoffs associated with moves that are preparatory to winning the battle.

An example from another area may serve to illustrate our point. Theoretically, it is possible to define a grand strategy to determine how to play chess in order to win. It is necessary only to consider all possible moves and opponent's countermoves, and then select that sequence which leads to winning the game. In practice, however, this is impossible because it would take even the fastest computer an astronomical number of years to consider all of the ways in which chess can be played. Consequently, those interested in programming a computer to play chess have found it necessary to analyze the game into sub-games and to assign to certain "intermediate" outcomes certain arbitrary payoffs: Taking a pawn is worth X points, taking a queen Y points, and so on. These arbitrary payoffs represent the analyst's estimates of how much a particular sub-outcome helps the player to achieve his main goal, winning the game.

It may be possible to make these arbitrary estimates fairly realistic in playing chess. But how firm can such estimates be when it comes to evaluating the capture of a strategic hill? Can one transform military decisions into a game in which capturing a hill is worth X points, destruction of a supply depot Y points, and so on? In a court battle, can one say how many points should be won when the lawyer discredits a particular witness? In a negotiation situation, is it possible to assign a value to keeping faith as opposed to breaking a commitment?

We cannot answer these questions. But we are convinced that attempts to reconcile the descriptive and normative modes of inquiry should be, and inevitably will be, made. It is one of the great challenges which the enterprise of model construction offers to the behavioral scientist.

CHAPTER 16

Construction and Function of Models

Having discussed a number of specific models in Parts II and III, we now turn to the questions alluded to in Chapter 1. Why should a behavioral scientist use mathematical models? What can he expect to gain from such models? And what losses are incurred in the process? As much as possible, we shall attempt to answer these questions by referring to the models discussed in previous chapters.

The advantages and shortcomings of models cannot be properly ascertained, however, without a clear understanding of the process of model construction. We shall not discuss specifics such as the problem of estimating free parameters, since enough attention was given to these matters when individual models were discussed. Instead, we shall consider the question of general strategy. When a simple model fails to fit the data, is it better to make the model more complex, or to investigate another simple model?

16.1 CONSTRUCTION OF MODELS

Some of the principles that should be followed when constructing mathematical models have already been discussed at various points in our book. For example, we emphasized that the builder of descriptive models should concern himself with establishing the empirical relevance of his model by determining whether the fit between it and the data is sufficiently good. We also noted that he should be alert to the possibility that he may need his empirical data both for constructing the model (for estimating free parameters) and for testing it, and we discussed in some detail how this problem can be overcome in a specific case.

There are other problems connected with testing a model. For example, the researcher should be aware that in showing that some implications of the model are empirically true he has not proved that the model itself is necessarily true. We have only touched upon the problem of testing the assumptions of the model itself. For example, there are various tests to determine whether a given set of data will allow the researcher to assume that the process is Markovian. We discussed the simple test of using the data to estimate two transition matrices, one for the early part of the process, the other for the later part. However, some other more efficient tests are available in the literature for this purpose.[1] Furthermore, we have not discussed at all the problem of a *time lag*. It may happen that a process is not a Markov chains process when very short time intervals are considered, but is Markovian when a longer interval is used—or vice versa.[2] Nor have we given systematic attention to the problem of estimating the parameters,[3] although we did discuss the trial-and-error and the mathematical approach to this problem in specific cases.

In order to acquire such technical skills, the reader will have to read other and often more advanced texts. There is one problem, however, which we would like to mention now. Should one explore many different models or only a few?

This problem is a very practical one. Quite often a researcher who wishes to construct a model of group behavior has only limited resources at his disposal. He must then decide how these limited resources can be used most efficiently. Should he select one theory, such as the Markov chains theory, and explore whether it fits his data, even if in doing so he must modify the theory so that it becomes

[1] See, for example, Anderson (1954), pp. 49–51.

[2] Goodman (1959) gives some statistical tests for Markov chains of mth order.

[3] For a good discussion of the various estimates of parameters in Markov chains models see, for example, Atkinson et al. (1965), Chapter 9.

more complex? Or, should he use a number of different mathematical theories, converting each into a distinct model and giving each model only a preliminary test?

Many of those who have given this problem systematic thought feel that *it is better, in general, to explore many models in a preliminary fashion than to explore one model in "depth."* Since we accept this principle, let us inquire into the possible reasons for following it. These reasons may serve as a guide in deciding when the principle should be followed and when it should be discarded.

Because we do not wish to discuss this problem at great length, we approach it through a simple analogy. It has been said that models are like gold mines: Some are rich in ore and rewarding over many years of digging; some are deceptive, yielding plenty of gold at the entrance but none further in; some are mediocre in that enough gold is there to make continuous digging profitable, but the returns are low; some are sterile.[4] In a sense, model construction in behavioral science is like the West Coast in the days of the gold rush. The results are exciting and tantalizing, but the territory is uncharted; we do not know how much gold there is, nor where to find it.

Granting that there is a similarity between a search for gold and a search for good models, let us pursue the analogy further. Imagine that a prospector has an opportunity for staking claim to two promising sites, one of which, he is assured, has an extensive gold deposit, but he doesn't know which one. Nor does he know whether the gold will be found close to the surface, or deep underground. Imagine, furthermore, that his resources are limited so that only two strategies are available to him: (1) He can choose one site (say, by flipping a coin) and excavate it in depth. (2) He can excavate the surface areas of both sites. Which strategy should he follow?

It is perhaps clear that whether the first or the second strategy is the wiser depends on whether gold usually occurs close to the surface: If it does, then he should construct one deep mine. To prove that this is so, let us conceptualize the gold prospector's problem as a decision problem under uncertainty, one in which the decision-maker has a choice of the two possible strategies and in which there are two "states of Nature": (1) Gold is close to the surface. (2) Gold is deep in the ground. Remember that there are two sites and that

---

[4] We borrowed this analogy from Inkeles (1964), p. 45.

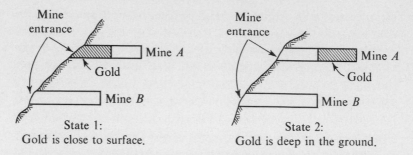

Figure 16.1. Two states of Nature in prospector's problem.

only one has gold in it. Hence the two states of Nature can be represented graphically as shown in Figure 16.1.

To convert our example into a decision problem under uncertainty, we have to assign payoffs to each outcome. Arbitrarily (but without loss of generality) we assign a payoff of 1 to the outcome "prospector finds gold," 0 to the outcome "prospector finds no gold." Now consider the payoffs associated with the first strategy available to the prospector. If the flip of the coin decides for him that he should excavate site A in depth, he strikes gold no matter where it is located (his payoff is 1); if he ends up excavating site B, he does not strike gold at all (his payoff is 0). Since each outcome occurs with probability of $\frac{1}{2}$ (assuming the coin to be fair), his expected payoff is $\frac{1}{2}$ no matter where the gold is located. If he follows the second strategy, he either strikes gold (if it is near the surface) or he does not (if the deposit is deep below the surface). Thus the decision problem can be represented as follows:

$$
\begin{array}{r c c}
 & \begin{array}{c}\text{Gold is close} \\ \text{to surface}\end{array} & \begin{array}{c}\text{Gold is deep} \\ \text{below surface}\end{array} \\
\text{Excavate one site in depth} & \begin{bmatrix}\frac{1}{2} & \frac{1}{2} \\ 1 & 0\end{bmatrix} \\
\text{Excavate both sites at the surface} & &
\end{array}
$$

Once the problem is formulated in this fashion, the solution is obvious. If the prospector is rational in the sense of wanting to maximize his (expected) payoff, he should (1) choose *one* site and excavate it in depth if he believes the gold to be deep below the surface (if the probability of state 2 is larger than $\frac{1}{2}$, $q_2 > \frac{1}{2}$), or

(2) excavate both sites at the surface if he believes the gold to be near the surface ($q_1 > \frac{1}{2}$).

Now to return from the gold prospector analogy to the problem of constructing mathematical models. It seems reasonable to apply this analogy because construction of many simple models is like excavating many sites close to the surface, modification of a model by making it more complex is like excavating in depth, and constructing a "good model" (e.g., one which fits the data well) like striking gold. Given these similarities, we see that, indeed, our advice to explore many simple models is predicated on the assumption that making a simple model more complex is not worth the effort if the simple model shows no promise to start with.

Thus our advice to the reader is to try as many different mathematical theories which can be transformed into simple models as possible. Some of the promising theories and their chief application to date are as follows:

1. Markov chains theory (for the study of group processes).
2. Matrix algebra (for the study of structures[5]).
3. Graph theory (for the study of structures and their balance[6]).
4. Difference equation (for the study of economic processes[7]).
5. Differential equations (for the study of classical economic models[8]).
6. Theory of linear and dynamic programming (for the study of many decision problems such as optimal allocation of resources[9]).
7. Theory of games (for the study of social conflicts).

We believe that a knowledge of these various theories and how they can be applied to the researcher's particular problem will greatly improve his chances of constructing a good mathematical model.

16.2 SOME REASONS FOR BUILDING MODELS

Most readers will agree that, ultimately, the usefulness of models has to be judged against the goals of all science. If model construction

[5] For an example, see Kemeny et al. (1957), Chapter 7, Sec. 7.
[6] For a good introduction to graph theory and its application to the study of structure see Harary et al. (1965).
[7] A good discussion of such processes is found in Beach (1964).
[8] *Ibid.*, Chapter 5.
[9] A good introductory statement is made by Sadowski (1965).

advances science at least as much as do other methods, and if its side effects are no worse than those of other methods, then its use is certainly justified. We shall now turn to the two main virtues of mathematical models; their "deductive fertility" and their "heuristic fertility."

Deductive Fertility

Even the most hard-headed empiricist will agree that gathering data cannot, by itself, advance science too far, that there is always a need to organize the findings into some meaningful system, a theory. The disagreement begins when we start to discuss the extent and the kind of organization that is desirable. Some behavioral scientists condemn extensive organization as "contaminating" the data; others are prepared to accept it. In this book we have implicitly defended a particular type of data organization, one that leads to the formation of a *deductive system*. What are the benefits of having data organized in this fashion?

Let us start by saying that mathematic theory is just one of a number of possible deductive systems. In fact, any system is deductive if it holds that (1) the sentences[10] which constitute the system can be divided into two subsets, and (2) the sentences of one subset can be logically deduced from the sentences of the other subset. The sentences from which the deductions are made are called axioms or assumptions and their set forms the theory "in the narrow sense"; the sentences that can be deduced from the first set are sometimes called theorems or the implications of the theory. Both sets of sentences together form the theory "in the broad sense." It is perhaps clear that each of the mathematical models we have considered is actually the theory "in the narrow sense". *A (mathematical) model is a set of assumptions (about the data) together with the rules of mathematical reasoning which permit us to deduce implications from the assumptions.*

The sentences and the rules that form a deductive system can be of various kinds. For example, the sentences can be of the classical

---

[10] Sentences are the basic units from which a deductive system is built. The language of these sentences may be plain English or it may be formal language such as mathematics.

logical variety such as "All men are mortal" and "Socrates is a man";
the rule may be "Whatever is true about the entire set is true also
about a member of the set." Given this rule, we conclude that
"Socrates is mortal." Or the sentences may be of the mathematical
variety. For example, when we dealt with Markov chains, the
sentences in the axiom set were, "The probability that the process is in
state k at time 0 is $p_k^{(0)}$," and "The probability that the process moves
from state i to state j in one step is p_{ij}," with $p_k^{(0)}$ and p_{ij} possibly being
specific numbers. The basic rule is

$$p^{(t+1)} = p^{(t)}P$$

Using this rule, we arrive at a number of sentences belonging to the
other set—the various theorems of the Markov chains theory.

It is easy to see that the extreme empiricist who objects to "contaminating" the data with logical reasoning has a point. The
deductive systems, and particularly the simple deductive systems
considered in this book, force the data into a straightjacket which
may not fit. But his objection becomes groundless if the model
builder follows the fundamental principle which we have emphasized
throughout our book. If the model is intended to describe reality,
it is not sufficient simply to formulate it; it is necessary to test it to
see how well it fits the data.

Two aspects of deductive systems are of considerable interest
to those who are concerned about the goodness of fit. When one
works with a set of independent hypotheses every one of them has to
be tested before they can be declared true; when one works with
hypotheses which form a deductive system (1) it is sufficient to test
only the assumptions of the theory, and (2) it is possible to test the
assumptions indirectly by testing (directly) their implications.

We have had ample opportunity to make use of the first property
of deductive systems. Recall that we considered in Chapter 8 a
number of models of social mobility and that we tested the basic
assumption that the transition matrix P remains the same for all t.
We found that this basic assumption was not supported by the data
and concluded that there was not much sense pursuing those models
further.

The second property was utilized by our models, too. As often
happens, several of our models were based on assumptions which

cannot be tested directly, or only with great difficulty. We circumvented these difficulties by testing the implications of such assumptions and then, by "backward" reasoning, we identified the "correct"
assumption. Two examples can be given. In the first place, recall that
Cohen's model of conformity presupposes that we know the state of
the subject at time $t = 0$. However, since this refers to the time before
the experiment begins, there is no easy way of determining $p^{(0)}$
empirically. We solved this difficulty by choosing the $p^{(0)}$ having
implications that fit the data best. The second example concerns
the bargaining games discussed in Chapter 14. We considered the
implications of several possible assumptions, and noted how well
these implications were supported by the data. We arrived at a
number of new assumptions, most notably, that the participants
know their opponents' payoffs only in a probabilistic fashion.

There are good reasons why we can never prove conclusively that
the assumptions of a model are correct. Even if all the presently
available data supports them, we cannot rule out the possibility
that future data may contradict them. Furthermore, the assumptions
are seldom, if ever, supported so strongly that we are absolutely
certain about their correctness. Thus, in practice, we test a model
by testing both its assumptions and its implications. By so doing
we permit deductive fertility to work for us in a somewhat different
way. Every piece of evidence, every item of observation, is utilized
with great efficiency. The more implications of the model we test
against the available set of data (always being careful not to use
correlated estimates, discussed in Chapter 7), the more confident
we are that our conclusions about the "goodness of fit" are correct.

So far we have utilized the deductive fertility of our models for
the purpose of testing the model empirically. We shall now consider
the advantages of deductive fertility after a model has been tested
and shown to fit the data well. Then the fact that we can deduce
implications from the assumptions can be used to accomplish two
all-important objectives of science: (1) prediction, and (2) explanation.

Scientists quite often use past findings to predict future events.
Most frequently, their prediction is based, usually implicitly, on the
assumption that an individual or a group will behave in the future
in the same fashion as they have in the past. For example, it is often
assumed that a person who voted Democratic in past elections will

vote Democratic in the future as well. It is truly amazing how often this simple assumption turns out to be correct. But two points should be made. First, some voters change their preferences and hence elementary[11] assumption of consistent behavior is, at best, a very rough approximation. In the second place, simple as is the assumption that things will remain the same, it nevertheless converts the data into a deductive system. True, it is a very simple system. For example, it may consist of such sentences as, "If a voter was a Democrat in the last election, he will be a Democrat in the next election." But a deductive system it is, and the prediction is possible only because it *is* such a system. We are making assertions about events that, in principle, cannot be tested empirically (since they are future events); hence, whatever weight the assertion has is carried by the process of logical reasoning. Assertions about future events thus fall into the same category as assumptions that cannot be tested directly. A deductive system permits indirect verification in both cases.

Mathematical models allow for prediction by making explicit assumptions about the future. For example, our Markov chains models assume that the past (time t) is linked with the future (time $t + 1$) in the fashion stipulated by the given transition matrix P. It is thus easy to see that a model based on the theory of Markov chains is ideally equipped to generate predictions. Recall that we can predict the distribution of responses $p^{(t)}$ for any time t from the theorem $p^{(t)} = p^{(0)}P^t$, and that we can predict a number of other events as well: the equilibrium distribution p^*, the mean number of steps before absorption, and so on.

But mathematical models can not only predict, they can also explain. We have noted that there are two chief ways in which this can be accomplished. In the first place, a model can enhance our understanding of behavior if it has a "built-in" behavioral theory in its assumptions. For example, our social stratification model derived its transition matrix P not from empirical data but from certain theoretical considerations. As a result, our conclusions about equality could be explained in terms of these original assumptions.

---

[11] We call "elementary" the assumption that behavior remains the same to emphasize that we are not referring to a more advanced assumption of sameness, such as the assumption that the probability of change in behavior (p_{ij}) remains the same.

For example, our (hypothetical) society tended to be equalitarian because (we assumed that) its members were all equally likely to meet and, having once met, tended to become dominant depending on status differences. More specifically, we showed that large societies had to become equalitarian (if our assumptions were met) in part because in large societies the "bias against reversal of dominance" had to be small.

But a model can explain behavior even if it has no built-in theory. For example, recall that we were able to explain why a reversal of the early trend toward conformity occurred under conditions of extreme conflict. We showed in Chapter 7 that whether or not such a reversal occurs depends on the starting vector $p^{(0)}$ and the transition probabilities p_{ij}. In particular, we showed that it can occur only if the probability of becoming an absorbed nonconformist is greater than the probability of becoming an absorbed conformist. The point is that this explanation was made possible by using our model. Without it, this reversal of trend, which occurred in extreme conflict but not in moderate conflict, would have been difficult to explain.

Heuristic Fertility

Most scientists will agree readily that the facility with which a theory can be tested against empirical data, its predictive power, and its ability to explain are of crucial importance. Less obvious, but, in our opinion, just as important, is the capacity of a model to suggest new observations, experiments, and conceptualizations. It seems to us that a theory which does not represent a challenge, which does not stimulate imagination, which does not attract scientists who wish to work with it, leaves something to be desired. Thus we turn to the facility with which models suggest new approaches—their "heuristic fertility."

Heuristic fertility is not as easily defined as deductive fertility. However, it is possible to identify two specific aspects of a model which determine just how heuristically fertile it is: (1) its free parameters, and (2) the range of situations to which it applies.[12] We shall discuss the role of these two aspects by considering some specific examples.

[12] We are indebted for these two items to Rapoport and Chammah (1965).

To start with, let us recall that a *free parameter* is a parameter that is not determined in a theoretical fashion and hence must be estimated from the data. And a model has heuristic fertility to the extent to which it is useful in considering the relationship between different situations and the variation in these free parameters. For example, we have seen that Cohen investigated two distinct situations in his experiments, the condition of moderate conflict and that of extreme conflict. We have also seen that a different transition matrix was associated with each of these two conditions. The question to be answered now is whether this change in transition matrices, which corresponds to a change in the situation, gives us new insights. If it does, then the model is heuristically fertile. We have already noted one interesting difference between the two matrices. Under moderate conditions, the transition probabilities are so arranged that subjects tend to become more and more conformist; under the extreme condition, however, this trend is reversed.

The work of Rapoport et al. gives us another example. We have already discussed their experiments with the Prisoner's Dilemma game and noted that they built various models to describe their data. The authors then proceeded to correlate the free parameters of their various models with various background factors. Their findings concerning the differences between men and women are particularly intriguing; they found that: (1) men cooperate more (are more likely to play C) than women do; (2) men reciprocate more (are more likely to play C when the opponent plays C, to play D when the opponent plays D) that do women; (3) men are likely to be locked in the cooperative (CC) responses, women in the defecting (DD) responses; (4) when men play against women, men play less cooperatively (than when playing against men); even then, however, men play more cooperatively than do women.

These findings are interesting in their own right, if for no other reason than that they cast some doubt upon our usual stereotype of man as the tough, competitive individual, and of woman as the soft, cooperative one. Women more nearly satisfy the "selfish" rationality of the theory of games than do men.[13] Of interest to us

[13] Recall that the defecting (D) response is said to be the rational way of playing the Prisoner's Dilemma. See Sec. 12.2.

here, however, is the fact that the results were obtained only *after* the plays of the Prisoner's Dilemma had been represented by a series of models, by investigating how the various parameters of the models vary with sex.

The second source of heuristic fertility is the *range of situations* to which a model can apply. The more generally applicable a model, the more likely it is to stir up the intellectual ferment we are speaking about. There is little doubt that the appeal of the theory of games lies in large part in its wide applicability. For example, its utility theory and its basic decision-making scheme have provided a challenge that psychologists cannot afford to ignore. Some psychologists, for example, Suppes and Atkinson (1960), have contrasted certain concepts of psychology (such as those of learning theory) with those of the theory of games; others have been moved to investigate new psychological problems (such as the problems of decision-making under uncertainty). We have seen that Anderson and Moore have been inspired by the game-theoretical approach to design new types of experimental environments and to explore a new type of logic. The affinity of the solutions of two-person zero-sum games with linear programming has been responsible in part for the current interest in linear (and dynamic) programming and its application to various administrative problems.[14] Finally, and perhaps most importantly for our purposes, the theory has given impetus to the current revival of interest in the area of social conflict and its resolution. We believe that it will be many years before the turmoil created by the theory of games will have run its course and lost its appeal for those wishing to understand group behavior.

One more point should be made about heuristic fertility. If we were to argue that a theory should be judged only with respect to its ability to predict and explain, we would imply that a researcher who has created a model without these properties has wasted his time. If we maintain, however, that heuristic considerations should also enter into the evaluation of a theory, then we have a basis for extracting some value from theories that have been failures from other points of view. For example, we have seen that our Markov

[14] For a discussion of linear and dynamic programming see, for example, Sadowski (1965).

chains models of social mobility have been incapable of yielding reliable predictions simply because the Markovian assumptions were not met. However, we did profit from those failures. First and foremost, we learned that some seemingly plausible assumptions about the mobility process are wrong. It is wrong to assume that the probability of moving from state i to state j, p_{ij}, remains constant for all time t. The point is that without spelling out this "intuitively plausible" assumption mathematically and without testing its implications against the data, we would still believe it to be plausible! In the second place, we made some "obvious discoveries"—obvious, that is, after we made our analysis, but by no means obvious before. For example, we learned that we cannot consider migration to and from California without considering migration in the rest of the world. Finally, we can learn much from examining the reasons why our models have failed. We have shown, in Chapter 8, how examination of the shortcomings has been instrumental in modifying the theory of Markov chains. In fact, it is precisely failures of this sort that can provide impetus for the development of new mathematical theories. When the social scientist demonstrates that the available mathematical systems do not apply to his problems, he is creating motivation for the development of new systems.

16.3   SOME DANGERS

It would be unwise to terminate this introductory discussion without scrutinizing our models for possibly damaging side effects. Some thoughtful critics have argued, for example, that emphasis on mathematics for social scientists may drive away the type of talent that is needed most: the creative and imaginative student who abhors mathematics.[15] Others have pointed to a number of specific dangers to which a model builder is particularly prone. One of the most recent, and best, discussions of such dangers is given by Kaplan (1964). Let us, therefore, see how his remarks apply to our models.

First of all, let us say that Kaplan (a philosopher of considerable

---

[15] See, for example, Etzioni (1965).

stature) is basically sympathetic to the enterprise of model construction. He says:

If the current fashion dictates the building of models, and perhaps even the kind of models to be constructed, it is not for that reason alone to be condemned. I have nothing against the current mode, but I trust that it is not shamefully oldfashioned to be interested still in what lies underneath: glamor isn't everything.... The intent of my head shaking with regard to models is neither to derogate what has been achieved nor to discourage further endeavor; to the contrary, I want to heighten awareness of possible shortcomings so as to make easier to avoid them....[16]

Turning to his specific warnings, let us consider the danger of *overemphasis on symbols*. A scientist who insists on translating English sentences into symbolic (mathematical) language is guilty of such overemphasis if nothing is gained through this translation. As we have stated already, our models express ideas that would be very difficult, perhaps impossible, to express in plain English. Moreover, by using the language of mathematics, we have gained "deductive fertility," the ability to derive many implications from a small number of assumptions.

The second danger is *overemphasis on form*. Essentially, this danger lies in our becoming so fascinated by the model itself that we have no time for, or lose interest in, the empirical evidence supporting it. The danger is very real. But we have tried to protect ourselves in two ways: (1) by dealing with simple models, and (2) by discussing the models always in connection with the process of their verification. By emphasizing simple models and by emphasizing the strategy of testing many simple models before making a commitment to one, we have attempted to discourage the reader from becoming interested in the model only for its own sake.

Thirdly, says Kaplan, one must be wary of *oversimplification*. The danger lies not in the fact that a model may be simpler than the reality to which it applies, but rather that it may be simplified in a wrong way, omitting features which are important for the purposes of the model. This is a danger to which we are particularly susceptible since our objective is the construction of simple models. It may be impossible in building them not to ignore important properties of the reality they are meant to represent.

[16] Kaplan (1964), pp. 276–77.

We have to admit to being guilty of considerable simplification in this book. We are guilty of assigning to our models names that are too ambitious in the light of what the models actually can do. For example, our model of "social stratification" answers only a few of the questions usually asked by students of social stratification. It tells us nothing about the differences in values held by the members of different social classes; it does not explain why the members of the middle class are more "conformist" than other citizens, nor why some societies have greater inequality than others. Similarly, our model of "conflict" tells us nothing about the social conditions that are conducive to a prolonged conflict or about the different types of conflict.[17]

On the other hand, let us note that while the models themselves do not answer many of the questions which can be legitimately asked, they can be used with advantage to answer them. As we have suggested, this can be accomplished by correlating the free parameters of our models with various background variables. Thus our shortcoming lies not so much in choosing wrong variables to be included in the model as with the decision to use simple models in areas that cannot be simplified without losing some of the traditionally included content. But perhaps, having explained the limitations of our models, we can be forgiven our ambitious names. We like those names since they serve to suggest the broad potentialities of the models. Let us quote Kaplan with respect to this problem:

There are models which, happily, take into account all the factors that are important for the existent stage of inquiry, models which are then improved upon or are honorably retired as inquiry moves ahead. There are other models which, though they neglect something significant, nevertheless provide a sufficiently good approximation to be of considerable scientific worth. In still other cases, the model may be serviceable even though what it omits in its simplification makes a big difference, provided we know at least the direction in which the outcome of the model must be corrected in order to be applicable to the problem at hand. . . .[18]

---

[17] Our model of conflict does specify the conditions under which a conflict will be prolonged, since the average time before absorption was shown to depend on the parameters of the model. However, it says nothing about the social conditions under which a given set of parameters is to be found.

[18] Kaplan (1964), pp. 282–83.

The fourth danger is *overemphasis on rigor*. In the construction of models, this problem becomes one of how "ambitious" our assumptions are to be. We have argued that stochastic models of group behavior are preferable to deterministic models, precisely because the stochastic models are more modest in their goals. In that sense we have avoided this particular danger when discussing descriptive models; with respect to the theory of games we had no choice but to present its main concepts in a deterministic fashion. We have argued, however, that in some cases to replace deterministic assumptions by stochastic ones may improve the realism of the model.

The fifth danger associated with the construction of models is that of *map reading*. A scientist falls victim to map reading if he assumes that everything true about the model must be also true about its subject-matter. For example, it would be erroneous to think that, in large societies, all pairs of members are equally likely to meet, even though we made such an assumption in our model of stratification. In fact, the very assumption underlying stochastic models is wrong from a realistic point of view. Although it is possible to assume, for example, that an average voter is exposed to random forces which mold his political opinions, we know full well that many forces impinging upon him are anything but random, and are instead deliberate attempts to influence him. We have tried to guard against this danger as far as possible by pointing out which features of our models were of doubtful realism.

The final danger mentioned by Kaplan is that of *pictorial realism*. This problem is the obverse of the map reading problem; it is the assumption that everything true about the subject matter must be also true of the model, that the model describes all aspects of the subject matter. This danger is sufficiently similar to the danger of oversimplification that the discussion given under that heading applies here also. The difference between the two, of course, is that the person guilty of oversimplification knows that he is simplifying but believes, mistakenly, that he is considering everything of importance; the person guilty of pictorial realism does not know in which ways his model is a simplification of complex reality.

We can think of no better conclusion to our discussion of simple models than to quote Kaplan's closing remarks on model construction:

That the behavioral scientist's interest in model building reflects the current fashion in science I have myself emphasized. But throughout the history of science we can discern cognitive styles distinctive of that period. Fashion does not necessarily stand in the way of scientific achievement; it may serve to give it form and color. And awareness of the danger that an established cognitive style may be repressive in its effect should not lead us to confuse mature emancipation with adolescent rebellion. The dangers are not in working with models, but in working with too few, and those much alike, and above all, in belittling any effort to work with anything else. That Euclid alone has looked on beauty bare is a romantic fiction.[19]

[19] *Ibid.*, pp. 292–93.

Estimating Transition
Probabilities in Cohen's Model

As is indicated in Chapter 7, it is possible to use mathematical reasoning to estimate the probabilities p_{ij} in Cohen's model of conformity, using as the basic data the transcripts in the form

$$(T)TTTFFT \cdots TFFF$$

where T stands for a correct response, F for an incorrect, (T) stands for the response the subject would presumably give before the experiment starts, the remaining T and F for his actual responses during the experiment.

As described in Chapter 7, each subject's transcripts can be divided into two segments, the initial and the final. (The final segment always contains an uninterrupted sequence of identical responses, either all T or all F.) For the initial segment it is possible to define the following quantities:

N_{TF}: number of switches from T to F
N_{FT}: number of switches from F to T
N_T: number of T-responses in the initial segment
N_F: number of F-responses in the initial segment

Now consider this question: What value does the mean number of F-responses in the initial segment, N_F/N, approach as the number of sequences (experiments) increases? This observable mean will approach the mean computed from the matrix P, that is, the theoretical mean. We do not know the theoretical mean number of F responses in the initial segment, but eq. 7.6 enables us to derive from P the mean number of trials n_{23} during which the subject is in state 3 (if he starts in state 2, as we are assuming). Consider the expression $n_{23} - f_{23}$, where f_{23} is the mean number of trials during which the subject is in state 3 (if he starts in state 2) during the *final* segment. Then, assuming that we can compute f_{23} from P, the expression $n_{23} - f_{23}$ gives us the theoretical mean of trials when the subject is in state 3 during the initial segment. But, in order to be in state s_3, the subject has to give an F-response. Hence $n_{23} - f_{23}$ gives us the theoretical mean of F-responses in the initial segment, and we can write that

$$(A.1) \qquad\qquad \frac{N_F}{N} \approx n_{23} - f_{23}$$

Our problem now is to derive f_{23} from the matrix P. Let us start by considering the probability that there are exactly m occurrences of state s_3 in the final segment, q_m. If the very last response of a sequence is T, then we know that, by definition, all responses in the final segment are T. Thus the probability that there are *no* F-responses in the final segment is the same as the probability that the process is absorbed in state s_1 (when it starts in state s_2), b_{21}. But, when there are no F responses in the final segment, the subject cannot, by definition, have been in state s_3 during the final segment at all; hence

$$q_0 = b_{21}$$

It is obvious that if the subject is in s_3 at time t, he will be in s_3 at time $t + 1$ only if the transition from time t to time $t + 1$ is from state s_3 to state s_3. Since this transition occurs with probability p_{33}, we can write that

$$q_{m+1} = p_{33}q_m \qquad \text{if } m > 0$$

Solving this difference equation,[1] we can write that

$$(A.2) \qquad\qquad q_{m+1} = p_{33}^m q_1$$

---

[1] For the solution of difference equations see, for example, Goldberg (1958).

Since q_m is a probability measure, it must be true that

$$\sum_{m=0}^{\infty} q_m = 1$$

It can be shown that $\sum_{m=1}^{\infty} p_{33}^m q_1 = q_1/(1 - p_{33})$,[2] and hence, adding the case when $m = 0$, we can write that

$$b_{21} + \frac{q_1}{1 - p_{33}} = 1$$

and

$$q_1 = (1 - p_{33})b_{24}$$

since $b_{24} = 1 - b_{21}$. Substituting the last expression into (A.2), we write that

(A.3) $$q_m = p_{33}^{m-1}(1 - p_{33})b_{24}$$

Remember that f_{23} is the mean number in state s_3 (in the final segment), while q_m is the *probability* that state s_3 occurs exactly m times (in the final segment). The reader should have no difficulty[3] in seeing that

$$f_{23} = \sum_{m=1}^{\infty} mq_m$$

Substituting (A.3) for q_m, we write

$$f_{23} = \sum_{m=1}^{\infty} mp_{33}^{m-1}(1 - p_{33})b_{24}$$

It can be shown[4] that this simplifies to

$$f_{23} = \frac{b_{24}}{1 - p_{33}}$$

Using eq. 7.7 to substitute for b_{24}, we obtain

$$f_{23} = \frac{p_{23}p_{34}}{1 - p_{33}}$$

---

[2] See, for example, Cohen (1963).
[3] Note that q_m is the probability that there are m F-responses in the final segment.
[4] See Kemeny and Snell (1962), p. 59.

Thus we have arrived at a way of computing the theoretical mean number of trials during which the subjects were in state s_3 in their final segment, f_{23}. Remember that to compute such quantities for the final segment was viewed as a major problem earlier. This problem now has been solved, and we thus can substitute this result into (A.1):

$$(A.4) \qquad \frac{N_F}{N} \approx \frac{p_{23}}{\Delta} - \frac{p_{23}p_{34}}{\Delta(1 - p_{33})} = \frac{p_{23}p_{32}}{\Delta(1 - p_{33})}$$

Using an analogous approach, we proceed to determine the mean number of T-responses in the initial segment N_T/N:

$$(A.5) \qquad \frac{N_T}{N} \approx \frac{p_{23}(1 - p_{33})}{\Delta(1 - p_{22})}$$

There is one quantity that can be derived from our model and can easily be estimated from the data, the probability that the process is observed in state s_4. We know from eq. 7.5 that this probability (given the assumption that the process starts in s_2) is b_{24}. If we designate the number of sequences that end in an F-response by t_F, then it is clear that $t_F N$ will be close to that probability, that is,

$$(A.6) \qquad \frac{t_F}{N} \approx b_{24}$$

Let us stop for a moment to see what we have done so far: We have succeeded in expressing directly observable quantities as functions the various p_{ij} of (7.1). So far, so good. But note that in order to estimate the four p_{ij} that form the free parameters of (7.1), we need four *independent* equations. The equations (A.4) to (A.6) are not independent, because it holds that

$$(A.7) \quad N_T = N_{TT} + N_{TF}, \qquad N_F = N_{FT} + N_{FF}, \qquad t_F = N_{TF} - N_{FT}$$

Thus we use these equations merely as an intermediate step.

To obtain the first of a set of four independent equations, we define a new absorbing Markov chain, one which arises when we fail to count transitions from a state into itself. In other words, we now define a process—as indeed we are free to do—in which we count only those trails that constitute transitions from a state to a different state. This procedure yields the following matrix:

$$
\hat{P} = \begin{array}{c} \\ 1 \\ 2 \\ \\ 3 \\ \\ 4 \end{array}
\begin{array}{cccc}
1 & 2 & 3 & 4 \\
\left[\begin{array}{cccc}
1 & 0 & 0 & 0 \\
\dfrac{p_{21}}{1 - p_{22}} & 0 & \dfrac{p_{23}}{1 - p_{22}} & 0 \\
0 & \dfrac{p_{32}}{1 - p_{33}} & 0 & \dfrac{p_{34}}{1 - p_{33}} \\
0 & 0 & 0 & 1
\end{array}\right]
\end{array}
$$

Rewriting $\hat{P}$ in canonical form and applying eq. 7.4, we obtain

$$
\hat{N} = \begin{array}{c} \\ 2 \\ \\ 3 \end{array}
\begin{array}{cc}
2 & 3 \\
\left[\begin{array}{cc}
\dfrac{(1 - p_{22})(1 - p_{33})}{\Delta} & \dfrac{p_{23}(1 - p_{23})}{\Delta} \\
\dfrac{p_{32}(1 - p_{22})}{\Delta} & \dfrac{(1 - p_{22})(1 - p_{33})}{\Delta}
\end{array}\right]
\end{array}
$$

Of particular interest is the quantity n_{23}. As before,[5] it is defined as the mean number of times in state s_3 if the process starts in s_2. However, note that, since transitions FF and TT do not occur in $\hat{P}$, the mean number in state s_3 happens to correspond with the mean number of switches from state s_2 to state s_3. But these switches (1) are identical with switches from response T to F and (2) can occur only in the initial segment. Hence we can write

(A.8) $$\frac{N_{TF}}{N} \approx \hat{n}_{23} = \frac{p_{23}(1 - p_{33})}{\Delta}$$

Noting that $N_T = N_{TT} + N_{TF}$, and using (A.5) and (A.7), we write

(A.9) $$\frac{N_{TT}}{N} \approx \frac{p_{22}p_{23}(1 - p_{33})}{\Delta(1 - p_{22})}$$

We now observe that $t_F = N_{TF} - N_{FT}$, and use (A.6) and (A.8) to obtain

(A.10) $$\frac{N_{FT}}{N} \approx \frac{p_{23}p_{32}}{\Delta}$$

[5] See Chapter 7, discussion explaining eq. 7.6.

Finally, noting that $N_F = N_{FT} + N_{FF}$, and using (A.4) and (A.10), we write

(A.11) $$\frac{N_{FF}}{N} \approx \frac{p_{23}p_{32}p_{33}}{\Delta(1 - p_{33})}$$

The four equations (A.8) to (A.11) are independent since the quantities N_{TF}, N_{TT}, N_{FT}, and N_{FF} each derive from a distinct set of data.

There is a technical problem we have to take care of before we can use the four equations to solve for four p_{ij}. These four relationships are not really equations, they are mere approximations, as signified by the fact that "$\approx$" instead of "$=$" is used. But this is not a major difficulty, since we can, in theory at least, consider an infinite number of experiments; under such conditions the theoretical quantities become equal to the observed quantities, and we can treat (A.8) through (A.11) as true equations. We can solve these four equations, and then again relax the assumption that we are dealing with an infinite number of experiments by replacing the equal signs with "$\approx$." Following this procedure, we obtain:

$$p_{21} \approx \frac{N_{TF}(1 - N_{TF} + N_{FT})}{A}$$

$$p_{22} \approx \frac{N_{TT}(1 + N_{FT})}{A}$$

$$p_{23} \approx \frac{N_{TF}^2}{A}$$

$$p_{32} \approx \frac{N_{FT}^2}{B}$$

$$p_{33} \approx \frac{N_{FF}N_{TF}}{B}$$

$$p_{34} \approx \frac{N_{FT}(N_{TF} - N_{FT})}{B}$$

where $A = (N_{TT} + N_{TF})(1 + N_{FT})$, $B = N_{TF}(N_{FT} + N_{FF})$

Bibliography

Anderson, Alan R., and O. K. Moore (1960), "Autotelic Folk-Models," *Sociological Quarterly*, I, 203–16.

——— (1962), "Logic, Norms, and Roles," *in* Joan Criswell et al. (eds.), *Mathematical Methods in Small Group Processes*, Stanford: Stanford University Press, pp. 11–22.

Anderson, T. W. (1954), "Probability Models for Analyzing Time Changes in Attitudes," *in* P. F. Lazarsfeld (ed.), *Mathematical Thinking in the Social Sciences*, Glencoe: The Free Press, pp. 17–66.

Asch, S. E. (1952), *Social Psychology*, New York: Prentice-Hall.

Atkinson, Richard C., Gordon H. Bower, and Edward J. Crothers (1965), *An Introduction to Mathematical Learning Theory*, New York: Wiley.

Bartos, Otomar J. (1966), "Concession-Making in Experimental Negotiations," *in* Berger et al. (eds.), *Sociological Theories in Progress*, New York: Houghton Mifflin.

Beach, E. F. (1964), *Economic Models*, New York: Wiley.

Berger, J., and J. L. Snell (1957), "On the Concept of Equal Exchange," *Behavioral Science*, II, 111–18.

Blumen, I., M. Kogan, and P. J. McCarthy (1955), *The Industrial Mobility of Labor as a Probability Process*, Ithaca: Cornell University Press.

Braithwaite, R. B. (1955), *Theory of Games as a Tool for the Moral Philosopher*, Cambridge: Cambridge University Press.

Brown, G. W. (1951), "Iterative Solutions of Games by Fictitious Play," *in* Koopmans (ed.), *Activity Analysis of Productivity and Allocation*, New York: Wiley.

Charlesworth, J. C. (June, 1963), *Mathematics and the Social Sciences*, a symposium sponsored by the American Academy of Political and Social Science, Philadelphia.

Cohen, Bernard P. (1958), "A Probability Model for Conformity," *Sociometry*, XXI, 69–81.

―――― (1963), *Conflict and Conformity: A Probability Model and Its Application*, Cambridge: MIT Press.

Coleman, James S. (1964), *Models of Change and Response Uncertainty*, Englewood Cliffs: Prentice-Hall.

Davis, Kingsley, and Wilbert E. Moore (1945), "Some Principles of Stratification," *American Sociological Review*, X, 242–49.

Dawson, Richard E. (1962), "Simulation in the Social Sciences," *in* Guetzkow (ed.), *Simulation in Social Science*, Englewood Cliffs: Prentice-Hall.

Etzioni, Amitai (1945), "Mathematics for Sociologists?" *American Sociological Review*, VI, 943–44.

Goldberg, Samuel (1958), *Introduction to Difference Equations*, New York: Wiley.

Goodman, Leo (1959), "On Some Statistical Tests for M-th Order Markov Chains," *Annals of Mathematical Statistics*, XXX, 154–64.

Harary, Frank, Robert Z. Norman, and Dorwin Cartwright (1965), *Structural Models*, New York: Wiley.

Haywood, O. G. (1954), "Military Decisions and Game Theory," *Journal of the Operations Research Society of America*, II, 365–85.

Homans, George C. (1961), *Social Behavior*, New York: Harcourt, Brace & World.

Horst, Paul (1963), *Matrix Algebra for Social Scientist*, New York: Holt, Rinehart & Winston.

Inkeles, Alex (1964), *What is Sociology?* Englewood Cliffs: Prentice-Hall.

Isaacs, Rufus (1965), *Differential Games*, New York: Wiley.

Kaplan, Abraham (1964), *The Conduct of Inquiry*, San Francisco: Chandler.

Kemeny, John G., Arthur Schleier, Jr., J. Laurie Snell, and Gerald L. Thompson (1962), *Finite Mathematics with Business Applications*, Englewood Cliffs: Prentice-Hall.

Kemeny, John G., and J. L. Snell (1960), *Finite Markov Chains*, Princeton: D. Van Nostrand Co., Inc.

Kemeny, John G., and J. L. Snell (1962), *Mathematical Models in the Social Sciences*, Boston: Ginn & Co.

Kemeny, John G., J. L. Snell, and G. L. Thompson (1957), *Introduction to Finite Mathematics*, Englewood Cliffs: Prentice-Hall.

Kuehn, Alfred A. (1958), "An Analysis of the Dynamics of Consumer Behavior and Its Implications for Marketing Management," Pittsburgh: Carnegie Institute of Technology, unpublished Ph.D. dissertation.

Landau, H. G. (1951a), "On Dominance Relations and the Structure of Animal Societies; I: Effect of Inherent Characteristics," *Bulletin of Mathematical Biophysics*, XIII, 1–19.

——— (1951b), "On Dominance Relations and the Structure of Animal Societies; II, *Bulletin of Mathematical Biophysics*, XIII, 245–62.

——— (1953), "On Dominance Relations and the Structure of Animal Societies; III: The Condition for a Score Structure," *Bulletin of Mathematical Biophysics*, XV, 143–48.

Lieberman, Bernard (1960), "Human Behavior in a Strictly Determined 3 × 3 Matrix Game," *Behavioral Science*, V, 317–22.

Lieberman, Bernard, and David Malcolm (1965), "The Behavior of Responsive Individuals Playing a Two-Person Game Requiring the Use of Mixed Strategies," *Psychoanalytic Science*, II, 373–74.

Luce, R. Duncan, and H. Raiffa (1957), *Games and Decisions*, New York: Wiley.

McGinnis (1966), "A Stochastic Theory of Social Mobility" (mimeographed report).

Moore, Omar K. (1963), *Autotelic Responsive Environments and Exceptional Children*, Hamden, Connecticut: Responsive Environment Foundation.

Mosteller, Frederick, Robert E. D. Rourke, and George B. Thomas, Jr. (1961), *Probability and Statistics*, Reading, Massachusetts: Addison-Wesley.

Nash, John F. (1950), "The Bargaining Problem," *Econometrica*, XVIII, 155–62.

Pool, Ithiel de Sola, Robert P. Abelson, and Samuel Popkin (1965), *Candidates, Issues and Strategies*, Cambridge: MIT Press.

Raiffa, H. (1953), "Arbitration Scheme for Generalized Two-Person Games," in H. W. Kuhn and A. W. Tucker (eds.), *Contribution to the Theory of Games*, Princeton University Press, pp. 361–95.

Rapoport, Anatol (1949a), "A Probabilistic Approach to Animal Sociology: I," *Bulletin of Mathematical Biophysics*, XI, 183–96.

——— (1949b), "A Probabilistic Approach to Animal Sociology: II," *Bulletin of Mathematical Biophysics*, XI, 273–82.

——— (1950), "Outline of a Probabilistic Approach to Animal Sociology: III," *Bulletin of Mathematical Biophysics*, XII, 7–17.

Rapoport, Anatol, and Albert M. Chammah (1965), *Prisoner's Dilemma*, Ann Arbor: The University of Michigan Press.

Rogers, Andrei (1965), "A Markovian Model of Interregional Migration," Berkeley: Center for Planning and Development Research (mimeographed report).

Sadowski, Wieslaw (1965), *The Theory of Decision-Making*, Oxford: Perganion Press.

Schelling, T. C. (1957), "Prospectus for a Reorientation of Game Theory," *Journal of Conflict Resolution*, I, 305–7.

Shelly, Maynard W., II, and Glenn L. Bryan, eds. (1964), *Human Judgement and Optimality*, New York: Wiley.

Spencer, Herbert (1877), *The Principles of Sociology*, New York: Appleton & Co.

Sumner, William G. (1906), *Folkways*, Boston: Ginn.

Suppes, Patrick, and R. C. Atkinson (1960), *Markov Learning Models for Multiperson Interactions*, Stanford: Stanford University Press.

Thibaut, John W., and Harold H. Kelley (1959), *The Social Psychology of Groups*, New York: Wiley.

von Neumann, John, and O. Morgenstern (1947), *Theory of Games and Economic Behavior*, Princeton: Princeton University Press.

von Wright, Georg H. (1951), *An Essay in Modal Logic*, Amsterdam.

Walton, Richard E., and Robert B. McKersie (1965), *A Behavioral Theory of Labor Negotiations*, New York: McGraw-Hill.

Weber, Max (1946), *Essays in Sociology*, Gerth and Mills (eds.), New York: Oxford University Press, pp. 196–204.

Wold, Herman O. (1964), *Econometric Model Building*, Amsterdam: North-Holland Publishing Co.

Index